Anthropological Papers
Museum of Anthropology, University of Michigan
Number 95

West African Early Towns

Archaeology of Households in Urban Landscapes

by
Augustin F.C. Holl

Ann Arbor, Michigan
2006

Cover design by Katherine Clahassey

The University of Michigan Museum of Anthropology currently publishes three monograph series: Anthropological Papers, Memoirs, and Technical Reports, as well as an electronic series in CD-ROM form. For a complete catalog, write to Museum of Anthropology Publications, 4009 Museums Building, Ann Arbor, MI 48109-1079.

Library of Congress Cataloging-in-Publication Data

Holl, Augustin.
 West African early towns : archaeology of households in urban landscapes / by Augustin F.C. Holl.
     p. cm. -- (Anthropological papers ; no. 95)
 Includes bibliographical references.
 ISBN-13: 978-0-915703-61-6 (alk. paper)
 ISBN-10: 0-915703-61-0 (alk. paper)
 1. Aoudaghost (Extinct city) 2. Excavations (Archaeology)--Mauritania. 3. Households--Mauritania--Aoudaghost (Extinct city) I. Title. II. Anthropological papers (University of Michigan. Museum of Anthropology) ; no. 95.
 GN2.M5 no. 95 H65 2006
 [DT554.9.A68]
 306 s--dc22
 [966
                                    2006000280

The paper used in this publication meets the requirements of the ANSI Standard Z39.48-1984 (Permanence of Paper)

Contents

Figures

Tables

Acknowledgments

The work published in the following pages was made possible by the sustained and skilled contributions of a succession of graduate students I have been honored to have as research assistants. Margie Burton from the University of California, San Diego, went through a series of archaeological monographs and edited report collections, extracted the maps, translated all of them into the same scale, and as such, set the foundations upon which all the latter work was done. Stephen Dueppen, Laura Villamil, and Min Li, from the University of Michigan, scanned, polished, and arranged the site maps into robust and flexible working tools. I am grateful for their enthusiasm and dedicated commitment. Kay Clahassey took good care of and polished all the illustrations published in this book, and Sally Mitani and Jill Rheinheimer took care of the tedious production work.

Introduction

This book is the realization of an old idea. The material from Awdaghost (also known as Tegdaoust) was an important part of my graduate school years. It was an essential component of the seminar "Recherches en cours en Archéologie Africaine" taught by the late Professor Jean Devisse at the Sorbonne in the late 1970s and early 1980s. I have a copy of part of the original manuscript of Tegdaoust III, three chapters of the "Conclusions Générales" from the 1983 volume, with Devisse's handwritten corrections. All the students enrolled in the 1979–1980 African Archaeology seminar were given a copy of these chapters in their final copyediting stage before publication, and were expected to read and comment on the original draft. As should be expected, none of us in the student group had a good grasp of the complexity and intricacies of the Tegdaoust/Awdaghost material at that time. The chapter on Tegdaoust palaeoenvironment was radically new, thrilling, and exciting. It was the main focus of the seminar discussions for at least three sessions. The glue that held all the distinct excavation units together was very clearly a chronological one. The spatial dimension was not ignored, but taken for granted and dealt with in terms of walls and their intersections. It was difficult to visualize, even in disparate fragments, the planes of the town's life, the organization of coherent habitation units and their links to the rest of the city's amenities, like streets and open places. There was always the confused impression that more could be done about the analysis of domestic space, but what? What would happen if contemporaneous levels were lumped within a single horizontal plan and analyzed as such? That was the simple idea that kept creeping in my mind. There was however no precise idea on how to proceed, or even how to try. The opportunity to write a book review of one of the volumes of the Tegdaoust collection (Holl 1988) reignited the old, almost forgotten, idea. And finally, the publication of most of the key archaeological projects conducted at Awdaghost/Tegdaoust made the project feasible.

The anthropological archaeology perspective adopted in this book focuses on the systematic analysis of the spatial organization of the inhabited space. It is anchored on the assumption that household internal space and structural patterning are responsive to demography, social standing and economic influences. The shaped and bounded spaces have a certain inertia and will tend to constrain activities and behaviors. Theoretically, then, the decision to erase a wall, or alter its course to reduce or increase the space size, is taken when the actual space is seen as unfit for the new emerging needs.

The chronological rearrangment of the material obtained from the medieval town Acropolis was a necessity. It was implemented through a narrow array of techniques and procedures that include stratigraphic considerations, radiocarbon dates, and datable imports. Instead of relying simply on the chronological tables published in the different Tegdaoust volumes, which appeared inadequate for a fine-tuned analysis of the household space, it was necessary to look for more precise common analytical units. Three such units were generated, the Building Sequence, the Habitation Complex, and the Household Unit. They are distinct levels of an inclusive spatial taxonomy: the Household Units form the Habitation Complexes, which in turn form in the Building Sequences.

The Building Sequence is the key stratigraphic level of analysis. It includes all contemporaneous constructions that are considered to have been inhabited and used during the same time segment. As the concept suggests, each new rearrangement of the architectural features that resulted in the addition or substraction of a spatial unit triggers the shift to a new Building Sequence. Fifteen such building sequences, numbered from the earliest to the latest (BS-1 to BS-15), have been identified in that part of the town under consideration in this book.

The Habitation Complex is a set of contiguous housing units with the common use of some of their walls. It is a self-contained architectural complex separated from the others by streets and open places. And finally, the Household Unit consists of connected rooms, corridors, and courtyard, inhabited more often than not by the members of a family unit, whatever structure (nuclear, extended, polygamous) and size it may have had during the medieval period in West Africa. The number of household units per habitation complex varies considerably, as is the case for the number of habitation complexes per building sequence.

"Awdaghost" is the Soninké name of the medieval town under consideration in this book. It is the only name of that place to be found in Early Arabic historical sources. The name of the medieval town was dropped and, to please the Mauritanian Moorish government, the ancient city was renamed "Tegdaoust," after the ethnonym of a Moorish tribe still inhabiting the area where they settled initially in the seventeenth or eighteenth century AD. Even if unintentional, this name reshuffle does do some disservice to the study of West African history; it conveys the subliminal false association between Awdaghost the medieval town, and the Tegdaoust, a Moorish tribe that settled in the area a few centuries after the abandonment of the city. Hence, in this book I have chosen to shift back to the original and authentic medieval name of the town.

This book starts with an exploration of what has been learned so far from approximately one century of archaeological research focused on West African towns. A number of recurring themes have sustained the enthusiasm of generations of researchers, mainly limited to looks at markets, trade, long distance exchange, and architecture styles.

The sociopolitical, economic, intellectual, and cultural context of emerging West African towns is very rarely fully acknowledged, much less investigated by most researchers. The two notable exceptions are the Niany and Kumbi-Saleh projects which make explicit links to an overarching state apparatus: Niani with the Mali Empire, and Kumbi Saleh with the Ghana Kingdom. Unfortunately, most of the other projects — Awdaghost, Azelik, Azugi, Gao, Jenne-Jeno, Marandet, Sincu-Bara — have paid little attention to the sociopolitical frame. It goes without saying that the question is a difficult one with no easy solution; in most cases, however, towns were critical nodes of larger political and economic systems.

As far as the internal organization of excavated West African towns is concerned, the usual small-scale probes constrain the access to the organization of housing complexes, quarters, and the general layout of the city. Access to such high-resolution spatial information is generally cumulative and predicated upon the excavation of large completely open probes. Despite all competing claims, the Awdaghost excavation is by far the most extensive, accurate, and finest archaeological field project ever conducted in West Africa. It is the only site that could provide the high-resolution material required for a foray into household archaeology.

The book is divided into nine chapters. Chapter 1 summarizes the data on ten West-African towns and singles out their similarities and differences as well as their potentials for an archaeology of household. Chapter 2 discusses the main theoretical and practical aspects of household archaeology and how it can be tailored to make the best of the material from Awdaghost. Chapter 3 describes the development and implementation of the Awdaghost archaeological project. It also outlines the appealing potential this well-published program offers for an archaeology of households.

Chapters 4 to 7 are the core of the book. They present the material excavated from Awdaghost Acropolis in light of the new methodology aiming at the fine-tuned analysis of domestic spaces. Chapter 4 deals with the early segment of Awdaghost settlement, with the significant shift from an undated pre-urban phase to the development of the town's urban layout in AD 900. Chapter 5 presents the material from the mushrooming town in 900 to 1000. Chapter 6 discusses the unstable plateau in the evolution of the town that lasted from 1000 to 1200. Chapter 7 investigates the downturn in Awdaghost settlement history, when the urban landscape disaggregates and the town was very likely abandoned, around 1500.

In Chapter 8, the archaeological reconstruction of Awdaghost settlement obtained in Chapters 4 through 7 is compared and contrasted with the Awdaghost described in early Arabic historical sources. Finally, Chapter 9 explores a range of interpretations for the patterns of space allocation discovered in the Awdaghost record.

In fact, this book presents another facet of what anthropological archaeologists do. Inferences have to be testable and propositions falsifiable, however difficult that may appear at first glance. There has to be a match between the research problem one wishes to tackle and the material record garnered to address the many facets of the selected questions, issue after issue. If we use the right approaches, archaeology should allow the West African past to speak for itself.

—1—

Archaeology of Early West African Towns

Introduction

What are the fundamental building blocks of West African early town landscapes? How were they shaped? How and why did they change—or not—through time? What can these building blocks tell us about social organization? These are some of the questions addressed in this book. Paradoxically, information on the fine-grained structure of most ancient West African towns is rare. There is an important record of published material on West African early cities (Bedaux et al. 2001; Bernus and Cressier 1991; Berthier 1997; Bivar and Shinnie 1962; Bocoum and McIntosh 2002; Connah 1981; Filipowiak 1979; Insoll 1996, 1997, 2003; Levtzion 1973; McIntosh and McIntosh 1980, 1984, 1993; S.K. McIntosh 1995, 1999; Moraes-Farias 1990; Thilmans and Ravise 1980). Some, like El Mina (Decorse 2000) and Begho in Ghana, Kong in Cote d'Ivoire, and Benin and Ife in Nigeria (Connah 1975), are too far south to be relevant for the case under consideration in this book. Others, like Birni Ghazzargamo (Bivar and Shinnie 1961; Connah 1981) or Timbuktu (Insoll 2000a; McIntosh and McIntosh 1986), are of later foundation, dating from the fifteenth or sixteenth century onward.

Africanist historians have devoted considerable skill and energy to the issue of urban development in West Africa during the last two millennia (Devisse 1993; Levtzion 1973; McIntosh and McIntosh 1984). In much West African archaeology, however, the focus on chronology and the desperate search for earliest evidence and unique material culture and trade items has generated a counterproductive approach. Authors jockey for the "earliest," "biggest," "largest," "richest" artifact/building/stratigraphy/artwork/site, ignoring their places in past West African social systems.

A number of urban sites have been subjected to archaeological investigation during the last century. The scale and scope of archaeological projects conducted in ancient West African towns vary considerably. Some important sites were visited, shallowly surveyed, and described but never tested archaeologically. Others were tested with one or a series of trial trenches which aimed to assess the thickness of the cultural deposits and, using these, the site's chronology. Others have been researched more ambitiously and systematically. A number of these works will be summarized below, and the most interesting cases will be singled out for further discussions.

Niani: The Debate

Despite its crucial involvement in the emergence and rise to primacy of the Mali Empire (ca. AD 1200 to 1400), the town of Niani, excavated in 1965, 1968 and 1973 by a Polish-Guinean research team (Filipowiak 1966, 1969, 1976, 1978), is still the object of a heated debate (Conrad 1994; Filipowiak 1978; Hunwick 1973; Insoll 2003; McIntosh 1998; Meillassoux 1972). Niani is located at 11°22'N and 8°23'W in the Sudano-Guinean climatic zone, at 370 m above sea level (Fig. 1). Filipowiak's excavation program dealt with an extensive mound complex at the confluence of the Sankarani and the Farakole rivers, both tributaries of the Niger River located in the Guinea Republic. The complex measures more than 2.5 km north-south and 4 km east-west and includes river shores, low hills, steep slopes, more than thirty scattered mounds, as well as caves, settled with fluctuating population from the early sixth to the seventeenth century AD. The earliest cultural deposit is dated to the middle of the sixth century and confined to the southwest of the archaeological complex. From its beginning to the ninth century, Niani was a small village measuring some 80 m in diameter with wattle and daub houses. The settlement went into accelerated growth in the ninth and tenth centuries. Arab merchants settled in Larabou-So northwest of the royal neighborhood and various compounds were dispersed throughout the landscape. Prime agricultural lands, hunting grounds, and fishing opportunities were all available within walking distance. Cabbage or turnip and lentils seeds were found in the ninth- or tenth-century level of Larabou-So. The different farmsteads were connected by a dense and intricate network of footpaths. The royal town included an audience room, a mosque, and a royal residence. *Pisé* or *banco* became the all-purpose building material. Iron production areas were also recorded in the Niani archaeological complex. From the tenth to the thirteenth century the main settlement seems to have shifted to the central part of the mound complex, in the area between the Farakole and Folonbadin rivers. The royal residence may have been located on Mound 6M1, the largest of the three large mounds (Filipowiak 1979:192, see map, Fig. 10). The eleventh-through thirteenth-century settlement was spread all over the mound complex. It included the mounds from Station 6, the newly developed Somonodougou (Station 5) and Krekréloudou (Station 14) neighborhoods, the extensive tell of Station 22, hamlets from Stations 42 and 45 upstream along the Farakole, and finally, iron smelter/blacksmith quarters on the west shore of the Farakole at Station 17 (Filipowiak 1979:193-94). The royal quarter excavated in the southwest of the Niani Mound complex and sitting on top of the pioneer small wattle and daub village may have been founded in the late thirteenth century and inhabited up to the seventeenth or eighteenth century AD (Filipowiak 1979:197-98). On almost every page of his book, particularly in the introductory chapter "L'histoire et l'état des recherches" (pp. 13-45), the conclusion "Niani—Capitale de l'empire du Mali" (pp. 296-306), and even a postscript on pages 307-8, Filipowiak insists heavily on the identification of the Niani he has excavated with Niani the imperial capital of Mali, mustering different strands of data to support his claims. On pages 40-41, specifically in notes 99-103, he develops a balanced and well-argued refutation of Meillassoux's (1972) and Hunwick's (1973) objections.

Meillassoux and Hunwick both were poorly informed of the results of the archaeological project in progress at Niani. They had access to a short report published in 1969 (Filipowiak 1969), but Filipowiak's late 1979 monograph offered a wealth of information with an acceptable summary of the archaeological findings to which they did not have access.

Hunwick (1973), Meillassoux (1972), and McIntosh (1998) have different views on the location of the Mali Empire's capital towns. Conrad (1994) is probably the most radical opponent to Filipowiak's (1979) interpretation of the Niani record. His position, shared by Insoll (2003:320-22), is that the Mali Empire had several capital cities rather than one. He bases this on two arguments. First, there is a significant chronological gap in the archaeological record. The radiocarbon dates obtained by the Guinea-Polish Niani Archaeological Project are distributed into two clusters, the sixth to tenth century at one end and the sixteenth to seventeenth at the other, resulting in a six-century gap. Second, long-distance trade items, particularly elements like beads, glass and glazed wares, "types of artefacts which may be expected from so important a site" (Insoll 2003:322), are virtually absent. Conrad (1994:377) suggests that the excavated Niani may have been a political capital in the sixteenth century, while earlier capitals should have been located in the area of Djakajalan.

Unfortunately, Djakajalan is a sacred place, presently out of archaeologists' reach. Insoll's conclusion summarizes the position of the new skeptics: "[I]t is safe to conclude that the capital of Mansa Musa and Mansa Suleyman await the archaeologist's attention, and it is not to be identified with Niani. Both the archaeology and its comparison with the historical description provided by Ibn Battuta make the Niani identification highly unlikely" (Insoll 2003:322). This may well be the case, but the argument developed here is very surprising. The purpose of an archaeological project is not to match the descriptions of an ancient writer, however prestigious he or she may have been. Ibn Battuta was commissioned by Sultan Abu 'Inan to travel in Western Sudan. He visited cities like Walata, Niani and Takkada between February of 1352 and December of 1353. Ibn Battuta's accounts were written later, in December, 1355, through February, 1356, by Ibn Juzayy, the Sultan's scribe (Levtzion and Hopkins 1981:279). Ibn Battuta may have had a phenomenal memory and his description of Niani is an important historical document, but it is one among many that also deserves to be looked at critically.

The arguments developed by Conrad (1994) and supported by Insoll (2003) are spurious, not to mention moot, since neither seem to have read Filipowiak's 1979 monograph seriously. Capital or dominant political centers can shift from one part of the country to another depending on political circumstances and the network of allies and support the rulers can garner at any specific time; this idea is discussed in the Filipowiak monograph. The dynamics of the mound complex delineated by Filipowiak solves the chronological gap identified by Conrad. Conrad's argument focused on the paucity of imported items and the reliability of Ibn Battuta's description of the imperial residence and reception hall, are even weaker. Despite its limitations, Filipowiak's monograph is the best that exists on all potential Mali capital cities. As the French saying goes, "la critique est aisée, mais l'art difficile."

Azelik/Takkada

Azelik—"Takedda," or "Takkada" to medieval Arab writers (Fig. 1)—is part of a late medieval settlement complex located southwest of the Aïr Mountains in central Niger. Azelik tell and the immediate periphery was investigated in the 1970s and 1980s by a series of French scientists (Bernus and Cressier 1991; Bernus and Gouletquer 1976; Grébénart 1985; Lhote 1972a). The settlement consists of two distinct parts: a set of mid-first millennium BC copper-smelting workshops, scattered over a surface of 8 ha located at some 300 m southeast of the tell with an occupation ranging from 540 to 90 BC (Grébénart 1985:219); and the main site, Azelik wan Birni, which dates from the thirteenth to the fifteenth century AD (Person and Saliege 1991:120).

Azelik archaeological tell is roughly crescent-shaped and measures 750 m in maximum length and 500 m in maximum width. An extensive geophysical survey and mapping program was implemented along with the excavation of two archaeological probes. The largest probe tested a surface of 300 m², 20 m in length and 15 m in width, and the smaller one, 144 m², 12 m by 12 m (Bernus and Cressier 1991:15). The limited size of the archaeological probes does not allow for an accurate reconstitution of the town's landscape and urban layout. The geophysical survey has nonetheless revealed the presence of important buildings and mosques. A particularly large and intriguing construction was found in the western part of the tell. The walls were indicated by lines of stone rubble delineating a rectangular building 90 m in length and 65 m in width. A series of narrow rooms and corridors seems to have been built along the southwest, south, and southeast sides, with the central and northern part left open (Bernus and Cressier 1991:158-60, Fig. 47). The use or function of this impressive building is still unknown, but in such a thriving Trans-Saharan trade town, a big caravansérail was probably not out of place. Three mosques were recorded and mapped. Mosque A, the largest and very likely the Friday or Cathedral Mosque, measuring 14 m in length and 8 m in width, was built in the northeast quadrant of the tell. Mosque B, slightly smaller and measuring 12 m in length and 7 m in width, is found in the southwest within the context of an extensive graveyard. And finally, Mosque C, located at some 200 m southeast of the town, is much smaller in size, 4.80 m in length and 3 m in width. As suggested by its location, Mosque C was very likely intended as a praying space for travelers. Imported items included glass beads, arm-rings and glazed wares. According to Ibn Battuta who visited the town in 1353 at the peak of its economic prosperity:

> the people of Takkada have no occupation but trade. They travel each year to Egypt and import some of everything which is there in the way of fine cloth [*thiyab*] and other things. Its people are comfortable and well off and are proud of the number of male and female slaves [*al-'abid wa-'l-khadam*] which they have. The people of Mali and Iwalatan are like this. [cited in Levtzion and Hopkins 1981:301-2]

The key socioeconomic activities of Azelik/Takedda were copper production from local native ore, salt production from brackish sources such as Guélélé and Tegidda-n-Tesemt, livestock husbandry, and interregional and long-distance trade. The find of 13 copper coins indicates that a local coinage operated during the fourteenth and fifteenth century AD (Bernus and Cressier 1991:145-47). Egypt appears to have been the key economic partner of Takkada

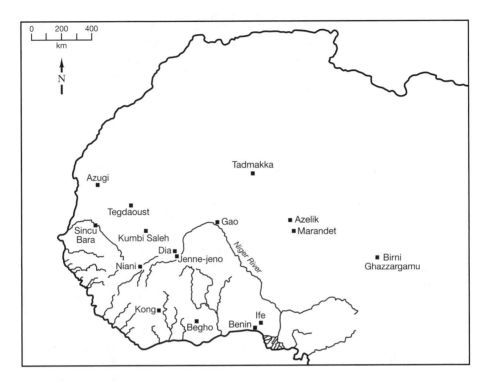

Figure 1. Medieval towns from West Africa mentioned in the text.

(Person and Saliege 1991:118). Paradoxically, North African material from Ifriqiya (Tunisia) and Morrocco are virtually absent. In fact, Takkada/Azelik was the dominant economic and political center of a medieval polity ruled by a Sultan from the thirteenth through the fifteenth centuries that comprised five settlements, known today under the names of Azelik wan Birni (Takkada), Tadraght in the east, Banguberi in the south, In-Zazan in the southeast, and finally, Guélélé in the west.

In summary, Takkada emulated Marandet and specialized in the intensive production of copper and salt that were channeled in the local, regional, and Trans-Saharan trade networks.

Azugi

Azugi is located next to the town of Atar in the Adrar region of northern Mauritania (Fig. 1). This site is strongly associated with the emergence and later expansion of the Almoravid revivalist movement of the eleventh century AD. In the 1960s, after its political independence, the Mauritanian government commissioned a series of archaeological surveys and excavations in and around Azugi. Land surveys on foot and automobile were conducted in

1968, 1971, and 1975 by S. Robert, D. Robert-Chaleix, and B. Saison. They were followed by an aerial photographic mission in 1980 by the French Institut Géographique National. These operations resulted in an improved knowledge of the landscape and its archaeological potential, as well as a more precise assessment of the Azugi ruins. Azugi is in fact an oasis situated at the confluence of two wadi courses, spread over some 63 ha, with date palm groves all along its east flank. It measures 900 m north-south and 700 m maximum east-west. The modern town developed to the south of the medieval one but was encroaching on the ruins in the early 1980s (Saison 1981). The town is divided into distinct zones, three of which have been singled out. First, the tell, located in the central part of the surveyed area, includes the highest density of medieval ruins. It is made up of a 100 by 70-80 m rectangular fortress built with two parallel walls and bastions, a series of collapsed and poorly preserved stone buildings spread over 1.6 ha (400 by 400 m), and a small cemetery with two distinct burial compounds, each with many graves. Second, the cenotaph of Imam el-Hadrami, a pilgrimage destination, is located at some 300 m northwest of the main tell. Finally, there is a rectilinear 25 by 12-15 m watchtower built on the cliff top at 800 m in the southeast of the tell (Saison 1981:69-70). Like the fortress, it is built with double parallel walls set slightly more than 2 m apart.

The 1980s were devoted to the excavation of the most promising architectural features. B. Saison organized two field seasons in June 1980 and June-July 1981. Three excavation probes were sunk in the north outer perimeter of the tell. A larger main excavation unit measuring 15 m by 10 m was opened within the confines of the fortress. The latter unit provided the archaeologist with a rewarding 2 to 3.5 m thick cultural deposit that was partitioned into four occupation levels. Level I deposit, recorded at 2.80 to 3.20 m, suggests a standard domestic occupation in an urban context with narrow streets, courtyards, rooms, and two wells. Level II, documented at 2.20 to 2.80 m, indicates a fully urban lifestyle with a habitation complex of two or three rooms, a latrine and two courtyards. Pottery, both local and imported, as well as metal artifacts in both iron and copper, and beads (carnelian, quartz and amazonite) are more abundant (Saison 1981:72). Level III deposit, at 1.60 to 2.20 m, presents evidence of a fire that destroyed the construction and charred the roof beams. The amount of portable cultural remains had shrunk considerably, with the material repertoire impoverished significantly. The quality of the architecture was also affected as the construction techniques were much less elaborate than those from the previous occupation. Finally, level IV deposit, recorded from the surface to 1.50 m below, is found only in the fortress area and is absent from the remaining parts of the site.

In chronological terms, Azugi appears to have been settled from the tenth century AD to the present. The earliest occupations I and II belong to the tenth through eleventh centuries. Occupation I is pre-Almoravid and occupation II coincides with the rise to regional primacy of the Almoravid revivalist movement. After the Almoravid, Azugi was not abandoned, but its urban status shrank to an intermittent settlement from the twelfth through the sixteenth century. A new revivalist and messianic movement preaching the return of the Almoravid emerged in Morocco and spread in the Adrar in the early part of the seventeenth century. This new movement "rediscovered" the tomb of Imam el-Hadrami, initiated a pilgrimage to the tomb of this holy man, and built the fortress that is part of the Azugi archaeological landscape. Contrary to all speculations that associated the Azugi fortress (*ribat*) with the emergence and development of the original Almoravid movement, the fortress was actually built 500 years later. This "decoupling" is one of the greatest achievement of the Azugi archaeological program (Saison 1981).

Dia

Dia, on the Diaka, a tributary of the Niger River, is found in the western edge of the Inland Niger Delta floodplain. It is an extensive 100 ha mound complex divided into three components of different size: the 49 ha Shoma, the archaeological site; the 29 ha present-day town of Dia; and finally, the 28 ha Mara which includes the cemetery and a soccer field (Bedaux et al. 2001). A new research program was launched at Dia in 1998 by a consortium of European universities collaborating with Malian institutions. The project ran from 1998 to 2004. Accordingly, what is available in print so far is very likely of a preliminary nature susceptible to change in the final report or site monograph.

The excavation program has focused on Shoma in the western part of the mound complex. Seven excavation units (A to G) were opened on the mound, six of seven (A, B, C, D, F, and G) sunk in the northern tip of Shoma. The tested sample measures 142.50 m^2: 50 m^2 for probe A and B (5 by 10 m); 25 m^2 each for probes C and D (5 by 5 m); 16 m^2 each for probes E and F (4 by 4 m); and finally, 10.5 m^2 for the trench of probe G (1.5 by 7 m). The uncovered mound deposit measures 3.5 m in thickness, for a site that appears to have been settled from the first half of the first millennium BC to the eighteenth century AD.

Dia settlement history has been segmented into five periods called horizons. The earliest Horizon I deposit belongs to a Late Stone Age site of remarkable size (Bedaux et al. 2001:841) with well-preserved floors. Bone tools and material culture elements that link the early Dia to the panregional Late Stone Age are well represented in the recorded assemblages. Iron artifacts are present at the end of the horizon, from 200 BC onwards. Horizon II occupation, bracketed between BC 300 and AD 300, appears to indicate a shift toward intermittent habitation during a particularly dry and arid period. The material culture repertoire is rather poor and for most of the cases appears to be a continuation of the previous Horizon I elements. Horizon III deposit, from AD 300 to 800(?), suggests the existence of a permanent settlement. The deposit was, however, seriously impacted by intrusive pits and burials from later occupations (Bedaux et al. 2001:844-45). House floors have nonetheless been recorded and mud-brick architecture seems to be represented. Horizon IV deposit was even more difficult to track as most of the sediment "has been removed by the subsequent erosional processes" (Bedaux et al. 2001:844). It appears to date from AD 800(?) to 1100, a time segment during which the area was turned into a cemetery. There is then a depositional hiatus or stratigraphic discontinuity resulting from the abandonment of the area and the ensuing erosion is documented to date from AD 1100 to 1400. Finally, Horizon V, dating from AD 1400 to 1700, attests for the existence of a large walled settlement. The city wall, visible from the surface along a 230 m stretch, consists of two parallel zigzagging 0.50 m thick walls with the 1-3 m interim space filled with rubble. Elongated rectangular houses or rooms were visible from the surface. The excavation probes A and B show these houses to be situated on both sides of a narrow street, with each of the probed rooms attached to a courtyard (Bedaux et al. 2001:839, Fig. 2).

The preliminary report from the new Dia archaeological program is interesting and raises a number of important issues. It is not known if the "horizon" is a simple adoption of the geomorphology and soils science concept or if it has any anthropological meaning. Does it correspond to an occupation episode or to a lumping of many occupations within a loose chronological bag? Either option is possible, and the report does not clarify. The time range of the reconstituted Dia horizons varies from 300 years (Horizon IV: AD 800-1100; Discontinuity: AD 1100-1400; Horizon V: AD 1400-1700), to 500 years (Horizon I: BC 800-300; Horizon III: AD 300-800), and 600 years (Horizon II: BC 300-AD 300). The Shoma mound buildup may have been a relatively slow process as suggested by its 3.50 m deposit that spans approximately 2,500 years, from BC 800 to AD 1700. But a mud or clay house floor used for 500 or 600 years would be really exceptional. Paradoxically, Dia Shoma was a cemetery and an abandoned part of the mound complex for the major part of the regional primacy of the Ghana and Mali states. It is as if the town's potentials were thwarted and diverted by more powerful neighbors from the ninth to the early fifteenth century when they were allowed to re-enter the scene.

Essuk/Tadmakka

Essuk—"Tadmakka" to medieval Arab authors (Fig. 1)—has never been probed archaeologically. As the name "Essuk" suggests, it was a thriving medieval market place visited by merchants and caravan crews from North Africa and the Sudan. It was visited and described by Mauny (1961) but its scholarly fame, other than the descriptions provided by medieval Arab authors (Levtzion and Hopkins 1981), accrues from the presence of epitaphed tombstones in some of its many cemeteries. This material recorded, presented, and discussed by Morias-Farias (1990) is considered to be the earliest extant writing of West Africa. The epitaphs from some tombstones, dated between AD 1000 and 1150, refer to kings and princesses.

According to Mauny (1961:487), Essuk/Tadmakka, along with Ghana/Kumbi Saleh, was one of the most important centers of the medieval Sahara. The ruins of the town are located in the west periphery of the Adrar-n-Ifogha at some distance north of the Niger River Bend (Fig. 1). The town is elongated, oriented north-south, and stretched along a series of low hills parallel to Wadi Essuk. The latter drainage divided the medieval town into three distinct parts. The main town is found on the eastern shore of Wadi Essuk. Limited on the east by low hills, it measures approximately one kilometer by 200 m in maximum width. A smaller component on an "island" measures 200 by 100 m. And finally, the western town on the west bank of the wadi measures 500 m by 200 m. Essuk ruins cover 32 ha and R. Mauny (1961:487) estimates that its population peaked at 3,000 inhabitants. The town is surrounded by six graveyards: west, east, southeast, southwest, northwest, and northeast.

The earliest mention of Tadmakka is found in Ibn Hawqal's *Kitab Surat al-ard* ("The Picture of the Earth") written in three successive versions between AD 967 and 988 (Levtzion and Hopkins 1981:44). The town is mentioned among many others, including Sidjilmasa and Awdaghost. It was one of the places with "water-points around which are tribes of unheeded Berbers who are unacquainted with cereals . . . and have never seen wheat or barley or any kind of grain" (Ibn Hawqal in Levtzion and Hopkins 1981:46). Ibn Hawqal described the Berber tribesmen as in a state of wretchedness, wearing sashwise pieces of cloth, and subsisting on milk and flesh. Later on, he referred to the "kings of Tadmakka" (Ibn Hawqal in Levtzion and Hopkins 1981:50) and speculated that their origins may have been Sudan but their skin and complexion turned white as they moved north, far from the land of Kawkaw (Gao). In the eleventh century Al-Bakri provided another interesting description of Tadmakka in his *Kitab al-masalik wa-l-mamalik* ("The Book of Routes and Realms"). The distances between the major Saharan and Sudan town are spelled out, as well as their dominant economic activities. For Al-Bakri (in Levtzion and Hopkins 1981:85), Tadmakka is the town that most resembles Mecca, a resemblance supported by its name which means "the Mecca-like." As Mecca, it is a large town in a mountainous landscape with ravines (Moraes-Farias 1999). Its inhabitants are veiled Berbers who subsist on flesh and milk, as well as wild and cultivated grains. They dress in cotton fabric and robes dyed in red and their king wears special accoutrements of blue trousers, yellow shirt, and a red turban. Their currency is a "bald" unstamped pure gold dinar. Al-Bakri's final comments revolve around Tadmakka's women and their "surprising" customs: "Their women are perfect beauty, un-equalled among people of any other country, but adultery is allowed among them. They fall upon any merchant [disputing as to] which of them shall take him to her house" (Al Bakri in Levtzion and Hopkins 1981:85).

Later references to Tadmakka found in writings of Ibn Hammad, Ibn Said, Al Dimashqi, and Al Umari, as well as the anonymous *Kitab al-Istibsar* and the Ibadi excerpts (Levtzion and Hopkins 1981), do not add significantly new information when compared to Ibn Hawqal's and Al-Bakri's descriptions. The town, ruled by a Berber king, was a commercial hub, where everything from slave girls to camels could be purchased and sold.

Gao/Kawkaw

With Kumbi Saleh, Gao ("Kawkaw" in the Arabic historical sources) is one of the most investigated urban sites of West Africa. It is a twin-settlement with Gao-Saney in the east and Gao-Ancien in the west on the left bank of the Niger River (Fig. 1). According to Mauny (1961:498), the town of Gao-Saney may have measured 800 m by 300 m, with the constructions built in *pisé* or *banco*. Gao-Ancien, the other center, was much more important, stretched on 2 to 2.5 km from the Sané tributary to the Niger River, with width varying from 300 to 600 m.

Gao and the surrounding land have been surveyed and tested archaeologically from the beginning of the twentieth century (Desplagnes 1907; De Gironcourt 1920; Insoll 1996, 2000, 2003; Lhote 1942, 1943; Mauny 1950a, 1951, 1952, 1961; Sauvaget 1950). A detailed summary of the history of archaeological research at Gao and its vicinity can be found in Insoll's 1996 and 2000a edited volumes. In the 1900s, Desplagnes (1907) and De Gironcourt

(1920) surveyed the area, recorded different kind of sites, and provided useful information relied on by following generations of researchers.

Lhote, Mauny, and Sauvaget took the research further, excavating different kinds of sites, uncovering Gao's medieval architecture, and deciphering the inscriptions from a sample of royal tombstones. Lhote (1942, 1943) excavated a carnelian bead workshop on the shore of the Niger River and reconstructed the bead-drilling techniques. Mauny (1950a, 1951, 1952, 1961) undertook an important excavation program at both Gao-Ancien and Gao-Saney. He found a 43.4 m long and 27 m wide mosque, probed the cemetery of Gao-Saney, and found material evidence indicating contact with medieval North Africa. Sauvaget (1950) worked on a sample of ten "epitaphed" tombstones found at Gao-Saney in 1939. According to the deciphered inscriptions, all the tombstones analyzed belonged to royalty burials ranging from the twelfth to the thirteenth century AD. In one case, the marble tombstone may have been ordered from Gao, carved in Almeria in Spain and shipped to Gao where it was erected on the tomb of the deceased. In another, skilled stone carvers from Spain were invited to come to Gao with the needed raw materials to carve the tombstones (Sauvaget 1950:429). The context of the finds was poorly documented, but Sauvaget (1950:440) claimed it was obvious that "when the site [is] investigated more thoroughly and systematically, a critical analysis of the recorded epigraphic texts will produce sensational scientific results."

Flight (1975a, b, 1979, 1981) and Insoll (1996, 2000b, 2003) implemented the latest phase of archaeological research at Gao and provided a broader and more detailed picture of the settlement history. The medieval occupation of the Gao settlement complex ranges from the sixth or seventh to the late sixteenth century AD. The complex developed locally even if "the earliest origins . . . are still largely unclear" (Insoll 2000b:150). Gadei appears to have been the earliest settlement in Gao, founded following a population move from Bentiya/Kukiya in the mid-first millennium AD (Insoll 2000b:26). The city grew considerably in the ninth and tenth centuries. Economic, religious, and cultural relations between Gao and the Islamic world reached its apex (Insoll 2003:232-50). A citadel surrounded by an enclosing wall with gateways, and including mosques, wealthy merchants' houses, and very likely the king's palace, was built at the core of Gao-Ancien. Gao-Saney was the Muslim settlement and manufacturing center. In the late eleventh or early twelfth century, Gao-Ancien acquired more of a cosmopolitan flavor, and developed into the Islamized neighborhood. The evolution of the town complex from the fourteenth century onwards, a period during which Mali was the regional "superpower," is still poorly understood. If the fame of Gao and its integration in the Mali Empire are taken into consideration, "the absence of imports and recognizable monumental architecture dating from the mid-fifteenth and the late sixteenth centuries is surprising" (Insoll 2000b:27).

In summary, as was the case with Niani and Jenne-jeno, the Gao settlement complex was a transshipment locality. Goods moving one way or the other had to be shifted from one mode of transportation to the other. On the northbound route, kola nuts, animal skins, slaves, and foodstuff may have been transferred from human carriers or dugout fleet to camel caravans. The opposite may have operated for the southbound trade, with goods unloaded from caravans to be reloaded on dugouts or human carriers.

Jenne-jeno

Jenne-jeno, Kaniana, and Hambarketolo, excavated by S.K. McIntosh and R.J. McIntosh (1980, 1995), are some of the largest mounds of an extensive mound-settlement system located in the floodplain of the Inland Niger Delta. Jenne-jeno at 13°53'20"N and 4°32'25"W is a teardrop-shaped 33 ha mound, 760 m long, 550 m wide, rising to 8 m above the surrounding plain (McIntosh and McIntosh 1980:63). Hambarketolo, immediately north of Jenne-jeno from which it is separated by a shallow water body, measures 8 ha in surface extent. Kaniana, on the other hand, is located at some 2-3 km northwest of the modern town of Jenne. It is the largest of the sites tested in the mound complex, measuring 41 ha (S.K. McIntosh 1995, 1999).

An archaeological sequence outlining the development of Jenne-jeno and its hinterland, based on a combination of careful excavation, stratigraphic correlation, radiocarbon dates, pottery seriation, as well as other material culture items, has been worked out. The sequence is divided into four phases (I to IV), ranging from 250 BC to AD 1400 (McIntosh and McIntosh 1980:188-98).

Phase I (250 BC-AD 50) witnessed the pioneer settlement of farmers equipped with iron tools, who raised cattle and goats, cultivated African rice, fished, hunted, and foraged in the relatively rich deltaïc environment. Their dwellings may have been made of wattle and daub. The size of the original site is not known. It is however very likely that distinct domestic units settled in this optimal zone during the dry spell of the end of the first millennium BC, the site developing progressively from the fusion of these built discrete spots.

Phase II, AD 50-400, witnessed a relatively fast growth of the site and accordingly its population. The subsistence base remained the same but intensified resource exploitation and production certainly took place. It is inferred that Jenne-jeno's size shifted from 12 ha in AD 100 to 25 ha in AD 400 (S.K. McIntosh 1999:70). There was no significant change in architecture, but iron, stone and a few glass beads of Mediterranean origin attest for the connection with local and interregional exchange networks.

Jenne-jeno reached its maximum extent of 33 ha around AD 800, during Phase III (AD 400-900). Mud architecture was adopted and dwellings consisted of round *banco* huts. The practice of urn burial emerged and a cemetery developed in the Jar-field 1 area. The deceased are nonetheless buried without grave goods. In addition to iron, copper and gold are present in the area archaeological record, suggesting a connection to the long-distance trade network. The size of the local population is inferred to have peaked during the later part of Phase III. Even if estimating population densities from mound size generally tends to inflate unverifiable population figures (S.K. McIntosh 1999:71-73), this does not diminish the relevance of Phase III settlement data if the tight correlation made between surface sherd scatter characteristics and chronology holds.

Phase IV, ranging from AD 900 to 1400, closes the developmental sequence of the Jenne-jeno town complex. It started with the construction of a 3 m thick and 2 km long fortification wall around the 33 ha site. Rectilinear buildings appear at the turn of the millennium in AD 1000 (S.K. McIntosh and R.J. McIntosh 1980:191; S.K. McIntosh 1999:71) with more frequent North African imports, such as brass, glass, and spindle whorls. In fact, building activities are shown to have been particularly intensive and impressive. In the Jenne-jeno Probe M2 Phase IV deposit, "houses 7, 4, and 3 were built and destroyed within a short period of time" (McIntosh and McIntosh 1980:191). However, the construction of three successive mud-brick houses on the same spot during a period of 150 years does not seem particularly unusual as it amounts to a remarkable 50 years use-life per building. From AD 1200 on, terracotta statuettes representing warriors became part of the Jenne-jeno cultural repertoire up to the final demise and abandonment of the site around AD 1400.

Despite repeated claims (S.K. McIntosh and R.J. McIntosh 1984, 1993; S.K. McIntosh 1995:360-98, 1999:77), the developmental trajectory outlined for Jenne-jeno does not seem to depart significantly from that of the other West African towns reviewed so far in this introduction.

Kumbi Saleh

Despite a long-lasting dispute, Kumbi Saleh (Fig. 1) is now accepted and recognized as the genuine capital of the Ghana Kingdom (Berthier 1997; Holl 1985). Located at 15°46'N and 7°59'W, it was "rediscovered" by A. Bonnel de Mezieres in 1914 (Mauny 1950b, 1961; Berthier 1997). According to R. Mauny (1961:481), the town archaeological complex consists of two distinct parts. One, the "upper city," is spread over 49 ha (700 by 700 m) and is entirely made of stone houses and located in the northeast. The other, the "lower city," spread over 35 ha (500 by 700 m) is found in the southwest; stone houses are isolated and dispersed within an extensive urban area that was very likely settled and built up with *pisé* and mud-brick houses with thatched roofs. For Mauny (1961:481), the upper city was inhabited by Arab and Berber merchants up to the time of its destruction by the Mali army led by King Sunjata Keita in AD 1240. The lower city was inhabited by native Soninké (Mauny's "Sarakolé"). Mauny's estimates for the population of Kumbi Saleh range from 15,000 to 20,000 inhabitants—according to him, the largest town that has ever existed in the medieval Sahara (Mauny 1961:482).

For Berthier (1997:1), the Kumbi Saleh archaeological complex consists of a large central tell, two main cemeteries, and numerous isolated tumuli distributed within a 25 to 30 km radius territory. The main tell is surrounded by a wall. The delineated space has a perimeter of some 2.4 km for a surface of 44 ha. The northwestern cemetery measures 1,600 m in length and 800 m in width; the southern one, where spectacular pillared tombs were found, is smaller, measuring 700 m by 400 m (Mauny 1961:482). Berthier (1997) focused exclusively on the "stone town."

A series of excavation projects were conducted at the Kumbi Saleh ruins from 1914 to 1981. In 1915, Bonnel de Mezieres sank four probes in the central part of the town. P. Lazartigues followed in 1939 with a single probe on the east flank of the large south plaza. R. Mauny, P. Thomassey and G. Szumowski excavated the central mosque and a series of houses in another probe in the south from 1949 to 1951. J. Devisse, S. Robert, and D. Robert-Chaleix conducted a new survey in 1968 and organized a short excavation project in 1972. Their four probes were in the southwest of the tell. And finally, S. Berthier organized four field seasons between 1975 and 1981 and traced the evolution of a household unit from the ninth to the fifteenth century AD.

Berthier's (1997:12) archaeological deposit is 6.25 m thick, divided into six occupation levels arranged into four periods. Period A, the pre-urban phase dated to the late ninth to late tenth century AD, is documented at the bottom of the sequence at a depth varying from 6 to 6.25 m. The settlement appears to have been ephemeral as suggested by the absence of solid constructions and the low density of other cultural remains.

Period B (AD 1000-1100) material is confined to level I at a depth varying from 5.60 to 6 m. It was the initial phase of urban growth, with the construction of a mud-brick and stone rectangular house. Period C (eleventh to fourteenth century AD) represents the peak of urban growth. It is documented in levels II, III, and IV and characterized by the construction of an elaborate stone house that was remodeled several times. Finally, Period D (late fourteenth through early fifteenth century AD) witnessed the demise of the town. The chronology devised by Berthier (1997:12-30) is too dependent on radiocarbon dating alone to be genuinely reliable for such a recent archaeological episode; radiocarbon method is too blunt a tool for historical archaeology. The suggestion that Kumbi Saleh, the capital city of the Ghana Kingdom, reached the peak of its urban growth in the fourteenth century AD, when the Mali Empire was reaching its maximum power, is intriguing and not necessarily surprising. However, the lack of supporting data garnered from a detailed analysis of the portable material culture elements, added to the significant range of variation of C14 dates obtained from each of the delineated occupation deposits (Berthier 1997:28-30), makes this chronological assessment doubtful.

The chronological issue raised above deserves to be spelled out in more detail. The number of charcoal samples collected from each of the occupation levels varies from three (levels I and III) to five (levels 0 and IV). Five samples collected from the pre-urban level 0, with one contaminated, range from AD 590 (LY-3146) to AD 1180 (LY-2533); three samples from level I range from AD 620 (LY-3147) to AD 1220 (LY-2534); four samples from level II range from AD 1070 (LY-2537) to AD 1360 (LY-1520); three samples from level III range from AD 950 (LY-1341) to AD 1240 (LY-2506); five samples from level IV range from AD 1170 (LY-2508) to AD 1510 (LY-1525); and finally, four samples from level V range from AD 930 (LY-2540) to AD 1720 (LY-1521). In all the levels, the minimum dates vary from AD 590 to AD 1170 and the maximum from AD 1180 to AD 1720, with a difference of 580 for the former and 540 for the latter. Berthier's (1997:103) decision to narrow the time range offered by the radiocarbon readings summarized above to a ninth- to fifteenth-century occupation of the part of Kumbi Saleh she has excavated is driven by nonexplicit assumptions.

Unfortunately, the pre-urban levels were not probed, but urban development appears to have peaked in the tenth or eleventh century AD. Most of the houses exposed in the excavation were built of stone. But none of the excavation probes was large enough to allow for the exploration of the patterns of settlement layout. All the houses excavated by Mauny and Thomassey (1951, 1956) and Berthier (1997) are elongated and narrow. All the excavation projects have focused on the main tell. The Soninké part of the settlement has not yet been probed. If the Soninké were indeed the natives and the founders of the site, which was inhabited by the king, their settlement may and should provide a more accurate indication of the very beginnings of the town history. According to Al-Bakri, writing in the middle of the eleventh century:

[T]he city of Ghana consists of two towns situated on a plain. One of these towns is inhabited by Muslims, is large and possesses twelve mosques, in one of which they assemble for the Friday prayer. . . . The king's town is six miles distant from this one and bears the name of Al-Ghaba. Between these two towns there are continuous habitations. The houses of the inhabitants are of stone and acacia wood. The king has a palace and a number of domed dwellings all surrounded with an enclosure like a city wall. [cited in Levtzion and Hopkins 1981:79-80]

Ghana kings and very likely many of the high ranking members of the kingdom did not convert to Islam: "in the King's town, not far from its court of justice, is a mosque where the Muslims who arrive at this court pray" (Al-Bakri in Levtzion and Hopkins 1981:80). The short chronology outlined by Berthier (1997) deals with the influx of Berber, Arab, and North African merchants who were part of the widespread trade diaspora that settled in Saharan and Sahelian towns from the ninth century onwards.

Marandet

Marandet (Maranda) is located south of Agades, in the eastern confine and at the foot of the Tigidit cliff in the Niger Republic. This medieval center is mentioned in most of the early Arabic historical sources. It is referred to by Al-Yakubi writing in the ninth century AD, Ibn al-Faqiq in the early tenth century, Al-Massudi and Ibn Hawqual in the middle of the tenth century, and finally by Al-Idrissi in the middle of the twelfth century AD (Levtzion and Hopkins 1981). Maranda was "rediscovered" by a French army officer, Lieutenant Prautois, in 1952. Prautois, based at Agades and following R. Mauny's suggestion, went to the area and found impressive archaeological remains of an ancient city being eroded by the meandering of the local intermittent stream, the Kori Marandet. Prautois sank a number of probes in the shallow archaeological deposit he found, the largest of which measured 50 m² (Grébénart 1985:350, 1993:375; Mauny 1953). But more important, he located a surprising accumulation of conical clay crucibles on the shore of the kori, scattered over an area of approximately one hectare, and clustered into about fifty workshops. Some copper ingots, 27 cm long and 1.5 cm thick, were collected from the same area. H. Lhote (1972b) visited Maranda in 1971 and 1972, tested several new spots on the site, and reported additional information on conical-shaped clay crucibles. He considered these pieces to have been used in gold working. But this inference was later shown to be inaccurate. D. Grebenart (1985, 1993) initiated a new archaeological project on Maranda in 1981. Marandet I, a small settlement that may have measured one hectare, developed on the shore of the Kori Marandet. The cultural deposit, partially destroyed by the stream, may have been more than 2 m thick. A number of pits and furnace remains (thirteen in total) inserted in the preserved archaeological deposit were exposed and many of them still contained a large amount of cone-shaped clay crucibles. By-products of metal production, including iron and copper implements, as well as traces of lead, are particularly noteworthy. "The total amount of these crucibles is particularly high. 42,500 specimens were counted, but the total amount may be around 200,000" (Grébénart 1993:376). According to Grébénart (1993), Marandet I was the craft quarter of a much larger town that developed at the foot of the Tigidit cliff. The set of radiocarbon dates obtained so far indicates the occupation of Marandet I to range from the third to the tenth century AD. "It is, however, only from the sixth century AD that the dated charcoal samples are associated with the crucibles, with the peak of metallurgical activities taking place in the ninth to tenth century AD" (Grébénart 1985:379).

Sincu Bara

Sincu Bara, at 15°42'N and 13°23'W, is an extensive site measuring 67 ha and located on the left bank of the Sénégal River in the Middle Sénégal Valley (Bocoum and McIntosh 2002; McIntosh and Bocoum 2000; Thilmans and Ravisé 1980). It was one of the major settlements of the Tekrur Kingdom even if it cannot be related to any of the Tekrur localities mentioned in the medieval Arabic sources (Levtzion and Hopkins 1981). The site was an aggregate of different mounds that were fused into a single archaeological locality. It has an irregular crescent shape, concave in the south, with tips in the west, southeast and northeast.

Sincu Bara was investigated in the 1970s by G. Thilmans and A. Ravisé. They conducted six excavation campaigns from 1973 to 1978 and published their monograph in 1980. They probed an area of 180 m^2 and exposed a stratigraphic sequence of some 3.56 m in thickness. The village appears to have been settled from the early fifth to the mid-eleventh century AD (Thilmans and Ravisé 1980:86-87). They made spectacular discoveries of alloyed copper artifacts such as disks, bells, and 7,500 brass viroles, as well as cowries, elephant tusks and an impressive assemblage of channeled and slipped wares. But their interpretation of the settlement history, according to which the whole archaeological sequence exposed at Sincu Bara attests to a single homogeneous occupation, was marred by postdepositional processes they were unaware of. A new project was launched by H. Bocoum in collaboration with S.K. McIntosh in 1991-1992. "The results of these excavations provide considerable new information about the chronology of occupation and metallurgy at the site, necessitating a substantial revision of the occupational history" (McIntosh and Bocoum 2000:3; Bocoum and McIntosh 2002).

Instead of one long and single occupation, the Sincu Bara archaeological sequence was divided into four phases based on an assortment of variables including radiocarbon dates, the site's stratigraphy, and a pottery sequence. Phase I material found at the bottom of test pit 3 is particularly loose and may have resulted from the redeposition by erosion agencies (McIntosh and Bocoum 2000:37). It is nonetheless suggested to "correspond to Phase Ia Iron Age Assemblage at Cubalel" which is dated from 0 to 250 AD (McIntosh and Bocoum 2000:39, Fig. 22). This early if loose occupation is followed by a hiatus that may have lasted for one and half centuries, from AD 250 to 400. The occupation of Sincu Bara resumed in Phase II, dated from AD 400 to 600. The exposed surface presents evidence for intensive iron smelting, organized into batteries of cylindrical furnaces. The settlement appears to have been a small mixed farming community, whose inhabitants reared cattle, sheep, and goats, cultivated millet, fished in the nearby river and seasonal ponds, and hunted and gathered wild resources. There are minor changes in the material culture during Phase III, dated from AD 600 to 800-900(?). The settlement was still inhabited by mixed farming and herding, potters, iron-smelters and blacksmiths. There is a significant increase in the frequency of hearths and pits documented in the archaeological record but the processes at work are still poorly understood. Finally, the Phase IV deposit at the top of the stratigraphic sequence includes some house remains, large pits, and gravel platforms. Brass and other alloyed copper artifacts

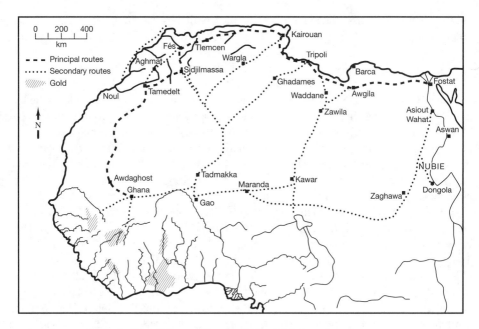

Figure 2. Trans-Saharan trade routes in the eighth through tenth century.

are more common. The deposit appears to date from AD 800-900 to 1100-1200(?) when the occupation of Sincu Bara seems to end. Surprisingly, the end of Sincu Bara occupation in the twelfth century appears to coincide with the peak of the Ghana Kingdom's power and influence. It is not stretching the evidence too far to suggest that this may indicate the end of Tekrur existence as an independent state.

Conclusion

The short review of the archaeology of a number of West African towns presented above focused on the Saharan, Sahelian, and Sudano-Sahelian zones. However, one must keep in mind that even in the best excavated cases the "unknown" by far outweighs the "known." This having been said, one is struck by the overwhelming locational and developmental similarities shared by most of the towns reviewed in this introduction.

Locationally, all the reviewed towns were built along the shores of an intermittent or perennial water course: Azugi in the confluence of a braided wadi, Awdaghost on the right bank of the Noudache, Niani on the Farakole and Sansandi, Dia on the Diarra, Jenne-jeno in the wetlands environment of the Inland Niger Delta, Gao/Kawkaw at the River Niger Bend, Essuk/Tadmakka on both shores of Wadi Essuk, Marandet on Kori Maranda, Azelik/Takkada in the middle of the fan-shaped headwater of the Azawagh drainage, and finally, Sincu Bara on the left bank of the Sénégal River. The location of Kumbi Saleh, far from any significant water course, has always intrigued many archaeologists (Mauny 1961).

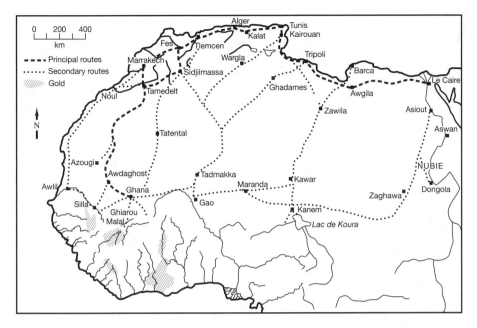

Figure 3. Trans-Saharan trade routes in the eleventh through thirteenth century.

In terms of developmental sequence, two towns, Dia and Jenne-jeno, were founded in the first millennium BC, Dia during the first quarter of the millennium around 800 BC, and Jenne-jeno during the last quarter around 250 BC. Both localities were settled with fluctuating populations up to the early fifteenth and seventeenth or eighteenth century AD. With the notable exception of Azelik and Azugi, most of the reviewed towns had their roots in the first half of the first millennium AD. The middle of the first millennium AD appears to have been particularly favorable for the emergence of urban centers, as is the case for Niani, Kumbi Saleh, Gao, Marandet, and Sincu Bara. The peak of urban growth occurred in the ninth to eleventh century AD, manifested by the acceleration of the pace of construction and reconstruction, and in the case of Dia, Jenne-jeno, Azugi, Kumbi Saleh, Gao, and Sincu Bara, the growth in size. At the very beginning of their different histories, each town seems to have been the center of a relatively small polity, ruled by a king. The intensification of local, regional, and Trans-Saharan social and economic relationships generated the influx of merchant and scholar diasporas from the Sahara, North Africa, and the Arabo-Muslim world (Fig. 2). The consolidation of political and economic power, peer polity competition, and the resulting expansion of the strongest polity, or polities, generated the rise and fall of a succession of states. The Ghana Kingdom, with Kumbi Saleh as the capital, emerged as the dominant regional power in the ninth or tenth century AD, and, with population fluctuations, lasted until AD 1200 when it fragmented into competing regional polities. The Mali Empire that emerged from the conquest of multiple regional polities toward the middle of the thirteenth century (AD 1230-1250) stretched from the Atlantic coast of the Senegambia

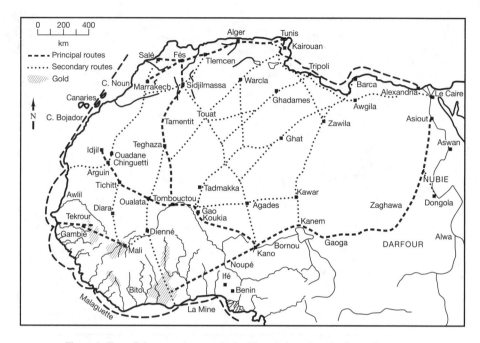

Figure 4. Trans-Saharan trade routes in the fifteenth through early sixteenth century.

to the Tilemsi Valley. Consequently, most of the towns reviewed in this introduction may have been at one time or another under the tutelage of the Mali (Mansa) kings. This was certainly the case for Niani, Kumbi Saleh, Jenne-jeno, and Gao. Dia seems to have been abandoned. Essuk would have remained an independent commercial hub, and Azelik was founded later, taking over the production of copper and salt that was previously dominated by Marandet (Fig. 3).

The decline of Mali and the expulsion of Muslims from Spain resulted in an eastward shift of the main trade routes. The fragmentation of the Mali Empire initiated another cycle of regional polity competition. The consolidation phase resulted in the emergence of the Songhai Empire centered on the Niger Bend in the fifteenth century. The Songhai emperors' power probably extended eastward to include Azelik (Fig. 4).

The towns were centers for social, economic, political and other activities. Their spatial layout is not always well known and the predominant domestic architecture is even less known. Kumbi Saleh and Gao were twin cities (Insoll 2003). Niani was an extensive mound complex. Azugi had a central fortress. Gao had a walled Acropolis with heavily built gateways. Dia had a series of narrow streets with rectilinear buildings with enclosed courtyards; mosques and an unusually large building are found at Azelik. The shape and structure of domestic units is more often than not completely unknown for most of the towns, with the exception of Kumbi Saleh, and a minor portion of Niani. Beside the presence/absence of imports that may range from regional craft products to sumptuary items from faraway lands, it is difficult to probe and assess the nature and characteristics of the transformations that may have been at work within each town society. Were the towns divided into socially/ethnically exclusive neighborhoods? What were the shape, size and structure of ordinary household units? How did these household units initiate or adjust to fluctuating social and economic circumstances? None of the simple issues raised above can be addressed using the record published from the archaeological work conducted in the sites reviewed in this introduction. Only the site of Tegdaoust—"Awdaghost" of the medieval writers, and the term which will be used in this book—allows for such a research project to be implemented, for reasons that will be clarified later in Chapter 3. This monograph is an archaeological analysis of households in a West African medieval town.

—2—

The Archaeology of Households
Theory and Expectation

Introduction

One of the fundamental building blocks of modern human societies is the core unit of socialization, where children are nurtured, groomed, protected, and educated to become full adult members of their communities. While standards of education vary considerably from society to society, the nurturing of children is universal. More often than not, the core social module in which people with kinship ties live in a more or less permanent daily interaction is coeval with their residential unit. The household, mono- or multifamily, is thus a core unit in the production and reproduction of any society. The fine-grained analysis of how households operate and adjust is crucial for any serious investigation of social change. The relevance of the household in the archaeology of social transformations is hard to dispute and does not need long and redundant justification.

The concept of "household" (*concession* or *maisonnée* in French) which is so common in sociology and ethnology has never taken hold in African archaeology and is not therefore a theoretical construct currently in use in West African studies. There are many reasons for this. The most important is the small size of most excavations. With a handful of exceptions (DeCorse 2000; Devisse 1983; Holl 1986, 1990, 1993, 2002; Polet 1985; Robert-Chaleix 1989), most of the excavation programs conducted in West Africa with a special focus on the last two millennia (cf. Berthier 1997; Insoll 1996, 2000) have used excavation units too small to provide the kind of spatial resolution needed for the archaeology of household. The material brought to light through the Awdaghost long-term archaeological project is thus unique not only by West African standards as will be shown later; it makes it possible to study the rise and demise of a West African medieval trade town through the lens of household archaeology.

What Are Households?

A functional definition of "household" is difficult because the characteristics of this social unit vary from one society to another (Blanton 1994; Deetz 1982; Kent 1990; Kramer 1982; Wilk and Rathje 1982). For Blanton (1994:5), *household* refers "to a group of people co-residing in a dwelling or residential compound, and who, to some degree, share householding activities and decision-making." For Hammel (1980:251), the household may be defined as "the smallest grouping with the maximum corporate function." Accordingly, if the different activities carried out by a household are conceptualized as constituting "activity spheres," we can see that these spheres overlap considerably. "A group that shares a living space (co-residence), a group that shares the activities of food preparation and consumption, and a group that socializes children often overlap completely; they are one and the same. Defining the household in a particular social setting does not require that each household has the same overlapping spheres of activity but that in each we find . . . the smallest groupings with the maximum corporate function" (Wilk and Netting 1984:5). Linares (1984:407) elegantly summarizes the difficulties involved in the precise definition of households.

> Households have been variously defined in the literature as co-resident domestic groups . . . , as places where individuals reside . . . , as agglomerations of "kin and non-kin ordered by norm specific to sex and marital status" . . . and as processes rather than facts. . . . Other scholars . . . have avoided definitions and typologies, emphasizing instead the polysemic nature of the word *household*, which may connote a physical space, the individuals residing in it, and the kinship ties binding co-resident domestic units. As a handy but imprecise word for an institution characterized by its flexibility, indeterminacy, and multiple functions, households are what households do.

Despite the polysemy and the extraordinary flexibility of the institution, households clearly perform five categories of activities: production, distribution, reproduction, co-residence, and transmission. The first two spheres of activities are directly related to socioeconomic organization, the third to the biological reproduction of individuals, the fourth to the structural features for habitation, and the last to the transmission of wealth and social position from one generation to the next.

The Economic Dimensions

The economic dimensions of households can be split into elementary components set in a spectrum from procurement through processing, distribution, and consumption of resources and goods. Accordingly, the household is at the same time a production and a consumption unit.

Units of production may be defined as minimal labor communities in which part or the total range of a production process is accomplished (Digard 1981:170). It is particularly difficult to translate such a definition into archaeological terms, due to the overlapping of varied and diverse activities within the same archaeological context. It is nonetheless possible to delineate clusters of artifacts into specific activity areas, to identify an archaeological feature with a specific function, or a site with a special purpose. These activity areas, archaeological features, or sites may indicate, for example, the procurement of raw material such as clay or metal ore, the processing of these raw materials in potters' or blacksmiths' workshops, or even the hunting or butchering of large animals in butchering sites. These archaeological remains reflect different units of production. If they are scattered all over the landscape, it will be difficult to assess the nature of the social entities that created the archaeological imprints. Matters are much easier if these activity areas and archaeological features are confined within well-delineated boundaries, as is the case for walled compounds. In this case, however, units of production overlap significantly with units of consumption.

Units of consumption are defined as the minimal social entity in which individuals interact daily and share food and other commodities, such as shelter. Analytical differentiation between production and consumption is theoretically valid, and based on the assumption that production is a precondition to consumption; however, there is always a part of one in the other. Situations of shared consumption of food and other commodities may vary from specific and strict social circumstances to more generalized and long-lasting ones. The use of space is palimpsestic in nature; repeated use of the same area for the same production or consumption activity results in the creation of detectable archaeological signatures. There is little doubt that site structure is patterned in the archaeological record. However, this patterning results from both past behaviors and site formation processes. In order to identify and understand past behavioral structures, the taphonomic integrity of archaeological contexts must first be established (Schiffer 1972, 1987) to avoid the "Pompeii premise" (Binford 1981). Two sets of problems should be considered when analyzing site structure if one wishes to infer both technological and social organization from the archaeological record (Oswald 1984:297-306): (1) the mechanical characteristics of activities, and (2) their sociotechnological contexts. The first category includes the procedures and material associated with all activities which cross-cut all social and ethnic affiliations and establish the basic requirements for every task. The second category limits the way in which space can be organized to accommodate the mechanical needs of any activity; it can also modify the spatial patterning but cannot override it. In summary, activities, whether part of procurement, processing, distribution, or consumption, have scheduling patterns that depend on basic characteristics such as frequency, periodicity, duration, number of participants, facility requirements, and bulk of the mobilized materials.

Production systems are either diverse, requiring the execution of different tasks simultaneously, or simple, with streamlined productive activities executed successively. Seen as a labor group, the household can be expected to face yearly fluctuations of workloads that may have strong influence on its optimal size. At some times of the year, the labor demand is low. At other times, it is very high and may generate activity "bottlenecks." The social unit needs coping strategies to handle variation in labor requirement and productive tasks. The coping strategy will have to integrate within the yearly cycle both the absolute timing of the productive tasks and their sequencing or ordering.

Some testable hypotheses about the direction and the nature of the household adaptation to differences in scheduling can be generated from the perspective sketched above. It can be expected "that the more simultaneous the labor requirements of major productive tasks within the yearly cycle, the more tendency we will see for larger household groups. Unless there is some other reason for large households to exist, [one will] expect that linear tasks arranged in a simple yearly cycle favor the small household as a productive group" (Wilk and Netting 1984:7-8).

Demographic and Social Reproduction Dimensions

Biological and social reproduction are intimately linked to the demography of households. During the life cycle of households, there are variations in demographic structure, number of members, social position, and economic status. Focusing on rural and peasant societies, Chayanov (1966; cf. Durrenberger 1984:39) has shown that there are sets of structural relations between the demographic composition of households, their potential labor force, their farming capacities and agricultural output. He has demonstrated that the same household is a different "working machine" according to its position in its life cycle. There are periods of increasing labor-force potentials followed by periods of decrease.

At the heart of Chayanov's approach to the analysis of peasant economies is the idea that, technology being constant, there is a natural limit to increasing output, determined by the balance or unstable equilibrium between the increasing drudgery of labor and the decreasing marginal return of output. For Chayanov (1966:5-6), the amount of labor product is determined mainly by: (1) the size and the demographic composition of the working household and the number of its members capable of work, then, (2) the productivity of the labor unit, and (3) the degree of self-exploitation through which the working members effect a certain quantity of labor units in the course of the year. He singled out some key variables, or mainly their intersections, to model the dynamics of peasant farm organization. These are: the *consumer/worker ratio*, which varies with the life cycle of the household, and the *marginal utility/drudgery ratio*, which limits the amount of labor input at certain levels. "Thus every family, depending on its age, is in its different phases of development a completely distinct labor machine as regards labor force, intensity of demand, consumer/worker ratio, and the possibility of applying the principle of complex cooperation" (Chayanov 1966:60). Through what he termed the "natural history" of the household, Chayanov developed the concept of demographic differentiation, according to which the size and the internal composition of households vary from the time of marriage of a young couple through the growth of their children to working age, and finally the marriage of this second generation.

Chayanov's findings present the researcher with robust and testable propositions. The fact that there is strong correlation between the demographic structure of a household, its size, its potential labor force, its wealth, its social position, and probably its spatial layout is amenable to archaeological model building. The household dynamics outlined above, linked to the process of generational segmentation, may be useful to understand the processes of change in the size and structure of domestic units, as well as settlement expansion or contraction at both intra- and inter-site levels.

A number of anthropologists have observed the dynamics of households in some of their case studies, at local and cross-cultural levels (Arnould 1984; Blanton 1994; Bohannan and Bohannan 1968; Dumas-Champion 1983; Hill 1982; Kunstadter 1984; Linares 1984; Netting et al. 1984; Sahlins 1969; Wilk 1984; Wolf 1984). In all the cases, kinship is the basic foundation of households, since very low proportions of members are unrelated to the household head, whether by consanguinity, marriage, adoption, or clientship. Depending on socioeconomic and historical circumstances, multi- or nuclear family households may predominate, one shifting into the other if necessary. Post-marital patterns of residence, virilocal, matrilocal, neolocal, or undifferentiated, are crucial to this type of analysis. Neolocal and undifferentiated post-marital residence favor the formation of nuclear family households. Virilocality and matrilocality tend to generate multifamily households. The latter category includes two main variants: one consists of the extended multigenerational family in which parents, their married children, and their grandchildren live together. The other is the polygamous family, with a household head living with multiple spouses. These distinctions may be blurred in particularly dynamic situations (Arnould 1984:138; Linares 1984:407).

In dealing with regions in India and northern Nigeria which are characterized by dry-grain farming, Hill (1982:91-92) observed that married sons find considerable difficulty in establishing independent, viable households that are dependent mainly on farming their own land, unless they receive some help from their fathers. But fathers generally prefer family to hired labor. Thus, they are usually anxious to retain the services of their married sons as much as possible, especially since the heads of large extended households are apt to be well respected by the village community. At the same time this generates tensions between generations. Bohannan and Bohannan (1968) have found the same feature among the Tiv, where a large compound with many wives and children is the optimal type of maximization for any individual Tiv, leading to prestige and wealth.

The Spatial Dimension

The household as a social unit can also be conceptualized in spatial terms as a microterritorial module. Space as considered in human interaction is not a given, static physical category. It represents sets of specific patterns regarding, for instance, activities, social distance, and relations of production. Once space has been bounded and shaped, it is no longer merely a neutral background; it exerts its own influence, it becomes, following Ardener's words (1981:13), a social map. The spatial dimension of households is the key element for any coherent archaeological study of these social units. The visibility of such units in the archaeological record is one of the stumbling blocks researchers have to deal with. The "co-residence" factor, while being one of its necessary conditions, raised a number of difficult problems (Kramer 1982a, b; Linares 1984). C. Kramer (1982a) advocates caution and warns archaeologists against the pitfalls of the reconstruction of households in archaeological sites. Deetz (1982:717) insists on the fact that "households" and "houses" are not always the same thing. Conditions of preservation, the extent of excavation, sampling error, and punctual analogy can generate serious shortcomings. However, even if the relations between households, house, and families are quite complex, it seems unquestionable that households are a real socioeconomic microcosm with a necessary spatial dimension. "Yet a doubt has been frequently raised as to the status of 'residence' as a criterion for the analysis of the family, whether comparisons are being made over space or through time. There are nonetheless perfectly sound reasons for considering that the knot of people who sleep and frequently, if not invariably, take meals together under the same roof constitute a unit for social analysis, and can form a basis for revealing inter-society comparisons, particularly if due attention is given to the means by which that unit has been brought together" (Smith 1984: ix).

Assuming adequate excavation methods have been implemented, the household presents many advantages as an archaeological unit of analysis for the study of past societies, at local, regional, and cross-cultural levels. First, this unit may be well delineated spatially, especially if the building material and architectural techniques are bulky. Second, patterns of distribution of activity areas in that spatially circumscribed unit may allow for an analysis of the internal structuration of the domestic domain. Finally, when the household is considered as the primary unit of social reproduction (Friedman and Rowlands 1977; Sahlins 1968, 1976; Tringham 1983:4), it may allow for a sound and empirically based discussion of long-term social change. Changes in construction techniques, building material, and dwelling layout more often than not reflect shifts in demography, wealth, and status; they are anchored on a shared cognitive module of what a "house" has to look like. "The spatial structure of any house, even one not overtly manifesting potent symbols, reinforces to some degree a customary pattern of interaction among its occupants and thus instills and reinforces a cognitive model" (Blanton 1994:19). As a built space, the household domain clearly takes into consideration the dialectic relationship involved in binary opposed concepts, such as public/private, insider/outsider, male/female, or parent/child. They are, however, part of a dynamic web of relationships that are shaped and reshaped according to circumstances. Blanton's (1994) comparative method, in which floor plans are graphs, illustrates differences in household strategies and their range of variation. It must, however, be paired with analysis of the shifting patterns of activity areas.

Expectations

Despite a certain amount of variability, households must be considered one of the core features of modern human societies. As far as archaeological investigation is concerned, the spatial dimension of households is principally what makes them amenable to systematic and empirically sound research. Depending on the nature of the building material used, household space may be more or less coherent, well delineated, and self-contained.

How are such units structured in the archaeological record? What is their range of variation and structural consistency? How and why did they change through time? One would expect a household to include a "generalized" activity area surrounded by special purpose spaces. Accordingly, the balance between "generalized" and "specific" activity areas may shift depending on demography, wealth, location, gender and age composition of the household membership, or a differential combination of any of the variables mentioned above. Household space is therefore a dynamic arena that may reflect the sociological profile of its members. Large and wealthy families can be expected to live in more segmented and internally differentiated household units. Increasing or decreasing general wealth is expected to impact the characteristics of household units. A longitudinal analysis of the shifting spatial organization of households is the most effective strategy to study past social change. The material from Awdaghost can be used to open a new research frontier in the archaeology of West African towns.

—3—

Awdaghost Archaeological Program

Introduction

The ruins of Awdaghost were found in the Noudache circus in the central part of the Hodh, in south-central Mauritania. They are located in the middle of a desert landscape, and it took significant time and energy, in addition to field logistics, to organize the Awdaghost archaeological research program. Not surprisingly for that time, none of the key members of the project was a trained archaeologist. They nonetheless shared a profound interest in understanding the West African past, and more precisely the segment during which Arabo-Moslems and Sub-Saharan Africans were pulled together in the same Islamic world system, the Dar al-Islam.

The excavation program of Awdaghost started in 1960 and lasted for fifteen years. The field component was followed by laboratory work, data analyses, and the publication of a series of books and articles (Robert et al. 1970; Robert and Robert 1970; Saison 1970, 1979; Vanacker 1975, 1979; Devisse 1983; Polet 1967, 1985). On all criteria, the program can be considered to have been successful. It is therefore interesting to recount how enthusiastic young scholars succeeded in launching a remarkable archaeological project in 1960.

The Early Stage

During the summer of 1960, there was an intensive correspondence between Jean Devisse from the Department of History at the University of Dakar and Raymond Mauny from the Department of Prehistory and Protohistory of the IFAN (Institut français d'Afrique noire). Devisse was in France for his summer vacation and Mauny had stayed in Dakar to follow up with the organization of the Awdaghost expedition. The letters convey a sense of urgency with the preparation moving along four major fronts (IFAN Archives, file XV-5-MAU).

1) The funding of the expedition. Funding was obtained through private sources of CED-DIMOM (Centre de documentation et de diffusion des industries minérales et énergétiques), an association of industrialists interested in the spread of science and technology in the educational system. CEDDIMOM funded the expedition through the club "Jeune Science" created by the University of Dakar Pedagogy Institute.

2) The organization of supplies, camping equipment, gas, tools, food, and drugs. The French army provided the expedition with all the needed camping material and field clothing and took care of the gas supply.

3) Field logistics. They were extraordinarily complicated and had to be coordinated by special request to Air France and the French Air Force for the transportation of the crew and to the army for freight trucks to carry the supplies from Dakar to Awdaghost via Tamchakett.

4) Diplomacy. Diplomacy was critical in 1960, when many of the former French colonies had acquired formal independence. Negotiations were conducted with Mauritanian officials for research permits, on issues such as the disposition of resulting archaeological collections, and for later export permits for study collections shipped to the University of Dakar and IFAN. In June, 1960, H. Masson, the rector (president) of the University of Dakar, sent a letter to the new Mauritanian Minister of National Education, informing the government of the archaeological project on the site of Awdaghost, referring to the institutions involved, the IFAN and the University, and specifying that the excavation was likely to take place at "Awdaghost, ancient city [in which ruins are] very likely next to the Tegdaoust well in the Rkiz, northeast of Tamchakett" (lettre de H. Masson, IFAN Archives, File XV-5-MAU*). At Aïoun-el-Atrous, the regional administrative center and the local landing strip, the expedition crew was welcomed and strongly supported by Mohamed Ould Dada, the district commissioner and cousin of the first president of the Islamic Republic of Mauritania.

Twenty-four students were enrolled in the expedition, supervised by a research crew of five faculty or research scientists: J. Devisse, S. Robert (both from the Department of History), and S. Daveau (Department of Geography) of the University of Dakar; and R. Mauny (Medieval History) and C. Toupet (Geography) from IFAN. The crew also included M.D.C. Quenum and M. Berger, representing CEDDIMOM, and Mrs. and Mr. Bracher, journalist and photojournalist. The expedition began on December 20, 1960, when the group of students boarded a train to Kidira. From there they drove a three-vehicle convoy with more than ten tons of supplies through Bakel, Selibaly-Kankossa, Kiffa, and to the rendez-vous point at Aïoun el Atrous. The research crew was flown from Dakar to Aïoun el Atrous on December 27, and met with the convoy there. The whole crew of students and staff drove from Aïoun el Atrous to Tamchakett on December 28, and Tegdaoust on December 29, 1960.

The first field season of the now launched Awdaghost archaeological program lasted from December 29, 1960, to January 10, 1961. The aims, achievement, and impact of this first expedition were widely publicized in newspapers and public lectures (*Afrique Nouvelle*, nos. 704, 712, 1961; *Dakar Matin*, May 21, 1963). The characteristics and extent of the research done during that first field season will be discussed later. Its political impact was much more important and palpable.

---

*This and the following communications and newspaper articles are in French. Translations are my own.

The public was informed of the launching of the Awdaghost archaeological campaign by the weekly paper *Afrique Nouvelle* in late January 1961 (no. 704). On March 29, 1961, the same weekly newspaper, the most important French West African weekly at that time and in its thirteenth year, published a stunning news story. The story covered the entire front page, the center spread on pages 8 and 9, and the last page, 16. For a well-circulated weekly paper to devote four of its sixteen pages to the story, it must have been a very important one. The organization of the display, the arrangement of sections and the structure of pages are instructive. The short editorial note set the tone and framed the context that explains the "media blitz" on the recent archaeological expedition of Awdaghost.

> We already had the opportunity to present the archaeological expedition conducted by a group of professors and students from the University of Dakar in the sands of Mauritania, in the search for the ancient African town of Awdaghost, which vanished in the 11th century.
> At a time when Africa, *now independent*, turns with passion to its past, for us this is an expedition of capital interest. Indeed, it appears that it allows for the veil that shrouded this historical enigma to be lifted.
> Here are the main elements of the Awdaghost dossier. [*Afrique Nouvelle*, No. 712, March 29, 1961: p. 8. Emphasis added.]

"Free" and "independent" Africa is emphatically presented as an equal partner, and the structure, organization, and selection and display of pictures aims to hammer this idea into the reader's mind. The articles are not signed but it is obvious that they were done by Mrs. and Mr. Bracher, the journalists who were part of the expedition staff. CEDDIMOM, as the industrialists' lobby and pressure group that funded the whole expedition, would have benefitted from such publicity.

There is a large 23.5 by 25.5 cm black and white photographic composition on the front page. The archaeological site of Awdaghost, with impressive architectural remains clearly visible, appears in the background with a group of four young men staged in the foreground (Fig. 5). The arrangement gives equal space to each of the selected crew members. The Europeans are young faculty members of the Department of History of the University of Dakar, and the two Africans are their students. The team of young adventurer-scholars are all dressed in army uniforms. The reader can feel the excitement of a major archaeological discovery.

The title in red running across the whole front page reads: "The discovery of Awdaghost." A more explicit and informative addition in black ink is written in the bottom right: "Twenty-four students and four professors from Dakar research African past in the sand." The staging of the front page intends to convey the thrill of adventure and the idea of commonality, mutual respect, and equality among those involved in this critical scientific venture. The key elements of the story are, however, found on pages 8, 9, and 16.

The spread on pages 8 and 9 is extraordinarily interesting. The title in red ink runs across both pages: "The Secret of Awdaghost—The Mysterious." A 17 by 18 cm black and white picture taken from the sandstone cliff east of Awdaghost with a view of the ruins is set in the upper left part of page 8. "Our Past" [*Notre Passé*] in bold uppercase letters runs vertically along the left margin of the photograph and connects the photograph with the editorial note.

Figure 5. Awdaghost on the front page of the weekly *Afrique Nouvelle*, March 29, 1961.

Excerpts from medieval Arabic sources, entitled "What History Says about It," are presented in the remaining four columns of page 8. These were compiled by the journalists, and consist of direct quotes from authors like Ibn Hawqal (before 977) and Al-Bakri (1067).

A two-column article by Raymond Mauny, entitled "Tegdaoust-Awdaghost," summarizes the purpose and achievement of the recent field season. He discusses the recent archaeological expedition, what Awdaghost was, its importance as a capital city, and finally, the surprising discovery of an unsuspected seventeenth-century town. Mauny concludes his paper by emphasizing the remarkable achievement of this short research expedition of only a few weeks' duration and reiterates the need for more research to be carried out in the future.

The student perspective is presented at the top of page 9 by Habibou Datt, a student of literature. He presents another complementary facet of the expedition, familiar to all those who have ever been involved in archaeological research in remote areas without roads. He describes the difficulties they had to overcome to drive the expedition's three-vehicle convoy to its destination. The heavy Berliet truck loaded with more than 10 tons of field gear and supplies was frequently stuck in the sand, usually more than ten times a day. It took eight days to travel 800 kilometers. He provides interesting glimpses into the daily life in the archaeological base camp that housed 24 students, 4 professors, a medical doctor, 13 workmen, 2 cooks and 2 guards. It is in Datt's piece that one learns that the field crew was supplied with fresh vegetables and extra food once a week by a French Air Force plane. Many other interesting details concerning daily schedule, meal routine and student work routines are described. He concludes by emphasizing the students' excitement and willingness to be part of future research expeditions in what promises to be just the beginning of an extraordinary adventure.

On the bottom left of page 9 is a view of the archaeological site, with a jumble of collapsed stone walls in the background and two students standing next to and sitting on part of a preserved wall. On the right is a compact summary of the outstanding preliminary results of the 1960-1961 field season, compiled by the paper's editorial staff, which makes three points. First, it mentions the discovery of at least two distinct towns, an early and a late one. The early one, it says, corresponds very likely to the medieval Ghana city of Awdaghost. Second, even if this discovered town is not Awdaghost, Tegdaoust (a Berber word) is a historical site inhabited for centuries, and as such worth excavating to improve the knowledge of that segment of West African history. Third, it mentions the unexpected discovery of the late town dating from the seventeenth century.

On page 16, the Awdaghost archaeological program is considered within the broader context of research in African history. The full-page article entitled "Professor Devisse Talks about Historical Research and Teaching in West Africa" is illustrated with a black and white photograph of Serge Robert recording the depth of an excavated feature. Jean Devisse calls for a serious scientific foundation of African historical scholarship. In his views, the best way to achieve a certain measure of success is to train and associate young students with ongoing fieldwork. He insists on the originality of the Awdaghost expedition, claiming it triggered an inter-institution and international collaboration, and put African students into the situation of doing archaeological fieldwork for the first time. He predicts that "in a thirty-year period, much progress will be made in this field [archaeological excavations] and many aspects of African past life will be known." For Devisse, the development of scholarship in African history has four complementary axes: (1) the systematic recording and analysis of oral traditions; (2) the systematic search, recording and protection of all written sources in order to create a "genuine corpus" of fundamental texts on Sub-Saharan Africa history; (3) the teaching of history in middle and high school as well as college level; and (4) the training of future historians and scholars in the "perspective of a serious 'Africanization.'" He advocates curricula reforms and highlights the achievements of the history department of the University of Dakar. Devisse concludes with a preemptive defense against the accusation of "perpetuating an anachronistic 'cultural imperialism.'" He makes a plea to "implement scientific and reasonable solutions. To put in this task *the best the culture we represent* [emphasis added] has to offer. Such are the goals of our provisional presence in Africa."

In an article published in the August-September 1961 issue of the magazine *Tropiques* (pp. 19-21) and entitled "The University of Dakar Excavations in Mauritania," R. Mauny presented views similar to those of Devisse and Robert. After the second field season of December 1962–January 1963, Serge Robert gave a public lecture at the University of Dakar, summarized and published in the May 21, 1963, issue of the daily *Dakar Matin*. He elaborates the achievements of the second expedition that confirmed the existence of an impressive archaeological deposit reaching some five meters in thickness in some places, as well as the existence of an extensive early town. He delineates the research program for the future expeditions: (1) to survey and probe on the field the importance of the ruins detected on air photographs; (2) to assess the size and extent of the archaeological site in the central depression of the Noudache stream and the neighboring cliffs; and (3) to implement systematic scientific research through the opening of many archaeological probes on the ruins known so far only from surface inspection. Robert acknowledges the difficulties of such a research endeavor and alludes to the uncertainties still plaguing the identification of the known ruins with the Awdaghost of Arab geographers. A new and significant suggestion was made at the end of the lecture when Robert alluded to the creation of a "field school": "the principal aim of the research expedition," he said, "is to train an African elite eager to discover its past, and to discover that past in the best conditions of efficiency and scholarly rigor, away from sentimental myths and literary approximations."

It is clear in the articles and documents discussed above that the end of the Colonial period, and the accession of Africans to "freedom" and political independence, were the subliminal forces behind the Awdaghost project media blitz. The Colonial establishment, still holding positions of power and influence, had its own cleavages and competing factions. Not everybody was entranced by the archaeological program and some used obstruction tactics to delay or halt field projects (Devisse 1983:5-6). However, the program did go forward and after some thirty years, from 1960 to 1989, produced an impressive scholarship and a remarkable body of new finds. The field program lasted from 1960 to 1976 with a number of African and French students. All of the French students, Denise Robert-Chaleix, Jean Polet, Bernard Saison, and Claudette Vanacker, completed their doctoral research and earned PhD's in French universities. Surprisingly, none of the African students went that far within the Awdaghost archaeological program.

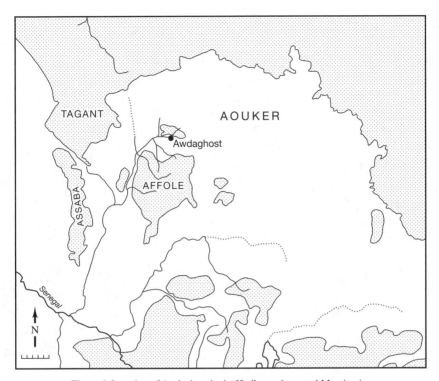

Figure 6. Location of Awdaghost in the Hodh, south-central Mauritania.

Encounters with the Ruins: The Early Field Seasons

The archaeological complex was found at 17°35' north latitude and 10°25' west longitude. It is located in the south flank of the Rkiz massif, in the Noudache circus (Fig. 6). The main site measures some 600 by 200 m, covering some 12 ha (Fig. 7). It is surrounded by many other sites and features of archaeological interest, including another settlement at approximately 1.2 km north, an exterior cemetery, a rock-art cave at Aguentour Labiod, and several used caves and rock shelters.

The first and exploratory field season focused on the most visible and well-preserved ruins in the west of the town. Jean Devisse supervised the excavation of an impressive building, a square measuring 40 by 40 m, with the hope that it would reveal the "Friday Mosque" alluded to by Al-Bakri (IFAN Archives: Mauny 1961, Interim Reports, pp. 1, 4). But the building happened to be a relatively recent seventeenth-century household unit with a large central courtyard and a maze of rooms. It was built on top of older buildings that seem to date from the medieval period. The probe was tested down to a depth of 4 m without reaching the sterile level. Mauny supervised the excavation of two probes. One probed the small mosque, 14 by 10 m, built with stone pillars and buttresses with the *qibla* at 91°, located a few meters north of the large central building. The other probe was 800 m northeast of the

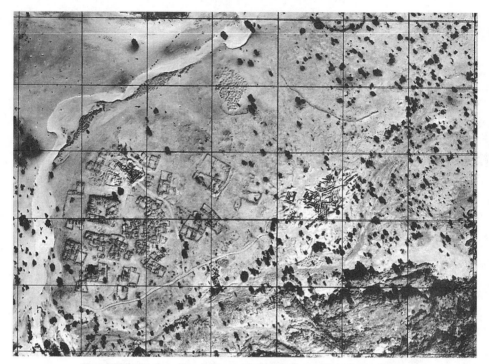

Figure 7. Aerial view of Awdaghost ruins with the Acropolis in the northeast.

main tell site: a large quadrangular 75 by 25 m "praying space" with the *qibla* at 94°, and a circular enclosure measuring 110 m in diameter, delimited by a 0.70 m thick wall made of sandstone blocks. The rock-art pieces from the Aguentour el Abiod cave that included some horse-drawn carts were also recorded.

It is clear from this summary of the first field season that the researchers were looking most carefully for archaeological evidence pointing to Islam. Archaeological probes were thus scattered around the best-preserved ruins. The problem of the archaeological identification of Awdaghost could hardly have been tackled with the material collected during that field season. Mauny was very well aware of that problem. He suggested a different tactic at the end of his interim report written on January 18, 1961: "more excavations have to be carried out, but this time in an area without the most recent ruins, and preferentially at the highest spot of the site, where there is a high probability of finding the thickest superimposed ruins deposit." Mauny's suggestion was adopted, and from 1962 onwards, excavations moved away from the recent ruins, shifted east, and focused on the main tell and its immediate periphery. Each excavation unit investigated by a French graduate student or the director of the expedition, Jean Devisse, was a coherent architectural unit.

The 1962-1963 field season lasted for only two weeks, from January 6 to January 19, 1963. In fact, genuine archaeological excavations were carried out for a maximum of eight days, January 12-19 (Devisse 1983:41). The excavation's intention was to uncover the stratigraphic sequence of the main tell in the northeast of the site. Two occupation levels were recorded at depths varying from the surface down to 2.00 m.

The 1963-1964 field season lasted from December, 1963, to January 16, 1964. Denise Robert and J. Devisse started to expand the excavation of the previous season. A coherent housing unit with a courtyard, a well, and four surrounding rooms was exposed and the probe was tested down to a depth of 3.80 m (Devisse 1983:61). At least five occupation levels are then documented. S. Robert, on the other hand, focused on the cemetery located in the north of the site, and with a group of students excavated a number of burials.

The 1964-1965 campaign lasted from December 29, 1964, to February 10, 1965. The excavation unit from the previous seasons was expanded to encompass approximately one-third of the Awdaghost Acropolis. The western and northern streets were fully exposed, providing an exciting vista into part of the town's structure and spatial layout. At the end of the season, a coherent quarter with three household units delineated in the west and north by two intersecting streets was exposed. The uncovered 2.80 m stratigraphy included seven or eight occupation levels (Devisse 1983:213).

Besides the Mauny and Devisse excavation probes tested in 1960-1961, at least four other excavation units were opened in different parts of the site and its immediate periphery between 1960 and 1965. C. Vanacker (1983) sank a 7.25 by 5.5 m test unit at some 300 m southwest of the main site. The uncovered archaeological sequence, some 2.50 m thick, attests to two major cultural deposits, the lower at 2.10-2.50 m below the surface, and the upper at 1.00-1.60 m. The lower deposit is interpreted as likely evidence of pastoral nomad presence (Vanacker 1983:297). The upper one is subdivided into three phases documented at 1.50-1.60 m below surface for phase A, 1.20-1.30 m for phase B, and 1.00-1.05 m for phase C. A small quadrangular house complex was built during the latest phase. It comprises a 5.50 by 4.25 m courtyard with two attached rooms along its west flank (Vanacker 1983:300). Most if not all the recorded cultural remains are of local origins (Vanacker 1983:301), making the relative dating of the site difficult at that stage of the research program.

S. Lebecq (1983) sank two excavation probes in a small isolated mound south of the main tell, on the left bank of the intermittent stream bed. Both probes, 45 m apart, were explicitly aimed at clarifying the site stratigraphy. Probe Z1 A was tested in a round house measuring 5.90 to 6.00 m in diameter and Z1 B in a rectangular two-room building measuring 7.30 by 5.60 m (Lebecq 1983:311). In both cases, the underlying sterile deposit was reached at 2.80 m below the surface. The cultural deposit consists of four occupation levels with the earliest level IV recorded at 2.50-2.70 m below the surface. Constructions with stone foundations appear in level III at 1.50/1.60 to 2.50 m as is the case for two 4 m deep pits claimed to be for refuse disposal (Lebecq 1983:315-16). The repertoire of cultural remains is particularly rich but the construction techniques are described as poor. Level II at 0.90-1.50 m documents an intermittent use of a spot that is devoid of architectural remains. And finally, level I, at 0.00-0.70/0.90 m, attests to the reoccupation of the area with the construction of two buildings: one a rectangular two-room house in the north and the other round, 5.90/6.00 m in diameter, with a central stone pillar (Lebecq 1983:322-23).

Thierno M. Bah participated in the 1963, 1964, and 1965 field seasons and used the material for his *maitrise* thesis at the University of Dakar. He supervised the excavation

of a house complex extended over a surface of some 100 m², the depth of the probe varying from 2.90 to 3.40 m (Bah 1983:327). The three-room house is rectilinear and oriented
north-south. It measures 10 m by 7 m, and was exposed in the topmost cultural level. An
elaborate drain channel was installed along the house's eastern wall. Neither the probe's
stratigraphy nor the sequence of finds from the earlier deposits were presented or discussed
in the 1983 report.

S. Robert excavated a series of medieval mosques in the northwestern part of the town.
These crucial architectural markers of the practice of Islam were carefully maintained and
preserved during the length of the field component of the research program.

In 1965, the medieval town uncovered in the Rkiz massif in south-central Mauritania
began to emerge. The material remains included a large portion of goods from North African
and Egyptian origins. After 1965, there was an organizational shift in the running of the field
operations. Each graduate student was given a coherent quarter to investigate, all resulting
in doctoral theses which, with a single exception, became books.

A Mature Field Program

The mature phase of the Awdaghost field project spans a period of ten years, from 1966 to
1976, when the excavation was discontinued because of subregional geopolitical unrest. D.
Robert-Chaleix and C. Richir surveyed a 10 km radius around Awdaghost to identify smaller
sites that were probably part of the town's social, economic and political catchment area.
They found three sites, Moulay Arbad, Sboueh Leadi, and Chigguettomi. All three appear
to have been settled by grain producers who colonized the hinterland of the big town where
prime agricultural land could be found. All three sites possessed large-scale storage facilities and a large number of caves. All of the surveyed caves were used for the construction
of large storage bins (Robert-Chaleix and Richir 1983:349).

Four major excavations were conducted during the years of the mature field program, all
by French graduate students. C. Vanacker (1975, 1979) excavated a craft quarter located at
some distance south of the main tell. Evidence for working metal, both iron and copper, and
for making pottery, beads, and many items, was found distributed among housing units. These
houses are generally small: one to two rooms with or without courtyards. The excavation
provided the material for a doctoral thesis presented at the University of Lille III in 1975.

B. Saison (1970, 1979) also excavated a craft neighborhood located in the southwest
and found a range of material record comparable to that from Vanacker's probe. Part of
the material was used for a *maitrise* thesis presented at the University of Lille in 1970. The
completed excavation provided the data for a doctoral thesis presented at the University of
Paris I in 1979.

The J. Polet and D. Robert-Chaleix probes were located on the main tell, later called
the Awdaghost Acropolis. The excavation unit supervised by J. Polet (1967, 1985) was
contiguous to the one excavated by Devisse in 1962-1965, and delimited in the east by
a north-south street. The area was part of an elaborate and sophisticated habitation zone,
with a stratigraphic sequence some 2.80 m thick. Part of the recorded cultural remains

were described in an "advanced degree" (*Diplome d'Études Supérieures*) thesis presented at the University of Lille III in 1967. The material from the completed excavation obtained after eight field seasons, from 1967 to 1975, was used for a doctoral thesis presented at the University of Paris I in 1980.

D. Robert-Chaleix's probe is contiguous to the Polet probe, and is located northwest of the Acropolis. It is delimited and connected to the rest of the town by a series of intersecting narrow streets. The probe was excavated in eight field seasons, from 1969 to 1976, and the collected data used for a doctoral thesis presented at the University of Paris I in 1985.

Finally, a number of students relied on their Awdaghost finds to complete their advanced studies or *maitrise* theses. S. Lebecq (1966, 1983) used the material from two houses he excavated in the south mound to write an advanced studies thesis presented at the University of Lille III. Cros (1968) used the material from the excavation of a house complex located in the northern part of the site for a *maitrise* thesis presented at the University of Paris I. Y. Babin (1967) excavated a house and presented an advanced studies thesis at the University of Lille III in 1967. J.B. Kiethega (1973) had participated in many successive field seasons from 1969 to 1974. He used the material from the excavation of a house he had supervised in the east of the site for a *maitrise* thesis presented at the University of Dakar in 1973.

The Devisse, Polet, and Robert-Chaleix excavation units, all located on the Acropolis, are contiguous. If combined, they provide an exceptional vista into the evolution of urban life and how that affected the structure of domestic space and household size.

The Awdaghost Program Major Publications

Beside training cohorts of students, the Awdaghost archaeological research program produced a number of monographs and edited volumes from 1970 onward. The series is entitled *Tegdaoust*, after the ethnonym of the most recent inhabitants of the area, an astute political but historically misleading decision.

Tegdaoust I: Recherches sur Aoudaghost is coedited by D. Robert-Chaleix, S. Robert, and J. Devisse (1970). The volume assembles most of the key Arabic historical sources pertaining to the town of Awdaghost in a long discussion termed "The Question of Audaghost." It includes a summary of the ongoing archaeological project and papers on the recorded rock-art sites. More recent ethnohistory of the "Tegdawost" is taken into consideration as well.

Tegdaoust II: Fouille d'un Quartier Artisanal, by C. Vanacker (1979), is a revised version of her doctoral thesis. She describes the spatial layout, architecture, and activities of a craft neighborhood.

Tegdaoust III: Recherches sur Aoudaghost is edited by J. Devisse (1983) with contributions from fourteen authors. It focuses principally on the 1960-1965 archaeological excavations in the east of the Acropolis, and the immediate periphery, with some regional survey material. The field archaeology is complemented by interesting and important specialists' reports. These include: a report on palaeobotany (by S. Van-Campo); an analysis of animal bones (by J. Bouchud and Devisse); an analysis of water table fluctuations tracked through changing well depth (by B. Moussié/Devisse); papers on glass weights, medal molds, and

Almoravid epigraphy on coins; and articles on typology and historical implications of decorated spindle-whorls and glass with geometric decoration. Another section discusses the problem of Awdaghost from an ethnohistorical perspective.

Tegdaoust IV: Fouille d'un Quartier de Tegdaoust, by J. Polet (1985), is a revised version of the author's 1980 doctoral thesis, focusing on the material and architectural evolution of the south-central part of Awdaghost Acropolis. The book presents a number of difficulties due to an over-emphasis on architecture (Holl 1988). Important archaeological features like wells, pits, and hearths are not described. Portable cultural remains are very rarely alluded to.

Tegdaoust V: Une Concession Médievale a Tegdaoust, by D. Robert-Chaleix (1989), is the fifth and last volume of the series. It is a revised version of her doctoral thesis dealing with the material and architecture of the western quarter of the Acropolis. The author seems to have taken advantage of the critical reviews of the previous volumes of the series and has presented an informative and well-balanced account of her research. There is an interesting attempt at stratigraphic correlation with a fourteen-page synthetic table. Local pottery and metal production are considered in the last two chapters of the book.

Conclusion

As graduate student at the Sorbonne, the author enrolled in Professor Jean Devisse's seminar "Current Research in African Archaeology." Awdaghost research was an important element of the seminar discussions. The Tegdaoust series was planned to include seven volumes that would have published all the doctoral theses. B. Saison's 1979 two-volume thesis was to be *Tegdaoust IV: Évolution Historique d'un Quartier Artisanal* (see Devisse 1983:2), but it was dropped from the series and remains unpublished. A seventh volume was intended to present the architecture and material from the north-central quarter of the Acropolis excavated from 1965 to 1975 by D. Robert-Chaleix and J. Devisse. This, too, was not published (see Devisse 1983:65). The published record from the Awdaghost archaeological program is by far the most remarkable achievement of French archaeology in West Africa. The size of the excavated sample is the most extensively and coherently exposed layout ever recorded in West Africa.

Because all these materials are still available in print, Awdaghost provides the perfect opportunity for addressing anthropological archaeology issues. In the Acropolis, with its large and continuous exposure combining three contiguous excavation probes, one can look at the structuring of household space and the dynamics behind the changes observed in the archaeological record.

—4—

The Pioneer Era
(AD 600-900)

Introduction

The earliest occupation of Awdaghost Acropolis is documented at depths varying from 2.30 to 2.80 m below datum in the east and southeast and 2.90 to 3.10 m below datum in the north and northwest (Table 1). The southeastern portion measures 85 m in length east-west and 31 m in width north-south. The surface consequently investigated covers an area of 1.736 m². The northwestern part is smaller, measuring 40 m in length east-west and 30 m in width north-south, with the excavated surface amounting to 1,200 m². The total surface exposed with archaeological evidence dating from the pre-urban phase is thus relatively important, amounting to 2,936 m².

The Prelude: Building Sequence 1 (Fig. 8)

The deposits at the bottom of the Awdaghost Acropolis archaeological sequence were unfortunately not investigated with the same level of dedication as the later urban ones. Numerous pits, postholes, hearths, and refuse dumps are mapped but poorly described. Diverse samples of artifacts were collected showing the settlement episode to have involved people with knowledge of copper and iron metallurgy. The precise dating of the first settlement phase is still a matter of debate. For Devisse (1983:554), "its duration is still undetermined. It ends in the nineteenth century at latest, and maybe before." Robert-Chaleix (1989:74), relying on a single radiocarbon date of 740±90 BP from a charcoal sample collected from a similar stratigraphic position in another part of the Acropolis excavation, suggests the mid-eighth century. The calibrated date however ranges from AD 610 to 1020. A similar range is documented for radiocarbon dates run on samples from the first two urban levels recorded above the pre-urban deposits (Robert-Chaleix 1989:87-189), making the mid-eighth century unlikely. The earliest mention of Awdaghost in Arabic historical sources comes from Al-Ya'qubi's *Kitab al-buldan*, a book he completed in 889-890. He described the geography of the Dar al-Islam with the location of the major urban centers. What he

Table 1: The new chronology of Awdaghost Acropolis

Stratigraphy	Building Sequence	Depth (m)	Date	Period
Level I	BS-1	3.10-2.30 bd*	? – AD 600	Pioneer
Level II	BS-2	2.80-1.90 bd	AD 600-800	
	BS-3	2.40-1.80 bd		
	BS-4	2.30-1.80 bd	AD 800-900	
Level III	BS-5	1.90-1.50 bd	AD 900-1000	Accelerated Growth
Level IV	BS-6	1.50-1.20 bd	AD 900-1000	
	BS-7	1.50-1.15 bd	AD 1000-1200	Unsteady Post-Climax
	BS-8	1.50-1.10 bd		
	BS-9	1.50-0.75 bd		
Level V	BS-10	1.20-0.60 bd	AD 1200-1400	Decline and Demise
	BS-11	1.20-0.60 bd		
	BS-12	0.90-0.10 bd		
	BS-13	0.10 bd-0.20 ad**		
Level IV	BS-14	0.20-0.45 ad	AD 1450-1500	
	BS-15	0.45-0.80 ad		

*bd = below datum.
**ad = above datum.

wrote about Awdaghost is not very informative but seems to refer to a pre-Islamic period: "Then the traveller will reach a town (*balad*) called Ghust which is an inhabited valley with dwellings. It is the residence of their king, who has no religion or law. He raids the land of the Sudan, who have many kingdoms" (Al-Ya'qubi in Levtzion and Hopkins 1981:22). What is evident here is that the town was already a well established one, with a king. The concept of king is however extremely vague and versatile in early Arabic historical sources and cannot be used to ascertain the existence of an Awdaghost (Awdaghust) kingdom in the ninth century. Al-Ya'qubi's description probably refers to an earlier period of Awdaghust history his informants were able to convey to him earlier in Khurasan and later in Cairo.

The most likely date for the origins of Awdaghost is probably around the middle of the first millennium AD. All things considered, the beginning of the seventh century seems the best option.

The discussion will focus on the mapped and described archaeological features, and when necessary will be expanded to consider artifacts. The spatial distribution of the recorded archaeological features will be used to look for patterns. The suggested patterns will then be used to hypothesize activity areas and structures. The reported artifacts' distribution will finally be used to test the strength of the inferred model.

The Refuse Dumps

Most of the mapped archaeological features present overlapping distribution. This is the case for hearths, pits, and refuse dumps that, nonetheless, present an interesting patterning. Twenty-two refuse dumps are documented on Figure 8. They are stretched on 50 m, along a northwest-southeast axis. The larger rubbish heaps are found at 10 to 20 m apart, with the largest specimen measuring 8 by 7 m and located in the southeast. One medium and fourteen small refuse dumps are found in the northwestern portion of the excavated probe. The smaller fourteen form a fan-shaped arrangement on the northern flank around the medium-sized one. It is as if trampling by humans and livestock combined with rearrangement by erosion had dismantled a larger refuse dump and scattered it. Six other refuse dumps are located in the central part of the probe; one is of medium size, oriented north-south, measuring 5 by 2 m. The northernmost specimen of the central cluster is relatively isolated but situated next to the northwestern cluster with smaller heaps located south at 5 to 10 m away. In this case, the refuse dumps appear to have resulted from distinct episodes of rubbish disposal on the periphery of a largely domestic space.

The Hearths

Hearths are distributed all over the tested probe. Forty-five specimens were recorded. Seven are located in the northwestern portion of the excavation, and are found more often in the western half of the tested unit. The distribution pattern of the southeastern portion's hearths is much more interesting and intricate. Two situations can be differentiated: in the east are 10 hearths, relatively isolated from each other, with the single exception of two close specimens in the center. The distance between nearest neighbors varies from 5 to 10 m. In fact, 7 m is clearly the modal distance recorded five times out of eight; 5 m, 6 m, and 10 m occur once each.

Conversely, the central part of the tested probe consists of 28 hearths arranged into dense microclusters of 2 to 8 specimens, all located on the perimeter of an elliptical space measuring 35 m northwest-southeast and 28 m northeast-southwest. Two microclusters of 2 and 3 hearths are found along the northern flank of the ellipse. A dense cluster of 8 hearths in a curvilinear arrangement is documented in the south. Finally, completing the southern flank of the ellipse is a string of four microclusters with 2 to 4 hearths. It is almost axiomatic that all the hearths documented at this phase of Awdaghost history resulted from a palimpsest of successive sequences of activities and very likely occupations. Many may have been used and reused, and some may have been used for a short period of time, or only once. Without a detailed and precise description of all the excavated hearths we cannot hope to sort out the use histories of these features.

The Pits

Thirty-six pits were recorded in the pre-urban level. Fourteen are located in the north-west portion and 22 in the southeast one. Most of these features were filled with refuse

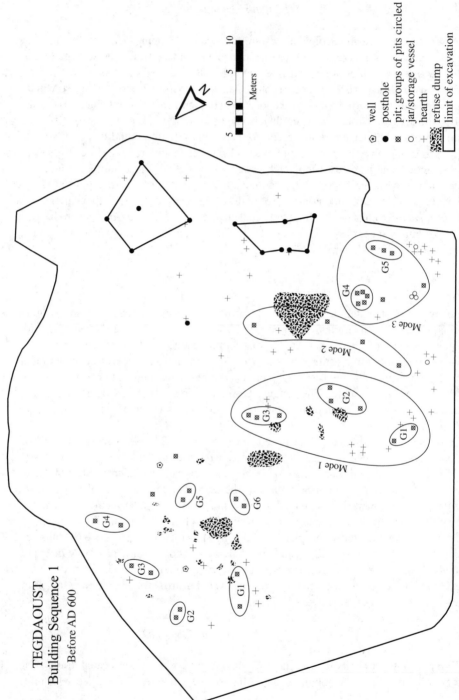

Figure 8. Building Sequence 1 constructions. Figure has been rotated so north, south, east, and west can be more easily described (i.e., what is described as "north" in text is actually closer to north by northeast).

and were accordingly indifferently characterized as refuse pits (Devisse et al. 1983; Polet 1985; Robert-Chaleix 1989). The spatial distribution of the recorded pits argues against a purposeful and exclusive use for refuse disposal. They were more likely used for the storage of products contained in large clay vessels. After their abandonment they were filled with rubbish, purposely or through deposition by erosion agencies, and then became de facto refuse pits.

Surprisingly enough, the eastern part of the excavated probe is devoid of pits. Nearest neighbor rationale allows for the organization of the northwest pits into six groups (see Fig. 8), each with two pits, with however two undecidable cases in the east. The relatively isolated specimens on the eastern flank are 7 m apart. It is remarkable that the distance between pit groups varies from 7 to 10 m, with a surprisingly balanced distribution: there are three occurrences of 7 m distances between groups 2 and 3, 3 and 4, and 5 and 6, and similarly three of 10 m distances between groups 1 and 2, 4 and 5, and 6 and 1. The tight patterning that seems to emerge from the spatial distribution of the northwest pits seems unlikely to have resulted from the random digging of trash pits.

The 22 pits exposed in the south-central part of the excavation totally overlap with the hearths. They are arranged into groups of 2 to 6 partitioned into three spatial modes (see Fig. 8). Mode 1 is found in the west. It consists of three groups of 2 to 3 pits each. Mode 2 is essentially a linear arrangement of four pits set along a southwest-northeast diagonal. Mode 3 has the densest pit concentration found in the southeast, consisting of a tight group of five pits in a circular arrangement, a group of three pits, and two singular pits.

The distance between groups of pits and even isolated specimens surprisingly ranges from 7 to 10 m. Group 2 is found at 7 m east of group 1. Group 3 is at 7 m north of group 2. The relatively isolated pits from the central diagonal are set at 7 m (pit 1 to pit 2), 7 m (pit 2 to pit 3), and finally, 10 m (pit 3 to pit 4). The triangular groupings in the southeast are also 7 meters apart. Such a structured patterning cannot have resulted from a succession of random pit-digging events.

The distribution of storage features appears to be strongly patterned. They may have been used to store supplies brought by groups of intermittent settlers using this location as a dry season camping area. The variations in the storage capacity documented may have depended on the size of each distinct group of settlers. Three additional sets of archaeological evidence can be harnessed to probe the seasonal camping hypothesis: wells, postholes, and storage vessels.

The Wells

Two wells were excavated in the northwestern portion of the probe. They are set at 16 m apart along a southeast-northwest axis, and measure slightly more than 2 m in diameter and 2.75 and 2.80 m in depth. They were not lined with cobbles or clay. Their sides may have been stabilized with tree branches. The sediment exposed all around the wells is greenish in color down to 0.20 m, suggesting intense use for watering purposes (Robert-Chaleix 1989:23).

The Postholes

Postholes are confined to the eastern part of the excavated unit. They form two geometric shapes, and one outlier (Fig. 8). The northern "shape" is composed of five postholes and the southern one, of seven. Precise descriptions of the postholes are not available, so the relationship of the postholes to each other is somewhat speculative. They may not be shapes at all, but merely the remains of random location of livestock tethering poles. But it seems unlikely that livestock tethering would have produced this pattern. Since there are no other archaeological features here that conflict with these shapes, the areas may well have been buildings of some sort: tents built with animal skins, or straw mats, or a combination of both, or light seasonal constructions. The same "foundations" may have been used successively for an unknown amount of time, or only once and never used again. The northern feature "substructure" is articulated on five postholes, delineating a "tent-pole" model. It is trapeze-shaped with a surface area of 60 m^2. The southern feature "substructure" is composed of seven postholes organized into two broadly parallel northeast-southwest lines. It measures 32.5 m^2. It is worth emphasizing that all the hearths documented in the eastern part of the probe are found out of the perimeter delimited by the postholes. It is as if fire represented a danger for the kind of material used in the construction of these dwelling features, and was consequently kept on the periphery.

The Storage Vessels

The remaining features of interest are a number of large clay storage vessels. They are all located along the southern flank of the excavated probe in strong association with hearths. The easternmost specimen, in the very south-southeast of the unit, is surrounded by four hearths. The central group is composed of three tightly clustered wares, located at 7 m west of the eastern specimen. And finally, a specimen was found some 10 m west of the central cluster along the same east-west axis. The single vessel was also surrounded, if more loosely, by three hearths.

Sedentary or Nomadic People?

The patterns of covariation in the spatial distribution of archaeological features from the pre-urban deposit suggest a well-structured occupation with some dominant and mutually exclusive activity areas. The palimpsest nature of the record precludes any simple assignment of archaeological features to a precise settlement episode. Water wells are confined to the northwestern portion of the excavated unit. Postholes from presumed dwelling features are confined to the opposite eastern end of the probe. Large storage vessels are confined to the southern flank of the exposed deposit. Refuse heaps, hearths, and pits overlap in their distribution. Artifacts include copper and iron objects and slag, potsherds, and a few animal bones, scattered, with preferential concentrations around hearths and pits. A heavy nonportable grindstone was found associated with the hearth and group 3 pits in the north of the northwestern excavation, providing strong evidence for food preparation activities at some distance from the shallow wells. The almost regular spacing between pit groups, the circular shape of the whole arrangement that measures 20 m in average diameter, and the overlapping distribution of hearths indicate the possibility for a well-organized seasonal camp with a central shallow well. The southeastern unit presents a very different patterning with clear distinctions in the use of space with dwelling installations confined to the east, and pits, hearths, and storage vessels to the west.

These differences between space usage in the northwest and southeast parts of the excavation do not allow for a clear characterization of the nature of the occupations under consideration. Were both areas settled at the same time? Was it a dry-season camp settled on a seasonal basis because of the presence of the nearby stream and a high watertable? Was it a sedentary and permanent settlement from the onset as suggested by the excavators (Polet 1985:26)? Did a seasonal camp and a sedentary community exist side by side (Robert-Chaleix 1989:25-26)? Or did the former precede the later? All these options are equally plausible. None of the available cultural remains favor any option.

Building Sequence 2 (Fig. 9)

The deposits from the earliest urban level, called Building Sequence 2, are exposed at depths varying from 2.40 to 2.80 m in the south, 2.50 to 2.10 in the northwest, and 2.30 to 1.90 m in the east. Mud-bricks and stone were used for the construction of dwellings. This building sequence inaugurates the segmentation of the Acropolis space into habitation complexes, with each complex divided into household units.

The eastern part of the excavated probe has a series of short walls that do not form a coherent space. Four of the short walls are built with mud-bricks. The longer specimens, 0.50 m thick and 2.5 to 2 m long, are found in the southeast and oriented east-west. The shorter ones, 0.30 m thick and 1 m long, are found in the north of the probe and oriented north-south.

Five stone walls are located in the south of the excavated unit: four east-west walls 3 to 3.5 m long and 0.35 to 0.5 m thick, and one north-south wall 1 m long. A longer isolated stone wall, oriented north-south, measuring 6 m in length and 0.5 m in width is found in the east.

Habitation Complex IV

An elaborate habitation complex, HC-IV, takes shape in the south. It was excavated and published by J. Polet (1985). Broadly rectilinear, oriented west-east, it measures 27 m in length, and 19 to 22 m in width. It is subdivided into three households units oriented north-south. Each household unit is articulated around a courtyard, with a varying number of rooms.

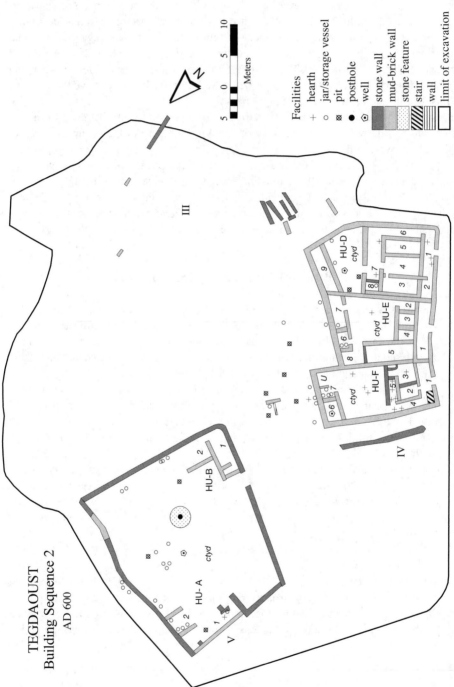

Figure 9. Building Sequence 2 constructions. Figure has been rotated so north, south, east, and west can be more easily described (i.e., what is described as "north" in text is actually closer to north by northeast).

Table 2: Building Sequence 2 constructions

Habitation Unit	Total Size (m²)	Courtyard (m²)	Rooms (m²)									Shape
			1	2	3	4	5	6	7	8	9	
Habitation Complex IV												
HU-IV-D	175.94	74.20	13.12	3.52	12.82	14.25	12.32	8.96	19.32	2.72	15.20	P
HU-IV-E	133.98	62.32	17.10	3.90	4.25	3.60	20.16	4.25	11.20	7.20		R
HU-IV-F	129.02	75.90	11.88	5.40	14.28*	7.08	4.08	7.04	3.36			R
Habitation Complex V												
HU-V-A	646.34	598	23.52	7.80								R
HU-V-B			17.50	12								

Key: H = Hexagonal; P = Pentagonal; R = Rectangular; T = Trapezoidal
*Probably a small courtyard.

Table 3: Variations in BS-2 room size (m²)

Habitation Unit	n	Minimum	Maximum	Mean	Range	Standard Deviation	Coefficient of Variation
Habitation Complex IV							
HU-IV-D	9	2.72	19.32	11.35	16.60	5.10	0.44
HU-IV-E	8	3.60	20.16	8.95	16.56	6.53	0.72
HU-IV-F	7	3.36	14.28	7.58	10.92	3.75	0.49
Habitation Complex V							
HU-V-A	2	7.80	23.52	15.66	15.72	7.86	0.50
HU-V-B	2	12	17.50	14.75	5.50	2.75	0.18

Household Unit D

HU-D at the eastern end is built almost entirely with mud-bricks and is shaped like an irregular pentagon. The enclosed surface area is 175.94 m², divided between a courtyard, corridors and rooms (Table 2). The main entrance door of the unit is found in the east half of the southern wall. Room 1, along the south flank of the unit, is a narrow space measuring 13.12 m², which would have been used to receive guests. The three recorded hearths may have been used both for making hot drinks and during cold nights to heat the space itself. The reception room is flanked in the west by the small room 2 (3.52 m²), probably a storage room. Room 5, the main sleeping room in this part of the unit, measures 5.6 by 2.2 m and is oriented northeast-southwest. Room 6 is a long narrow corridor (8.96 m²) set along the eastern flank of HU-D. It leads to room 7, the central and large reception/eating room of the unit. It is 8.4 m long east-west and 2.3 m in maximum width, with two hearths set 5 m apart. The western hearth was probably used for routine cooking purposes. It is found next to the small storage room 8, 2.1 m in length and 1.3 m in width, demarcated by a stone wall. The eastern hearth could have been used to make hot beverages and for heat. Room 7 gives access to room 4 on its south flank. Room 4 is the third largest room of the unit, measuring 5.7 m by 2.5 m. Room 3, on the west flank, accessed through room 4, has the same north-south orientation and measures 5.6 m by 2.2 m. Trapeze-shaped room 9 set along the north of the unit measures 6.9 to 8 by 1.9 m. It is the second largest room but its function is unclear. It may have been used as a sleeping space, warehouse, or both. Finally, the courtyard, covering 74.20 m², is the center of household life. It is out of sight from the streets, in the most private part of the household space. This one is shaped like an irregular pentagon, measuring (clockwise, beginning with the south wall) 10 by 3 by 8 by 3.5 by 3 m. Two pits are dug in the west, abutting the south and west walls and set 2 m apart. Two storage jars were also recorded in the northeast, along the north and the northeast walls, 3 m apart. The well is slightly west of the center and is shaped like a truncated cone, 0.8 m in diameter at the mouth, 1.20 m in diameter at the bottom, and 3 m deep, its walls lined with wadi cobbles.

In summary, HC-IV/HU-D is divided into a relatively large courtyard, one corridor, three elongated and transversal rooms, and three smaller north-south oriented rooms. The unit architectural blueprint seems to have consisted of two distinct components.

The southern component is a square with sides measuring 12 m. It was divided into three parallel and transversal space blocks, a southern, a central, and a northern one. The central space was then divided into four smaller spaces, rooms 3, 4, and 5, and corridor 6. The west end of the southern and northern blocks consisted of small rooms, used for storage, cooking, or both. The southern component appears to consist of two functional units connected by corridor 6. The core of the private domain, probably used by the household head, consisted of sleeping rooms 3 and 4, reception, living, and eating room 7, and storage/cooking room 8. The smaller functional unit, in direct contact with the outside, includes the reception room 1, the storage room 2, and finally, the sleeping room 5. It may have been used by junior members of the household, or for guests.

The trapeze-shaped northern component consists of the courtyard and the northern large room of unknown function. The northern component appears to have been used as the main area for domestic and maintenance activities. From this perspective, room 9 was very likely used for the storage of household equipment and tools.

Household Unit E

HC-IV/HU-E is set along the west flank of the HU-D. It is a trapeze-shaped unit extended over 133.98 m², built almost exclusively with mud-bricks, and divided into a courtyard and eight rooms. The southern side measures 9 m in length; the northern one, 11 m; the western, 15 m; and finally, the eastern, 18 m. The poor preservation of the remaining walls did not allow for the determination of all the door locations (Polet 1985:42), making the identification of the intrahousehold circulation pattern uncertain.

Room 1 is an elongated (9 m by 1.9 m) transversal space found along the unit's southern flank. It is clearly a reception room that controlled the access to the core of the domestic space, and may also have been used as the eating/living space. Despite the absence of clear evidence, it can be suggested that room 2 was a small 2.6 by 1.5 m corridor, providing access to the courtyard, the inner sanctum of the unit. The courtyard is trapeze-shaped and extended over 62.32 m². The hearth is almost central and surrounded by rooms on the southern, western, and northern sides. Rooms 3 and 4 are small. Their doors may have opened into the courtyard, and if so, may have been used as sleeping rooms by younger household members. Room 5, the largest of the unit, measures 7.2 m long north-south and 2.8 m wide and is set along the west wall. Its northern wall is, surprisingly, built of stone, and it appears to have been the main sleeping room. A complex of three rooms, all with doors opening on the courtyard, is located along the northern wall. Room 7, on the eastern half, measures 11.20 m². A large storage vessel in clay was found at the northwest corner of the room, suggesting a dual function as a sleeping and storage space. Rooms 6 and 8 share the western half of the complex. The former is a small room (measuring 2.5 m by 1.7 m) that was used for storage; two large storage clay vessels were found disposed along the room's west wall. Finally, room 8 at the west end (7.20 m²) might have been the "bathing room."

The architectural blueprint of HU-E has many things in common with that of HU-D. Construction is articulated on three elongated transversal space blocks with widths varying from 1.9 to 2.5 m. The southern space block served as a reception/eating/living room. The northern block was divided into three sub-units. The central block consisted of a short corridor, two small sleeping rooms, and one large sleeping room. The household very likely consisted of parents with grown dependents, children, or servants.

Household Unit F

Household unit HC-IV/HU-F is located at the western end of the complex. It is almost rectangular in shape and oriented north-south. The longer east wall measures 20 m and the west, 19 m. The difference is greater between northern (9 m) and the southern (6 m) walls.

The unit total area is 129.02 m², divided into a courtyard and seven or eight rooms (Table 2). Three of the internal walls are made of stone. The longest (6 m) is oriented east-west. The shorter ones (3 and 1 m) are oriented north-south. The unit's entrance is set in the middle of the southern wall and opens on the reception room 1. It is a long and narrow 11.88 m² room (6.4 to 6.6 by 1.8 m) with a "staircase" leading to the roof or the upper rooms at the southwest corner. Room 2, reached via room 1, is a small 5.4 m² space that may have been used as a sleeping room. Room 3, or more precisely "space 3" (14.28 m²), may have been a small courtyard and was very likely unroofed (Polet 1985:44) because of the limit on the length of date palm beams used for roof support in this non-wooded area. If this were the case, reception room 1, sleeping room 2, and small courtyard 3 probably form a coherent functional sub-unit. There is a stone-paved sunken surface in the northeast corner of courtyard 3 and a hearth at its center. The sunken surface was very likely the sub-unit "bathing area." Room 1 leads to the upper floor and the remaining part of the unit. The possibility of an upper floor is suggested by the existence of three stone walls in the central part of the household unit. They may have been built there to support the additional weight of one or two upper rooms as will be discussed later. Room 4 is in fact a narrow corridor (5.9 by 1.2 m) oriented north-south and leading to the northern half of the household unit. It gives access to the main courtyard and room 5. Two hearths were uncovered in the corridor, set along the west wall and next to the entrance of room 5. Room 5, located east of the corridor, is a narrow 4.08 m² room (3.4 by 1.2 m) with no less than four hearths. It is probably a cooking area that may have been extended to the corridor. The large courtyard measures 9 to 10 m in length and 7.5 m in width, with two hearths in the center and one next to the east wall. Two rooms and a small space block of unknown use are found along the north flank of the courtyard. Room 6, the "well room" found at the northwest corner (7.04 m²), is paved, resulting in a raised platform that was part of the well installation. The well *stricto-sensu* measures 0.70 m in diameter at mouth, 1.15 to 1.25 m in length and width at its oval-shaped bottom, and is lined with wadi cobbles down to 3.20 m. The very bottom of the well was documented at 3.20 m (Polet 1985:46). It is unlikely to have been roofed. The floor of room 7, east of the well room, is 0.30 m lower. Small (3.36 m²), it contained four large storage vessels. These large clay vessels were most likely water containers, perhaps to cool drinking water or store bathing water. The small space next to it may thus have been used as a "bathing area."

So far, HC-IV/HU-F appears to consist of only one tiny sleeping room 2, with reception room 1, a small courtyard 3, the kitchen room 5 with an unusual number of hearths, an elaborate well in room 6, and water storage in room 7. The possibility of an upper floor with additional rooms is suggested by the limited range of living facilities documented on the ground floor, especially when compared to HU-D and HU-E. Despite some superficial similarities, such as long transversal space blocks at both south and north ends, a north-south corridor, and a central room block, HU-F significantly departs from the structural consistency documented in HU-D and HU-E. It may have been a special housing unit for travelers, traders, and scholars. In other words, it was a kind of inn; the guests would have slept in rooms 2 and 3, their drinking and bath water pulled from the well and made available in large clay vessels, and their food cooked in the small kitchen.

Many features of archaeological interest were exposed in the west and along the northern flank of Habitation Complex IV: two tiny T-shaped walls at 6 to 7 m north of the HU-F north wall, and a 14 m long north-south stone wall delineating a "street" along the HU-F west wall. Large clay vessels are distributed in two loose groups: four vessels along the north wall of HU-F, and two vessels along the HU-E north wall. Two other isolated vessels were also found, one associated with the T-shaped walls and the other some 7 m north of the HU-E north wall. Some pits and a hearth were also found in this area.

Habitation Complex V

Habitation Complex V (HC-V) is located in the northwest of the Acropolis, 15 m north of HC-IV. The complex covers an area of 646.34 m² and is shaped like an irregular trapeze and oriented east-west, with the entrance located in the eastern half of the south wall. The southern wall, entirely built of stone, measures 27 m. The eastern wall, also stone, is 25 m. The northern wall, mostly stone with a small segment in mud-brick, measures 30 m. Finally, the west wall, the shortest, measures 18 m. The complex can be divided into two parts, the larger (HU-A) in the west and the smaller (HU-B) in the east, with a common entrance and courtyard.

Household Unit A

HC-V/HU-A, in the west of the complex, consists of two or three rooms set along the west wall and the northwestern corner. Room 1 (9.8 by 2.4 m) is roughly rectilinear and oriented north-south and was probably used as a sleeping/storage area. One large storage clay vessel was exposed within a stone installation in the southern part of the room. A large pit, in fact a storage bin, was recorded to the north of the center, a few meters from a short stone wall. Room 2, to the east, has no southern wall. Both east and west walls are built in mud-brick. The area was probably used for storage: four large storage clay vessels were uncovered there (three along the west wall, on an ashy layer from the hearth underneath, and the fourth in the northeast corner). A third partly walled space is found at the southwest area of the complex. It measures 6.5 m in length and 3 m in width. It is not known if the area was roofed or not: a tent or woven mats may have been used to create a useful sheltered reception area. The presence of a hearth supports the hypothesis of the use of this area as a reception room.

Household Unit B

HU-B is located in the southeast area of the complex, and comprises two or three rooms built with four distinct mud-brick walls. Room 1, the largest, is oriented east-west and covers an area of 17.5 m² and has a demarcated smaller component at the west end. This smaller room with a door on the southeast side was probably used for storage. The main room 1 has a door in the north, and was most likely a sleeping room. To the north of room 1 is room 2, oriented north-south, and open on the north side. The room's dimensions are 4.5 by 3 m. It may or may not have been roofed; considering that roof beams seem to have been limited to 2.5 m (Polet 1985), the 3 m beams that would have been needed to roof this area may have been rare but occasionally available. Whatever the case however, roofed or unroofed, the delineated space may have been used as a reception or meal-taking room.

A pit is located at 1 to 2 m north of the west wall of room 2. Five large clay vessels are arranged along the east wall in two distinct groups.

The extensive courtyard would have been shared by the members of HU-A and HU-B. Two important archaeological features are located in the central part of the courtyard: a well and a shelter. The well, dug during the previous building sequence (BS-1), was kept in use without any significant modification. A circular shelter was exposed at 3 to 4 m east-southeast of the well. It measures 3 m in diameter and consists of a central posthole, 10 cm in diameter and 15 cm deep (Robert-Chaleix 1989:37), and a perimeter of stones with the entrance in the west. A handful of locally made sherds were found scattered on the shelter's floor. The most significant finds were iron and copper slag, pieces of broken crucibles, and an amazonite fragment. These metal-working by-products suggest this may have been a blacksmith's workshop.

One pit and five large storage vessels are clustered at some distance from the well. With the well so close, it's unlikely these vessels were used to store food; more likely they were used to store water pulled from the well.

HC-V appears to have been inhabited by households of craftpeople. The housing facilities, set in opposing corners, are small, consisting mainly of a roofed or unroofed reception area/room, a sleeping area, and a storage/cooking area. The forge workshop is closer to HU-B.

Eleven clay vessels (not all shown in Fig. 9) of different shapes and sizes were found stored in the southern end of HU-A room 1. Robert-Chaleix (1989:33) suggests two scenarios to explain this pattern. In scenario 1, the whole set can be considered to have been part of the domestic kit of the household; the presence in the sample of a pot with a thick tar deposit tends to support this idea. In scenario 2, the wares may have been part of a pottery production stored in the room while waiting to be sold. This scenario is based on the strong association between blacksmiths and potters documented in West African caste-like societies (Conrad and Frank 1995; McNaughton 1988). Generally, the potters are wives of the blacksmiths (Tamari 1995). This material may well be a very early occurrence of the "endogamous caste-like" social arrangement. However, according to the most detailed analyses (Tamari 1992, 1995), such a development, at least in the Manding world, "began to form in the thirteenth century, partly as a result of the Sosso-Malinke conflict" (Tamari 1995:82, note 27). The pottery assemblage was probably part of the domestic equipment of the HU-A household.

Summary

At its very beginning, Awdaghost may have been settled by numerous groups who built their dwelling facilities in different parts of the future town, as yet undiscovered. The settlement may then have consisted of scattered household estates. Excavated evidence nonetheless suggests that the Acropolis has the longest archaeological sequence so far, and we can use it to document the shifting patterns involved in the rise and demise of this West African medieval trade town.

During Building Sequence 2 (BS-2), two habitation complexes were built in the Acropolis area. The northwestern one appears to have belonged to a group involved in craft production, who were sharing a well and courtyard. The southern complex was divided into three architecturally more elaborate household units, each with a secluded courtyard, the number of rooms varying from 7 to 9. The size of the courtyard, which varies from 62.32 m² for the smallest in HU-E to 74.20 (HU-D) and 75.90 m² (HU-F), highlights similarities in the structure of domestic space. The room size varies considerably from one household unit to the next (Table 3).

If we group room size into 5 m² classes* there is no clear pattern to the units. There are eight class 1 rooms: two in HU-D and HU-F, and four in HU-E. There are six occurrences of class 2 rooms varying from one to three per HU. Seven class 3 rooms were recorded, ranging from one to four per HU. Four class 4 rooms were found distributed through four units, one or at most two per HU. And finally, there is a single case of a class 5 room recorded in HU-E (see Table 2).

Throughout HC-V, room size and arrangement are similar. The total room space amounts to 31.32 m² in HU-A and 29.5 m² in HU-B. The largest room in HU-A measures 23.52 m² while the largest room in HU-B is 17.50 m². The smallest are 7.80 m² and 12 m². Clearly, in HC-V inhabited by specialized craftpeople, the architecture is much less elaborate.

We can see by Table 3, on the other hand, that within HC-IV, the household units vary from *each other*: HU-E is characterized by fairly dramatic variations in room size. Room size is more balanced in HU-D with three transversal and elongated east-west and three rectangular north-south rooms. HU-F is notable for its small rooms.

The layout of HU-F departs so significantly from that of HU-D and HU-E that it is suggested that HU-F may have been a sort of inn for travelers, traders, and scholars during their visit at Awdaghost. It is interesting to note that at this early stage of the town's history, approximately AD 600-800, there was no spatial segregation between craftpeople and the rest of the society. Glazed wares from north Africa, copper and iron objects, and predominantly locally made pottery were recorded in varying proportions in all the excavated habitations.

Building Sequence 3 (Fig. 10)

The archaeological deposits assigned to Building Sequence 3 (BS-3) were exposed at depths ranging from 1.90 m to 2.80 m. The Building Sequence 3 archaeological level measures 0.40 m in thickness in all the tested excavation units but was reached at different depths, varying from 2.40 to 2.80 m in the south, and 2.10 to 2.50 m in the northwest, to 1.90 to 2.30 m in the east. The building and the occupation of BS-3 features probably happened between AD 650 and 750. HC-III in the east is at this time still lacking significant construction, existing mainly as the same series of short stone and mud-brick walls seen in BS-2. HC-IV, on the other hand, has been extended significantly on its northern flank with two new household units, and the previous ones altered. HC-V has been slightly reshaped but still preserves its basic bipartition. In general, there is an increased reliance on stone as a building material.

---

*Class 1: < 5 m²; class 2: >5-10 m²; class 3: >10-15 m²; and so forth in 5 m² increments.

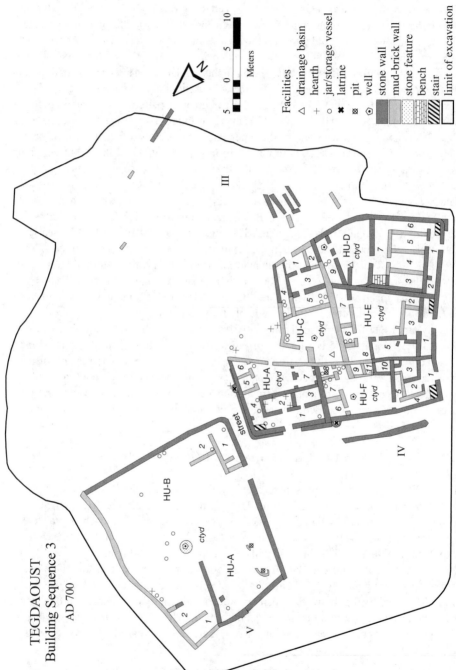

Figure 10. Building Sequence 3 constructions. Figure has been rotated so north, south, east, and west can be more easily described (i.e., what is described as "north" in text is actually closer to north by northeast).

Table 4: Building Sequence 3 constructions

Habitation Unit	Total Size (m²)	Courtyard (m²)	Rooms (m²)												Shape
			1	2	3	4	5	6	7	8	9	10	11	
Habitation Complex IV															
HU-IV-A	110.06	34.72	25.08	8.8	8.0	8.36	3.96	5.94	15.2					T
HU-IV-C	120.32	67.08	10.08	4.16	14	11.2	14.00							R
HU-IV-D	169.01	70.00	13.12	3.52	12.32	14.25	12.32	8.96	22.04		15.2			P
HU-IV-E	139.97	62.32	17.10	3.90	.12		18.04	4.25	11.20	11.16				R
HU-IV-F	115.80	47.04	11.88	5.40	14.28*	7.08	4.08	5.76	6	3.08	3.60	4.8	2.8	R
Habitation Complex V															
HU-V-A	627	598	29	7.80										R
HU-V-B	—		17.50	12										R

Key: H = Hexagonal; P = Pentagonal; R = Rectangular; T = Trapezoidal
*Small courtyard.

Table 5: Variations in BS-3 room size (m²)

Habitation Unit	n	Minimum	Maximum	Mean	Range	Standard Deviation	Coefficient of Variation
Habitation Complex IV							
HU-IV-A	7	3.96	25.08	10.76	21.12	6.67	0.61
HU-IV-C	5	4.16	14.00	10.64	9.84	3.57	0.33
HU-IV-D	8	3.52	22.04	12.37	15.80	4.33	0.35
HU-IV-E	7	3.90	18.04	13.46	14.14	8.84	0.65
HU-IV-F	11	2.8	14.28	6.25	11.48	3.65	0.55
Habitation Complex V							
HU-V-A	2	7.80	29.00	18.40	21.20	5.75	0.24
HU-V-B	2	12.00	17.50	14.75	5.50	2.75	0.18

Habitation Complex IV

The new units, HU-A and HU-C, are built on the northern flank (see Fig. 10).

Household Unit A

HU-A is a trapeze-shaped building measuring 110.06 m^2 in surface area. It is mostly built with stone with mud-brick walls confined to the eastern side. The western and northern walls are double, both measuring 13 m in length. The shared southern wall is 10 m long; the east wall, 14 m long, is built with mud-bricks. HU-A has two entrances, one in the west and the other in the east, and includes a courtyard and seven rooms. The courtyard measures 34.72 m^2. It is located in the eastern half of the unit and is accessed immediately from the street. It is flanked in the south by a pillared gallery (room 7) measuring 15.20 m^2. The roof was supported by six pillars, providing the household members with a comfortable sheltered reception room 2.8 to 3.8 m wide and 4 m long. Two small rooms with walls made of mud-bricks are set along the north side of the courtyard. Room 5 is the smallest of the unit (3.96 m^2), providing access to the latrine. Room 6, in the east, small and irregularly shaped, is entirely paved with stone, suggesting this space was used for bathing and showering. Room 4 is located along the remaining west portion of the north wall (8.36 m^2). It has one door giving access to the courtyard and another leading to the corridor in the west. Two large storage vessels were found set against the room's south wall. Room 4 may have been used predominantly for sleeping and the storage of some household supplies. Room 1 (25.08 m^2) provides access to a staircase set in the northwest corner. Three large storage vessels were found in room 1: one in the southwest corner, and two in the northwest next to the stairs. The staircase provides access to the roof, which could have been used for sleeping during the warm nights of the dry-season, and to dry laundry, grain, or other products. Or, HU-A may have been a two-story building. Rooms 2 and 3, both oriented north-south, open in the corridor. The former, measuring 4.4 m by 2 m, was very likely the kitchen of the household unit as indicated by the four hearths exposed. Two are located along the room's east wall; a third is found in the southwestern corner, and the fourth is set against the north wall. Room 3 is slightly smaller (4 m by 2 m) and was probably one of the sleeping rooms of the unit.

The presence of a staircase and the very existence of unusually thick double stone walls delimiting the south, west, and north of the house suggest that the unit may have been built with an upper floor, and the thick walls designed to support the extra weight of the upper floor structures.

Household Unit C

Household unit C is set transversally across the habitation complex. It is irregular, somewhat of an elongated trapeze. The unit has an area of 120.32 m^2 partitioned into a large courtyard and five rooms (Table 4). Its southern (18 m) and western (11 m) walls are shared with the surrounding buildings. Most of the unit walls are built of mud-bricks, with the exception of four short stone walls that are part of the eastern half of the building.

The 67.08 m² courtyard is located in the western half of the household unit with an entrance in the northwest. Two major archaeological features were found as part of the courtyard facilities. A well was dug almost at its center, but was not excavated in detail. A shallow drain to collect rain water, 1.20 m in diameter and 1.00 m deep, its sides lined with stone, was dug near the western wall. Two large clay storage vessels were found at the northwestern corner of the unit, leaning against the northern wall.

The unit's eastern half is partitioned into five rooms of different shapes and size. Room 4 (11.2 m²) in the north is a long east-west corridor connecting the complex of rooms to the courtyard. The western and southeastern sides are low thin walls. East-central room 1 is a hallway regulating the movement of people in and out of the house unit. Its north wall is thin and low, allowing access to the corridor room 4. One entrance is set in the east wall, connecting the unit with the outside on its eastern side. The other door, set in the west wall, provides access to the inner sanctum of the household unit. Room 2 is located along the southern flank of the hallway room 1. It is the smallest room of the unit, measuring 2.8 to 3.2 by 1.3 m. It was probably accessed from the west as suggested by the presence of a thinner and lower wall. Rooms 3 and 5 are almost the same size, rectangular and oriented north-south. Room 3 was very likely the living/reception room where meals would have been served to household members. Two serving wares, a large carinated jug and a large glazed green hole-mouth bowl broken into numerous sherds found on room 3's floor (Polet 1985:118-19), were probably used for serving beverages and food. A door in the west wall of room 3 provides access to the sleeping area of room 5. Three large clay vessels were set in the floor in the south end of room 5. They were full of light-gray ash and the floor around was fire-hardened (Polet 1985:120). They were probably used as heaters, very likely during the relatively cool nights of the rainy season.

HU-C can be seen as having two functional halves. The west half is made up of the unroofed courtyard with an exit in the northwest. The east half is the roofed segment of the building with a long corridor, a vestibule opening on the east street, a reception/living/eating room, a sleeping room and a smaller (probably storage) room. This partitioning of the domestic space outlined above suggests HU-C was inhabited by only one family, possibly composed of parents and young children.

Household Unit D

During Building Sequence 3, the size of HU-D remained the same but there were some significant changes. Almost all the walls are built with stone, with the exception of the sleeping room complex. A staircase providing access to the roof was built at the unit's southeastern corner. The outer side of that corner was buttressed with another thick but short stone wall to stabilize the construction. The former room 8 was filled with a mud-brick low platform that served as a bench or a sleeping platform. This new facility was part of the refurbished reception and living room 7. The most extensive addition to the unit was made in the northern half, in the courtyard and room 9. The well from the previous BS-2 household unit was turned into a drain for rainwater, connected to the wall by a "drainpipe" oriented east-west. A new well was dug in room 9, at the eastern end, 1.10 m in diameter at mouth, 1.55 to 1.70 m at bottom, and 2.85 m in depth. Its sides are lined with wadi cobbles from the mouth to a depth of 2.45 m, with the well's bottom found 0.30 to 0.40 m deeper. The well's margin is made of a raised and paved platform. Two doors were set in room 9's south wall. One provides access to the new well, and the other to what may have been used as a bathing/showering room. A wooden panel that may also have operated as a door was set between the "new well room" and room 9 (Polet 1985:86). Two large clay vessels were found in the bathing/showering room 9; they were probably part of the bath facility, filled with water pulled from the well, and ready to be used when needed.

In summary, HU-D had preserved its original structure from the previous Building Sequence 2, but with very significant improvements of the daily life facilities. It can be divided into three segments. One segment is the reception room 1, small storage room 2, and sleeping room 5, perhaps used by the younger generation of household members, dependents, or even servants. Another segment includes the long corridor room 6, the relatively large reception/living room 7 with a new comfortable raised bench at the west end, and sleeping rooms 3 and 4. This segment was very likely that of the household head's family. The third segment, consisting of the courtyard, the well, and the bathing/showering room 9, was confined to the north of the unit. The access to the roof added some additional space to the unit, but it is difficult to find evidence suggesting the construction of an upper level.

Household Unit E

HU-E witnessed some important transformations during Building Sequence 3. The general shape and size of the unit were preserved, but the room arrangement and the construction materials differ. Stone was used to build approximately half of the walls of the unit, located in the south and west, and a small portion of room 7's south wall in the northeast.

All the walls from the reception room 1 in the south were built in stone. A staircase, providing access to the terrace roof, was set in the southeastern corner of the room. A larger room 3, measuring 4.8 by 2.5 m, with a small niche in the west, opens in the reception room through a new door, probably making it the principal reception/living room with room 1 serving as a vestibule. The short corridor room 2 in the east provides access to the courtyard and the rest of the unit. The courtyard and all the rooms along the north wall are for the most part built with mud-bricks, with their shapes and sizes unmodified. Room 8 may have been the bathing/showering room; room 6 may have been used as a kitchen as well as storage, as suggested by the presence of two large clay storage vessels set along the west wall. And finally, room 7, with a small portion of its south wall built of stone, may have been used as a sleeping room. The large room 5 (18.04 m^2) located along the west wall of the unit went through a change of shape and size. It is a combination of a 5.4 by 2.6 m rectangular space in the north with a smaller 2 by 2 m square in the south end. This makes the BS-3 room 5 slightly smaller than the 20.16 m^2 BS-2 room 5.

In summary, HC-IV/HU-E may have housed two to three family units; one may have used room 1 for reception and room 3 for sleeping. Another may have used the same reception room 1 and the large room 5 for sleeping. A third may have used reception room 1 and sleeping room 7. The whole household group shared corridor room 2, kitchen/storage room

6, and the probable bathing/showering room 8. Additional terrace roof space would have been accessible through the newly constructed staircase.

Household Unit F

HC-IV/HU-F went through an extensive restructuring (Fig. 10). The south, west and north walls were built in stone. The southern part of the unit with the reception room 1, the staircase, the sleeping room 2, the small courtyard 3, the corridor room 4, and finally, room 5 were kept unaltered, with two minor modifications. The short south wall of the sleeping room 2 was built with stone while the short east wall of room 5 previously in stone was rebuilt with mud-bricks. All the new construction was along the eastern and northern sides of the courtyard that is now smaller (47.04 m²).

Four additional rooms were built along the east wall. Room 10, at the south end, is entirely closed in by four stone walls. It may have been used as a sleeping room. North of it, room 11 is a narrow (2 by 1.4 m) room, perhaps a kitchen. Room 9, north of it, is entirely built of mud-brick walls; a 3.60 m² trapezoidal space, it may have been a sleeping room. A storage area (2.8 m²) set along the north wall of room 9 contained three clay storage vessels.

Three new rooms were built along the north wall. Room 6 at the west end is a stone-paved bathing/showering room with an attached latrine (5.76 m²). Its door is narrow and set in the west part of the south wall. Room 7, in the middle, is rectangular in shape, opening on the courtyard through a door set in the south wall. The 6 m² space was very likely a sleeping room, partly used for the storage of household supplies. Three large clay storage jars were found in the room, two along the north wall, the other leaning on the east wall. Room 8, next to room 7, has a narrow door set in the south mud-brick wall. It was clearly a storage area as suggested by the presence of a storage pit as well as a large storage vessel.

The courtyard, confined to the west and center of unit, is extended over 44.24 m² excluding the storage extension. A new well was dug in the northern part of the courtyard. It measures 1 m in diameter at mouth and 1.20 m in diameter at bottom. The sides are lined with wadi cobbles down to a depth of 2.4 m, with its margin's platform raised 0.50 m above the courtyard level.

In summary, HU-F consists of a series of small rooms scattered all over the unit's space. A bathing/showering room with an attached latrine was added, bringing more comfort to the unit's inhabitants. The restructuring of the unit's architecture suggests a change in the nature of the users; it may then have been inhabited by an extended or polygamous family. If an extended family, the household unit may have been partitioned into three subsets: one in the south composed of the reception room 1, the sleeping room 2, the small courtyard 3 and its small attached paved bathing/showering space; another would be the rooms along the east wall, also connected to the reception room 1, and comprising sleeping rooms 10 and 9, and the attached storage area 11; the third subset also includes the reception room 1, the sleeping/storage room 7 and storage room 8. Common to all members of the household would have been corridor room 4, the courtyard, the kitchen room 11, the latrine, and the main bathing/showering room 6, as well as the staircase and the terrace roof. (It is difficult to assign room 5 to any of the subsets outlined above due to its location and shape.)

A polygamous family could also have fit in the partitions described above, with each wife sharing a subset with her children, and the husband moving from one to the next, or having his apartment in the upper floor.

Habitation Complex V

Along with the new HU-A at the northwestern end of Habitation Complex IV, there is now a narrow 2 m wide street oriented east-west between HC-IV and HC-V. The architectural modifications implemented in HC-V during Building Sequence 3 are moderate. Most of the complex's north wall, previously made of stone, was rebuilt in mud-brick, and two-thirds of the west wall is made of stone. The complex is still divided into two household units with most of the extensive courtyard still shared (Table 4).

Household Unit A

HC-V/HU-A, in the west half of the complex, witnessed the most extensive architectural transformations. A stone wall measuring 10 m in length and oriented east-west was added to the unit. Two rooms are located in the northwest, while the southwest houses an extensive courtyard delimited by three stone walls.

Room 1 in the northwest corner is made of mud-brick on three sides, with the south wall built of stone. This north-south rectangle, with an area of 29 m^2, was probably the sleeping room of the unit. Its door is set at the southern end of the room's east wall. Room 2 was built along the east flank of room 1 with the south left open. It was a roofed and sheltered area (7.80 m^2) that may have been used as the reception/living room. The small courtyard next to room 2 was partly disturbed by pit-digging from later occupations but it nonetheless contains significant evidence for metal working, iron as well as copper: a relatively large amount of crucible fragments with vitrified surfaces, iron and copper slag, one copper fragment, and a small copper ring (Robert-Chaleix 1989:43).

Two storage bins of sun-dried clay were found in the courtyard along the south wall. The preservation is poor, with the evidence consisting of the bottom of the bins with a few centimeters of the original walls. The larger specimen, in the west, is roughly circular, 1.55 m in maximum diameter. It was partitioned into two parts by a poorly preserved dividing wall. The smaller bin, 3 meters east, is oval-shaped, 0.85 m in maximum diameter and 0.70 m in minimum diameter (Robert-Chaleix 1989:49). A hearth was exposed along the north wall where it is associated with two storage vessels. Two additional storage vessels were found in the southern part of the courtyard, 6 m apart near the west wall. HU-A was still, very likely, the dwelling unit of craftpeople. Metal-working debris was conspicuous in the documented archaeological record. The presence of the two storage bins is ambiguous. There is no evidence suggesting that these features were used for the storage of grain or other foodstuff. They may well have been used to store clay, making this a potter's workshop.

Household Unit B

HU-B of HC-V remained much the same architecturally. Five storage vessels are scattered all over the unit. One is located in the southeastern corner of room 1; another is found in the southwest corner of room 2; two are set against the east wall, a few meters north of room 2; and finally, the remaining and fifth vessel is found at the center of the northern half of the courtyard.

The well in the center of the complex could be used by both HU-A and HU-B household members. This well was not excavated in detail; its characteristics, diameter at mouth and bottom, depth, lined or unlined, are unknown. The outer diameter of its margins is 1.50 m. Three large clay vessels are set in a fan-shaped arrangement along the northeast quadrant of the well. They were very likely used to store water pulled from the well.

In summary, the Habitation Complex V was still inhabited by craftpeople during Building Sequence 3. Evidence of pottery making, even if not overwhelming, appears to be suggested here.

Summary

During BS-3, the settlement on Awdaghost Acropolis still consisted of two habitation complexes, separated by a short street oriented east-west. There are significant if different architectural modifications in both habitation complexes. Two new household units were added to Habitation Complex IV, with very interesting restructuring of the three already in existence. The new units, HC-IV/HU-A and HC-IV/HU-C, have two characteristics in common: they are built with two entrances, one in the west and the other in the east, and tend on the average to have fewer rooms (Table 4).

Variation in household unit size and room number is minimal in Habitation Complex V. In this complex, HU-A and HU-B are two-room units sharing an extensive courtyard with a common well. Habitation Complex IV, on the other hand, witnessed very interesting transformations during BS-3. The number of household units shifted from three to five, and range in size from 169.01 m^2 for HU-D in the southeast to 110.06 m^2 for HU-A in the northwest.

Interestingly enough, at this stage there appears to be a trend toward decreasing size in the household units. The space allocated to the courtyard varies from a maximum of 70 m^2 in HC-IV/HU-D (41% of the unit's area), to a minimum 34.72 m^2 in HC-IV/HU-A (31%). The number of rooms varies from 5 in HC-IV/HU-C to 11 in HC-IV/HU-F. The early units, HC-IV/HU-D and HC-IV/HU-E, have eight and seven rooms respectively, and on average, the rooms are larger. Mean size varies from 12.37 to 13.46 m^2; ranges from 15.80 to 14.14; standard deviation from 4.33 to 8.84; and finally, coefficient of variation from 0.35 to 0.65 (Table 5). HC-IV/HU-F, one of the earliest-built units, is an unusual unit: it has a high number of small rooms. HU-F room mean size is 6.25 m^2, with a range of 11.48, a standard deviation of 3.65, and a coefficient of 0.55. The units built later, HU-A and HU-C, have 7 and 5 rooms respectively, with an almost similar room mean size, varying from 10.64 to 10.76 (see Table 5). Variations in range (21.12 and 9.84), standard deviation (6.67

and 3.57), and finally, coefficient of variation (0.61 and 0.33), are significant. The virtual similarity in room mean size thus appears to be an artifact of descriptive statistics, without any architectural or social meaning.

Building Sequence 4 (Fig. 11)

Building Sequence 4 deposits have been recorded at depths varying from 1.80 to 2.30 m. The major construction event is the addition of a sixth household unit, HU-B, to the northern end of the Habitation Complex IV, which now has the shape of a hexagon, 36 m north-south and 30 m east-west, with the sides measuring 27 m in the south, 15 m in the southeast, 30 m in the northeast, 19 m in the north, and 30 m in the west. There were, in addition, a few minor architectural modifications in some household units. Nothing was added or removed from Habitation Complex V that altered its BS-3 organization and structure.

Habitation Complex IV

Household Unit A

HU-A was slightly rearranged without noticeable architectural modifications. The courtyard and room size, number, and location remained unchanged. The storage vessels previously spread out and distributed in four distinct spots are now regrouped in room 6 in the northeastern corner. Surprisingly, the number of these vessels, six, is identical in both BS-3 and BS-4 occupations. In BS-4, all six are set along room 6 walls, clearly the main storage space of the unit. The kitchen also shifted from room 2 in BS-3 to the northern half of the reception/living room 1. This time, three instead of four hearths are set in a triangular arrangement. Room 2 was then turned into a sleeping space. HU-A thus consisted of a courtyard with an entrance to a neighboring unit, one pillared main reception room 7, one bathing/showering and latrine room 5, one storage room 6, a cooking space in room 1, a hallway room 1, and three sleeping rooms 2, 3, and 4, with the possibility of an upper floor accessed through the staircase.

Household Unit B

HU-B is the latest and the smallest of the household units built at this stage of the development of Awdaghost Acropolis. It covers a surface of 97.76 m², divided into a 65 m² courtyard and three rooms. It is shaped like an irregular trapeze (15 m in the south, 7 m in the north, 8 m in the west, 13 m in the east). The unit's entrance is set in the southeast end of the eastern wall, with the courtyard opening immediately on the street. All the new walls are built with stone, with the room complex located in the west half of the building. The courtyard is triangular in shape with the sides measuring 10 m in the south, 11 m in the west, and 13 m in the east. A circular well was dug in the east of the unit, next to the wall; it is 1.40 m in outer diameter, 0.40 m in inner diameter, and 3.70 m in depth (Polet 1985:136). It is lined with wadi cobbles down to 2.50 m, with the margin's platform raised at some 0.62 m above the courtyard surface. Two hearths and one large storage vessel were exposed in the western part of the courtyard, along the room's east wall.

Room 7 in the north of the unit is a narrow corridorlike space (2 to 2.1 m long, 1.2 to 1.4 m wide), open at both west and east ends and connecting the courtyard to room 1 and the staircase. Rooms 1 and 2 are roughly rectilinear, parallel, and oriented northeast-southwest. Room 2 covers 13.02 m². Both may have been used as sleeping rooms, with room 2 also functioning as a reception and living space. Room 1, 15.80 m², has a staircase to the roof in its northwest corner and three doors. There is an alcovelike space in the northwest flank of room 1. It has a curvilinear wall and measures 3 m in length and 1.5 m in maximum width. This small area may have been used as the bathing/showering space. The thick interior walls and the presence of a staircase providing access to the roof suggest that the house may have had an upper floor. If that were the case, the available room surface may have been twice as much as indicated in the archaeological record.

Household Unit C

HU-C witnessed some significant modification in its west half, with the east half left unchanged. The room distribution remained identical but the arrangement of portable features was different. All the storage vessels are found in the west half: two in the courtyard, each set against a wall, and the remaining two in the newly built hallway, room 6, connecting HU-A and HU-C. Room 6 is an upside-down L-shaped space, 36.8 m², 7.6 to 8 m long and 1.6 to 4.6 m wide, resulting in a significant increase in the size of the building complex to 157.12 m² (from 120.32 m² in BS-3). HU-C is divided into a courtyard with a rainwater drain and a well; hallway room 6 partially used for the storage of food or liquid supplies; reception room 1 opening onto the street; a reception/living room 3; a sleeping room 5; and very likely, a bathing/showering space in room 2.

Household Units D, E and F

Household units HU-D and HU-E were left unchanged. HU-D room 9 kept its function as a well room, but no water storage vessels were found this time. HU-E room 6, which previously contained two storage vessels, had none this time. It may have been turned into a dedicated sleeping room. Household unit HU-F was slightly rearranged in its northern half, with rooms 7 and 8 made into a single larger room. Four storage vessels are clustered in the west end of the rectilinear 9.08 m² space that may also have been used as a sleeping room.

Summary

At the end of BS-4 occupation, probably toward the end of the ninth century, two habitation complexes found on the Acropolis present very sharp contrasts in architecture, internal organization and room layout. Habitation Complex V in the northwest remained a largely

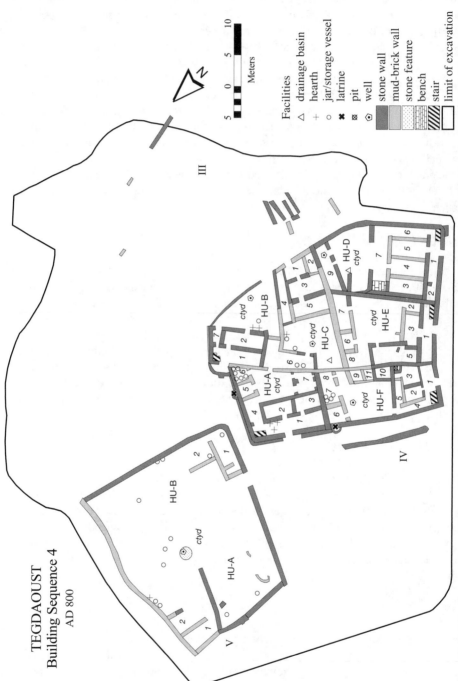

Figure 11. Building Sequence 4 constructions. Figure has been rotated so north, south, east, and west can be more easily described (i.e., what is described as "north" in text is actually closer to north by northeast).

Table 6: Building Sequence 4 constructions

Habitation Unit	Total Size (m²)	Courtyard (m²)	Rooms (m²)											Shape
			1	2	3	4	5	6	7	8	9	10	11	
Habitation Complex IV														
HU-IV-A	116.02	34.72	25.52	8.8	8.0	8.36	3.96	5.94	15.2					T
HU-IV-B	97.76	65	15.80	13.02					2.94					P
HU-IV-C	157.12	67.08	10.08	4.16	14	11.2	13.8	36.80						R
HU-IV-D	169.01	70	13.12	3.52	13.52	14.25	12.32	8.96	22.04		15.2			R
HU-IV-E	139.97	62.32	17.10	3.90	12		18.04	4.25	11.20	11.16				R
HU-IV-F	115.58	47.04	11.88	5.40	14.28	6.86	4.08	5.76	6	3.08	3.60	4.8	2.8	R
Habitation Complex V														
HU-V-A	627	598	29	7.5										R
HU-V-B	—	—	17.50	12										R

Key: H = Hexagonal; P = Pentagonal; R = Rectangular; T = Trapezoidal

Table 7: Variations in BS-4 room size (m²)

Habitation Unit	n	Minimum	Maximum	Mean	Range	Standard Deviation	Coefficient of Variation
Habitation Complex IV							
HU-IV-A	7	3.96	25.52	10.03	21.56	6.70	0.66
HU-IV-B	3	2.94	15.80	10.58	12.86	5.52	0.52
HU-IV-C	6	4.16	36.80	15.00	32.64	10.27	0.68
HU-IV-D	8	3.52	22.04	12.37	15.80	4.33	0.35
HU-IV-E	7	3.90	18.04	9.33	13.20	4.22	0.45
HU-IV-F	11	2.80	14.28	6.23	11.48	3.48	0.55
Habitation Complex V							
HU-V-A	2	7.5	29	18.04	21.20	5.75	0.24
HU-V-B	2	12	17.5	14.75	5.50	2.70	0.18

open courtyard shared by two households of craftpeople. The dwelling of each of the craft households consisted of two-room sets built at opposite northwest-southeast corners of the walled habitation complex.

Habitation Complex IV in the south, on the other hand, is a packed space divided between six household units, two of which, HU-A and HU-C, shared a common hallway in room 6. Four wells were available; the one in HU-C was very likely shared with HU-A. The excavated household units range in size from 97.76 m^2 for the smallest (HU-B) to 169.01 m^2 for the largest (HU-D). The courtyard ranges from 29% (HU-A) to 66% (HU-B) of the walled space. A remarkable pattern differentiates the early from the late buildings. The variation in size of the courtyard is extreme between the late-built units HU-A and HU-B. Its range is surprisingly narrow for the four early-built units, with 40% for HU-F; 41% for HU-D; 42% for HU-C; and finally, 44% for HC-IV/HU-E.

If room 6, the hallway connecting HU-A and HU-C, is excluded, the number of rooms varies from a minimum of three in HU-B to a maximum of eleven in HU-F. The modal number of rooms appears to range from six to eight (Table 6). They are divided into two to four classes.* Classes 1 and 3 with, respectively, 10 and 14 occurrences are the most frequent. Their frequencies vary from 1 (HU-C and HU-D) to 5 (HU-F) for class 1, and 1 (HU-B) to 4 (HU-C and HU-D) for class 3. Rooms larger than 20 m^2 are rare. Room size appears more compact, with means ranging from 9.33 to 12.37 m^2, if both extremes (HU-C with room 6 hallway and HU-F with its many cell-like rooms) are excluded from consideration. The coefficient of variation is nonetheless quite spread out, ranging from 0.35 to 0.66 (Table 7), suggesting the absence of any template as well as the lack of standardization.

Conclusion

The Pioneer era of the growth of the Acropolis, and by extension the town of Awdaghost, may have lasted for one and a half to two centuries, from the very beginning of the seventh century to the early ninth century. The Acropolis urban layout then consisted of two habitation complexes that were built incrementally in four archaeologically detectable sequences. It is not assumed that the time interval between one building sequence and the next was the same; in fact, it was certainly not. The growth and modification of buildings depended on such factors as demography, wealth, occupation, and social status.

For the whole duration of the Pioneer era, Habitation Complex V was inhabited by two households of craftpeople. The investment in dwelling facilities was minimal with the emphasis on the collectively managed working and living space of the courtyard with its well and workshops. Habitation Complex IV, on the other hand, changed considerably from one building phase to the next. Three households were built during BS-2, with mud-brick as the predominant building material. These three units set the southern limit of the complex that would later expand northward. Two additional household units were added during BS-3. The complex then consisted of five building units, with slightly more than half of the walls

---

*Class 1: < 5 m^2; class 2: >5-10 m^2; class 3: >10-15 m^2; and so forth in 5 m^2 increments.

(33 of 61) built with stone. A sixth household unit was added to the complex during BS-4. Stone was by then the predominant building material used in the construction of dwelling structures. Habitation Complex IV displays much more architectural sophistication and diversity, suggesting a distinct and different social status for the household members. From BS-3 onward, standards for comfort are on the rise, with the addition of latrines and specially designed bathing/showering rooms.

In summary, there are clearly two distinct social groups sharing Awdaghost Acropolis during the Pioneer era: one composed of craftpeople and the other probably of wealthier citizens, merchants, scholars, or town employees, with, on the average, larger family units.

—5—

The Accelerated Growth
(AD 900–1000)

The Pioneer era was followed by a phase of accelerated growth of the town that took place in the tenth and eleventh centuries. Regular commercial long-distance connections with both North Africa and the more humid and tropical West Africa brought more wealth to the town. Trade diasporas that may have included both North African and Sub-Saharan elements settled in the town and may have triggered its "cosmopolitan" Muslim outlook (Devisse 1983:162). The Acropolis was then covered with elaborate buildings divided into five habitation complexes separated by narrow winding streets (Robert-Chaleix 1989:55). Unfortunately, all the material excavated so far is not yet available in print. This discussion will then be based on the material available from three of the excavated habitation complexes, HC-III in the east, HC-IV in the center-south, and HC-V in the northwest. Awdaghost Acropolis's accelerated growth spanned two building sequences, BS-5 and BS-6, bracketed between AD 900 and 1000.

Building Sequence 5 (Fig. 12)

The Building Sequence 5 deposits were exposed at depths varying from 1.50 to 1.90 m and very likely date to the tenth century. A new habitation complex (HC-III), made up of three household units, was built in the eastern part of the Acropolis excavated probe. Habitation Complex V (HC-V) in the northwest was remodeled and emerged as an elaborate architectural construction. The tremendous difference with the previous BS-4 constructions, in terms of complexity as well as elaboration, suggests the ownership of the complex shifted to more affluent community members. Habitation Complex IV (HC-IV) in the center-south witnessed significant rearrangement of some of its household units.

Habitation Complex III

At first glance, this new complex is very distinctive. Rounded corners are replaced by sharp angles, and habitation space appears more compact and confined to a single large building with subdivisions. This house archetype is new in Awdaghost. Devisse (1983:161-64), even if cautiously, argued for the origin of its blueprint in the Circum-Mediterranean Muslim world of Spain, Iran, or North Africa. He quotes published archaeological evidence from Fustat and Sadrata in Egypt, Sabra Mansuriya in Iran, and Medinat-az-Zahra in Andalusia (Spain).

The complex is pentagonal in shape, extended over 618.74 m², and built almost exclusively with stone. The south wall is the shortest, measuring 10 m in length. The western wall, oriented north-south, is 30 m long, the northern one oriented east-west, 25 m, the eastern one 20 m, and finally, the southeast side, which is not strictly speaking a wall, also measures 30 m in length. The walled space is divided into three household units with size varying from 151.96 m² for the smallest (HU-B) to 217.08 m² for the largest (HU-C).

Household Unit A

HU-A is located in the northwest of HC-III and is shaped like an irregular polygon. The west wall measures 13 m in length, the north one 11 m, the south one 10 m, the southeast 6 m, and finally, the east wall is composed of two segments each 7 m long. The space is partitioned into an extensive courtyard in the south and five rooms of varying sizes and shapes. The unit is accessed through a narrow entrance set in the middle of the east wall, leading to the neighboring household unit. The door opens in room 4, a narrow elongated 7.36 m² space that served as a hallway. Its south flank was open, providing access to the large courtyard and its well. The well is 5.1 m deep with a stone-paved circular margin raised above the courtyard level.

Room 5 is the kitchen (2.88 m²), in the southwest corner of the household unit. It is delineated by west, south, and east walls and measures 1.8 m in length and 1.6 m in width. A tree stump with roots traced 2 m down was found in this area, associated with a large clay vessel. The vessel may have been used for the storage of bathing/showering water pulled from the well and left under the tree shade to cool. In general, however, the presence of this tree suggests that some of the courtyard may have been "landscaped" with bushes and trees to provide a cooler atmosphere.

A triangular corridor room 3 leads northward to the domestic inner sanctum. It measures 6 to 6.2 m in length and 2.8 m in maximum width, ending with a narrow doorway to room 1. Trapezoidal room 1 (33.04 m²) is found on the north side of the complex. It was a roofed space that may have been used as a reception and living room. A doorway in the middle of the room 1 south wall provides access to a set of three sleeping rooms (room 2), a large 39.10 m² space with what must have been a heavy roof, supported by a system of seven stone pillars. Room 2 is divided into three segments: the central one, almost a square, is 20.24 m²; the east segment is 8.28 m²; and the west segment is 9.66 m².

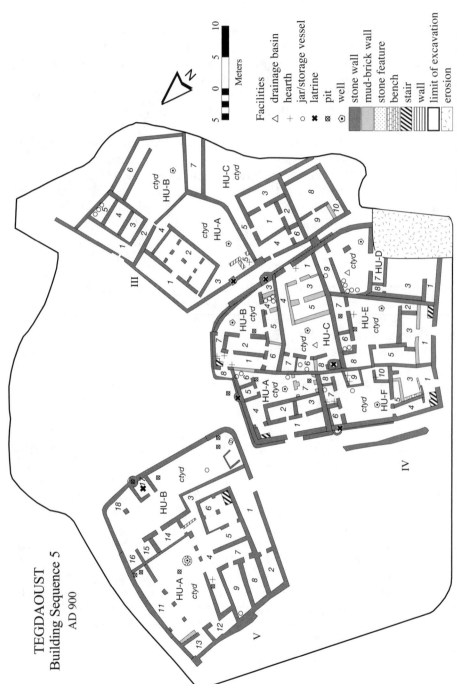

Figure 12. Building Sequence 5 constructions. Figure has been rotated so north, south, east, and west can be more easily described (i.e., what is described as "north" in text is actually closer to north by northeast).

Table 8: Building Sequence 5 constructions

Habitation Unit	Total Size (m²)	Courtyard (m²)	1	2	3	4	5	6	7	8	9	10	11	12	13	Shape
Habitation Complex III																
HU-III-A	190	74.48	33.04	39.10	17.36	7.36	2.88									H
HU-III-B	151.96	69.60	27.04	7.56	8.40	10.56	8.80	20								H
HU-III-C	217.08	67.50	20.16	6.72	13.20	16.40	17.60	3	18	30	12.5	3				H
Habitation Complex IV																
HU-IV-A	110.50	34.72	25.52	8.8	8.0	8.36	3.96	5.94	15.2							T
HU-IV-B	102.24	38.40	15.8	13.02	4.32	4	10	8	4.2	4.5						P
HU-IV-C	122.60	46.40	16.8		14	11.2	13.8	6	4.8	9.6						R
HU-IV-D	127.84	70.00	8.32		25.92				6	2.4	15.2					P
HU-IV-E	139.97	62.32	17.1	3.9	12		14.04	4.25	11.2	11.16						R
HU-IV-F	137.46	59.80	11.8		33.6	6.72	4.08	3.36	5.40	3.20	4.62	4.8				R
Habitation Complex V																
HU-V-A	319.81	104	35.38	11.7	21.38	29.04	11.82	22.54	11.5	12.4	16.4		27.28	8.93	7.8	R
			14	15	16	17	18									
HU-V-B	210.96	167.24	10.12	5.28	5.72	4.6	18									R

Key: H = Hexagonal; P = Pentagonal; R = Rectangular; T = Trapezoidal

Table 9: Variations in BS-5 room size (m²)

Habitation Unit	n	Minimum	Maximum	Mean	Range	Standard Deviation	Coefficient of Variation
Habitation Complex III							
HU-III-A	5	2.88	33.04	14.44	30.16	10.45	0.72
HU-III-B	6	7.56	27.04	12.47	19.48	7.34	0.58
HU-III-C	10	3.0	30	14.95	27	7.07	0.47
Habitation Complex IV							
HU-IV-A	7	3.96	25.52	10.82	21.56	6.80	0.62
HU-IV-B	8	4	15.80	7.98	11.80	4.27	0.53
HU-IV-C	7	4.8	16.80	9.17	12	4.91	0.53
HU-IV-D	5	2.4	25.92	11.56	23.52	8.30	0.71
HU-IV-E	7	3.9	17.10	9.70	13.20	4.73	0.48
HU-IV-F	9	3.20	33.60	8.62	30.40	9.16	1.06
Habitation Complex V							
HU-V-A	12	7.8	35.38	17.40	27.58	8.50	0.48
HU-V-B	5	4.6	18	8.40	13.40	5.55	0.66

HU-A, inhabited by more affluent community members (Devisse 1983:168), was clearly partitioned into two functional blocks: the courtyard with its well, the kitchen room 5, and the bathing/showering space with the latrine, and the restricted-access reception/living room 1 and the complex of three sleeping rooms.

Household Unit B

HU-B is an irregular polygon located in the eastern side of the complex. It has seven sides and covers a surface of 151.96 m², partitioned into a courtyard and six rooms. It has seven sides, measuring (clockwise, starting with the north wall, see Fig. 12) 13 m, 8 m, 10 m, 7 m, 9 m, 7 m, and 7 m. The unit's entrance is in the west end of the north wall, providing access to the reception/living room 1, a rectilinear 27.04 m² space. The pattern of internal circulation is difficult to delineate because most of the rooms' doorways are not mentioned explicitly in the excavation report (Devisse 1983:172-76). Room 1 provides access in its southwest to the narrow corridor room 2 (7.56 m²), which leads to the courtyard. Rooms 3 to 5 were very likely used for sleeping. The larger central room 4 (10.56 m²) is flanked in the east and west by smaller rooms 3 (8.4 m²) and 5 (8.8 m²). Based on architectural consideration, the doorway to room 4 was probably set in the north wall, opening in room 1, with smaller rooms 3 and 5 accessed through room 4. Room 5 may have doubled as a storage room as indicated by the presence of the bases of three storage vessels found along the east wall (Devisse 1983:174).

The courtyard is shaped like a pentagon with the sides measuring (clockwise, beginning with the north wall) 6 m, 12 m, 4 m, 7 m, and 9 m. The well, located in the center-southwest, was not fully excavated. Room 6 is a trapezoidal 20 m² space, 2 m wide, built along the eastern side of the courtyard. Archaeological features that may provide clues on the function of this room were not found; it could have been used for storage, cooking, sleeping, or any combination of those. Cooking was most likely done in the courtyard, but the downslope and the accumulated ashy refuse makes it difficult to pinpoint precise places.

HU-B has strong similiarities with HU-A. Like HU-A, the courtyard is found in the southern half, with room complexes in the north. HU-B and HU-A communicated through a narrow doorway, and appear to share the same gate to the outside (through room 1 of HU-B). In both cases, the courtyard was arranged to be far removed from outsiders' view and access. The unit thus consists of the reception/living room 1. From there one can move to the sleeping room complex accessed very likely through a doorway to room 4, which may have commanded the access to rooms 3 and 5. The corridor room 2 at the west end of room 1 leads to the courtyard where most of the domestic tasks may have been performed.

Household Unit C

HU-C is located in the south of the complex and shaped like a fan oriented southward. Unfortunately, the household unit was not entirely excavated (Devisse 1983:176). It is difficult to assess the size of the unexcavated portion along the southeastern flank of the probe. The limit of the excavation cuts across the courtyard, of which slightly more than half appears to have been exposed. The excavated portion of HU-C measures 217.08 m², delimited by five stone walls measuring 16 m (west wall), 10 and 6 m (north walls), 8 m (northeast), and 9 m (south). The space is divided into a 67.5 m² main courtyard, two smaller courtyards, and eight rooms and corridors. According to Devisse (1983:176), the excavation of this unit was particularly delicate and difficult because of the diversity of the associated architectural components. Unfortunately, some key elements that may have allowed for the reconstitution of the pattern of circulation within the unit, such as the location of doorways, were not published.

The household unit can be partitioned into three components. The first component, with the most elaborate architecture, is located in the northwest of the complex at what may have been the unit's entrance and consists of rooms 1 through 6. The unit is rectangular in shape, measuring 10 m in length west-east and 9 to 10 m in width north-south. From the street, one enters room 4, an elongated 16.40 m² trapezoidal space, very likely the reception/living room with an attached small storage room (room 6, 3 m²). The corridor room 5, 1.6 to 2 m in width and 8.8 m in length, leads east to the main courtyard. The precise location of the doorway allowing access to room 1, a smaller courtyard, is not known. It could have been set either in the west or more likely the north wall (Fig. 12). Courtyard room 1 is a rough square, 20.16 m². This well-secluded space may have been the core of the domestic domain, commanding access to rooms 2 and 3, which were very likely sleeping rooms. Room 2 (6.72 m²) may have been a sleeping room for children. Room 3, on the east side of the courtyard, is significantly larger (13.20 m²). It was most likely the sleeping room of the main family.

The second component, south of the first component, comprises two rooms and a courtyard. It is smaller in size, and trapezoidal (11 m and 9 m on north and south, 8 and 6 m east and west). The two rooms are found along the west wall. Room 9 is a rectangular 12.5 m² space, very likely used as the main sleeping room. Its south wall is the only mud-brick wall in the whole complex. Room 10, located at the southwestern corner of the component, is a tiny 3 m² space, with its east side open. It may have been used as a kitchen or a storage space with unimpeded access to the courtyard room 8. Courtyard room 8 measures approximately 30 m², 6 m in length and 5 m in width, and extends over two-thirds of the component where it reaches the limit of the excavation probe. It is not known how the component was accessed. Room 9 may have communicated with the narrow street to the west, but most likely the component was reached through the main courtyard.

The third component includes the main courtyard and room 7. The courtyard could be accessed through the corridor room 5, but it is not known if there was another entrance in the unexcavated southeast. Whatever the case, the main courtyard is a rough triangle (67.5 m²). Room 7, located along the northeastern flank of the main courtyard, was not exposed entirely, but the excavated portion measures 9 m in length and 2 m in width. There is an interruption in its southeastern end that may have been the doorway. The function of this room is unknown. It was large enough for sleeping, or storage, or both at the same time.

HU-C appears to have been inhabited by at least two distinct social units. The first component with four rooms, a secluded courtyard, and a long communication corridor very likely belonged to the founding household members and may have included the household head's family. This sub-unit controlled the access to the household unit. The second component with a single room, a storage or cooking area, and a courtyard may have been inhabited by dependents or younger but adult members of the household. And finally, the third component with the main courtyard and the elongated northeast room may have been used by all the members of the household. There was probably a well somewhere in the southeast, in the unexcavated portion of the courtyard. HU-C was clearly a multifamily household; unfortunately, it is difficult to decipher the kind of large family units represented. It may have been an extended family with the parent generation living side by side with the generation of adult and married children, or a polygamous family, consisting of the household head with his wives and children.

Habitation Complex IV

Habitation Complex IV in the center-south of the excavated Acropolis reached the peak of its growth during Building Sequence 5. There was some significant rearrangement of the internal space in a few of the household units in the northern half of the complex. In general, however, each of the units had its own well.

Household Unit A

HC-IV/HU-A in the northwest of the complex has preserved the same number of rooms and the basic organization of living facilities from BS-4, but with some significant improvements. All the walls, with the exception of those from the sleeping room 3, have been painted red (Polet 1985:164). The entrance is still in the middle of the west wall, as in BS-4. A small staircase with three steps and a low platform has been built at the northwestern corner of the unit, in the reception/living room 1. Combined with the use of ladders, this low staircase provided access to the roof. Rooms 2 and 3 remained unchanged, as did room 4. In room 4, however, a water drain oriented north-south and covered with flat stone slabs was dug along the east wall. The bathing/showering room 5, connected to a latrine, has been paved with flat stone slabs. Room 6 was used as kitchen and still contained two large storage vessels, set in the northeast corner. A pit, used later for the disposal of kitchen refuse, was found next to the kitchen entrance. A well was dug in the courtyard. It was located closer to the large pillared room 7. It is not known if this well was entirely excavated or not. No details are available. One large storage vessel, probably used to cool the water pulled from the well, was exposed leaning against the east wall. The six pillars from room 7 were rebuilt in mud-brick, and a pit, very likely used for fire, was dug in the floor, next to one of the central pillars.

During BS-5, HU-A presented unmistakable signs of increased opulence. Numerous small but critical improvements were added to the unit, enhancing its comfort for the household's members. The pillared room 7 may also have been used as a prestigious reception patio. The fire pit may accordingly have been used to warm the room up during cool evenings and nights.

Household Unit B

HC-IV/HU-B in the northeast of the complex witnessed large-scale remodeling, shifting from a three- to an eight-room unit. Its size was increased with the inclusion of a south-

western room built in an area previously part of the HU-C unit during BS-4. The 102.24 m²
area is surrounded by stone walls. The eastern wall consists of three partially overlapping
walls. The unit entrance is located in the west side of the north wall, providing access to
the reception/living room 1. It is a rectilinear space oriented north-south, covering 15.8 m².
Three hearths were found in the northern half of the room. They may have been used for
heating, hot beverage-making, or both. The reception/living room 1 appears to have been
a crucial node in the structure of HU-B domestic space. It provided access to no less than
four rooms. Room 8, on the northwestern flank, is a small area of 4.5 m². It may have been
used for the storage of domestic equipment other than food and cooking gear. Room 6,
along the south side, was accessed through rooms 1 and 2. This new addition of 8 m², its
east wall built with mud-brick, was taken from HU-C to which it belonged during BS-4. It
was very likely a sleeping room. Room 2 is also a communication node providing access to
three distinct spaces: the reception/living room 1 in the west, through a doorway set at the
north end of the west wall; the sleeping room 6 in the south, through a doorway set in the
middle of its south wall; and finally, the courtyard in the east, through a large doorway set
in the middle of east wall. Room 2 is rectangular in shape and oriented north-south. It
covers 13.02 m² and may have been used as a sleeping room.

Space (room) 7 located along the northern wall is a short corridor, 4.2 m², oriented west-
east, connecting the reception/living room 1 to the courtyard and the eastern part of the unit.
The 38.40 m² courtyard is comparatively small (Table 8) and triangle-shaped (8 m, 7.2 m
and 9.6 m). A new well was dug in the north with stone-paved margins raised 0.5 m above
the occupation surface. Unfortunately, no details are available on the main characteristics
of this new well, not even its diameter or depth (Polet 1985:168). There is also a new pit
filled with refuse near the room 2 wall.

Three contiguous rooms were built along the south wall. Room 5, probably a sleeping
room, is a trapezoidal 10 m² space. It opens into the courtyard and also communicated with
room 4 in the east. Room 4 was a food storage area, 4 m², with two doorways. It included
four large clay storage vessels found in a 0.5 m thick ash deposit, and set along the east wall.
The unusually large amount of ash found in the storage room 4 is puzzling. The excavator
suggested it was a kitchen that was never cleaned, thus allowing for an extraordinary accumulation of ash (Polet 1985:168). One wonders, however, how food could be cooked in
such a thick ash deposit. The documented ash accumulation was more probably caused by
a fire that may have burnt the roof supporting beams. These beams were generally made of
split date-palm tree trunk, a material that can produce a large quantity of ash. Room 3, at
the southeast end of the unit, is a trapezoidal 4.32 m² bathing/showering room combined
with and providing access to the latrine.

Household unit B presents an unusually high degree of connectivity, with a high redun-
dancy in the intra-unit circulation pattern. The reception/living room 1 has four doorways,
in the northwest, south, east and northeast; the sleeping room 2 has three doorways, in the
northwest, south, and east; room 6 has two doorways, both in the north wall; room 5 has
two doorways, in the north and east; and room 4 has two doorways, in the west and north.
Room 8 in the northwest and the bathing/showering room 3 in the southeast have one doorway each. There are, at least, three different options to reach the courtyard from the unit's
main entrance in the northwest: (1) from the entrance through the reception/living room

1, then the corridor 7, to the courtyard; (2) from the entrance through room 1, then room 2, to the courtyard; and (3) from the entrance through room 1, then room 6, room 2, to the courtyard. Such an "openness" is clearly unique so far and indicates an alternative way of structuring the domestic space.

Household Unit C

HC-IV/HU-C was also significantly remodeled during BS-5. All the unit's demarcation walls are now built with stone, with most of the mud-brick walls confined to the eastern set of rooms. The 122.60 m² of the walled domestic space is partitioned into six rooms, a courtyard and a relatively long corridor, with the main entrance set in the east wall. The building complex is accessed through the reception/living room 1 in the east end of the unit. It is an elongated 16.8 m² trapezoidal room, oriented north-south. A hearth was uncovered at the main entrance, set close to the red-painted east wall. It may have been used for both hot beverage-making and warming the room during the cool evenings and nights. From the reception/living room 1, one has access to a relatively long corridor in the north and to a set of rooms in the west. Room 3, to the west, shares the same north-south orientation. Three of this room's walls are built with mud-bricks and delineate a 14 m² rectilinear space. It was probably one of the unit's sleeping rooms, and was part of a three-room set including the reception/living room 1, and the sleeping rooms 3 and 5. Room 5 is accessed through a doorway set in its east wall. Three of this room's walls were built of mud-bricks. It is a roughly rectangular space, similar in size to room 3.

The remaining part of the unit is accessed through the 8 m long corridor (room 4), which provides the only access to the courtyard. The courtyard is a pentagon-shaped 46.4 m² space (sides measuring 8 m, 5.8 m, 3.6 m in the north, 4.1 m, and 4.8 m). Two features were uncovered in the courtyard: a rainwater drain and a well. Both are located along the central east-west axis of the courtyard, with the well dug closer to the east wall. The rainwater drain system utilizes the former well that probably dried up. The new well was then dug a few meters east.

Three rooms were built along the west wall, in a north-south arrangement. Room 7, at the northern end, is a small roughly square 4.8 m² space. All its walls were built with stone. The inside walls are painted in red, and an oil lamp in glazed ceramic was found on the floor at the foot of the wall (Polet 1985:170). Despite its small size, this room may have been used for sleeping. Room 6, in the middle, is trapezoidal and measures 6 m² in surface area. Three of its walls were stone; the south wall was built in mud-bricks. The room was accessed through a doorway opening in the courtyard. Its floor is ashy but no hearth was uncovered. Two large clay storage vessels were set against the north and east walls. Room 6 may thus have been used mainly as a storage space, with possibly intermittent utilization as a cooking area. Room 8, at the southern end of this block of rooms, measures 9.6 m² in surface area and consists of two distinct sub-units; the northern half had no special installation but was very likely used as bathing/showering space. The southern half was a latrine.

HC-IV/HU-C can be divided into two architectural components of almost equal size. The eastern component that commanded the entry to the unit consists of four relatively large rooms; the reception/living room 1 was the gateway. From there, one can be admitted to the sleeping rooms 3 and 5 or walk to the courtyard through the corridor (room 4). The western component comprises the courtyard with its well and rainwater drain, and a row of small rooms, 6, 7, and 8, utilized for a range of functions that included sleeping (room 7), storage and possibly cooking (room 6), and finally, bathing/showering and latrine (room 8). The rear or west part of the household unit was therefore the main service area. In that context, room 7 may have been the sleeping space of the household servant(s) or slave(s), or both. The front or east part was clearly that of the household head and family.

Household Unit D

HC-IV/HU-D in the southeastern corner of the complex was seriously impacted by erosion and later construction activities. Approximately one-third of the southern half of the building complex was destroyed. Despite these unfortunate circumstances, it is still possible to identify a major trend toward simplification in the remodeling of the unit during BS-5. All the preserved walls are built in stone. The main entrance was probably set in the south wall. If that was the case, household unit HU-D had two courtyards and four rooms. All the recorded rooms are arranged into roughly parallel bands. Room 1, located in the south, may have been the reception/living space. The exposed portion measures some 5.2 m in length and 1.6 m in width. It provided access to the southern courtyard, the excavated portion of which measures some 25.92 m². The southern courtyard, here termed room 3, was previously part of a three-room complex. It is not known if there was a room or a corridor along the east wall in what was the eroded part of the household unit. In any case, the southern courtyard was serviced by at least three doorways, two along its north side, and one, from the reception/living room 1, on its south side. Room 7, along the north side of the southern courtyard, is a narrow elongated space, of which 6 m² has been preserved. It controlled the access to the second, northern courtyard to which it was connected through a doorway, and may have been used as a combined reception/sleeping room. The inner side of room 7's north wall was painted in red as was the small room 8 (2.4 m²) at its west end. A low thin wall divides rooms 7 and 8, 0.15 m thick, made of stone slab masonry (Polet 1985:173). Room 8 has a doorway opening in the south courtyard and was very likely used as a storage space for the household members' belongings that may have required permanent supervision.

The northern courtyard is trapezoid and covers 70 m². It appears to have been the core of HU-D domestic activities. It had three fixed installations: a rainwater drain in the northwest, a small gallerylike construction, and a well. A description is available for the rainwater drain (Polet 1985:174) but not for the other two installations. The drain system was connected to the old abandoned well; the mouth of the old well was raised to the level of the occupation surface, and the sides lined with wadi cobbles and clay mortar. The small gallerylike construction, 1 to 2 m north of the well, included a number of small hearths and may have been used as the main cooking area of the whole household unit. The new well was dug in the southeast of the northern courtyard.

A storage area was exposed at the northwestern corner of the northern courtyard, in a thick ash deposit. The storage equipment consisted of five large clay vessels, three set along the west wall and two along the north wall. One would expect the food supply to be protected from the elements; the storage area may have been under a roof made of woven mat or any other biodegradable material. The ash deposit could have resulted from cleaning the storage area, a process that may have involved burning dry grass and twigs to eliminate pests. This seems to be corroborated by the two or three out-of-use clay pots used as supporting devices for the exposed storage vessels (Polet 1985:173). Alternatively, the ash deposit may have consisted of the burnt remains of the light roof material that was documented by "a thin layer of white ash, difficult to detect in an ashy context as this one" (Polet 1985:174).

Room 9, along the northern side of the unit, runs the length of the housing unit, as was probably the case for rooms 1 and 7. Its floor, extended over 15.2 m², is slightly ashy. It is a trapezoidal space with a doorway giving access to the north courtyard set in the eastern side of the south wall. A large storage vessel was found in the central part of the room, suggesting that it may have functioned as an opportunistic storage area as well as a sleeping room.

In summary, household unit D was an iterated replication of a smaller module that consisted of a transversal and elongated room combined with a courtyard. With the exception of the tiny storage room 8, all the other larger rooms, the reception/living room 1 in the front, the reception/living/sleeping room 7 in the middle, and the sleeping/storage room 9 in the rear, were very likely versatile and multi-functional. They were probably used flexibly to face the different needs of the household members. Though there is hardly any material evidence to support such an assertion, the southern courtyard, which does not contain any built feature of archaeological interest, may have been used for corralling livestock at night.

Household Unit E

With the exception of the reception/living room 1 north mud-brick wall, all the unit's walls are now built of stone. The pattern of circulation from the south entrance remained the same, but a well was dug in the southeastern portion of the courtyard. No details are provided for the main characteristics of the unit's new well, which is given only a passing mention (Polet 1985:175). It is flanked on its southern side by a short wall devised to keep the spilled water away from the corridor (room 2).

Two new features were set along the courtyard's northern side. One is a shallow pit, 0.60 m in diameter and 0.20 m deep, dug along the wall, and claimed to have been used for refuse disposal. The shallowness of this feature does not seem to fit with the garbage disposal function. There are no indications suggesting any impact from erosion agencies or other attritional forces that may have reduced the original size and depth of the courtyard pit. It is probably safer to consider this pit function unknown. The other feature is a relatively large hearth made of three hearthstones set in a triangular arrangement at the bottom of a shallow pit located at the very doorway of the sleeping room 7.

A shallow pit of undetermined function was also dug at the center of the 11.2 m² sleeping room 7. Its light ash content suggests that it may have been used as a heating device, and also possibly for pest control, to keep mosquitoes and other insects away from the room.

The remaining modification took place in the 4.25 m² kitchen in room 6: two large storage vessels set along the room's west wall.

In summary, during BS-5, the solidity of the household unit HC-IV/HU-E building was enhanced by an extensive use of stone as the main building material. The addition of a well would have increased the autonomy of the household members. The access to the unit's inner part was strongly constrained by the mandatory passage through the reception/living room 1 and corridor (room 2). Room 1 also provided an access to the roof through the staircase located at the southeastern corner.

Household Unit F

HC-IV/HU-F at the southwestern corner of the habitation complex went through a re-modeling program that resulted in fewer rooms, though it has preserved the same overall shape and size, 137.46 m^2 partitioned into eight rooms and two courtyards, with all the walls but one built with stone.

The unit was accessed from the south through the main entrance set at the middle of the south wall. Room 1 was very likely just a hallway that may have been infrequently used for informal reception. The staircase, leading to the rooftop and located at the southwestern corner of the hallway, was expanded with the addition of a smaller north-south segment. This addition created a very narrow passage to the inner part of the household unit. From the hallway (room) 1, one could move to a relatively small courtyard, to the rooftop, or to the inner part of the unit. The small southern courtyard was concealed from view from the outside by a thin short stone wall measuring 3 m in length and oriented east-west. The ir-regular-shaped courtyard (room) 3 (33.60 m^2) has two lateral closetlike appendages in the northeast. A low bench, made of stone slabs laid flat atop a clay platform, was built along the west and south walls. This installation suggests the southern courtyard to have been used as a kind of meeting place, a Koranic school for example.

The narrow passage to the inner part of the household unit is located at the northwest corner of room 1, leading to the corridor (room) 4. It is a long and narrow 6.72 m^2 rectangular space, with doorways at both ends and the wall painted red. The corridor provides access to the 59.8 m^2 main central courtyard, a trapezoidal space with sides measuring 5 m in length in the north and south, 8 m in the west, and 9 m in the east. A second thinner stone wall was built along the west wall to enhance its stability, and a new well was dug in the southwest. One large clay storage vessel was found in the center-northeast of the courtyard, leaning on the wall. This specimen is one of a set of three large storage vessels arranged along the wall. The missing two were represented by their unfired clay supports (Polet 1985:179).

A series of small rooms were built along the south, east and north sides of the courtyard. Room 5, on the southern side, is a narrow elongated 4.08 m^2 space accessed from the courtyard through a doorway located at the west end of the room's north wall. Its south and east walls were built with mud-brick. This cell-like space, with the inner wall side painted in red, may have been used as a sleeping area for a single individual. Room 6, in the northwest corner of the unit, is attached to the latrine and was used as the bathing/showering space. It is a 3.36 m^2 rectangular-shaped room, accessed through a doorway opening in the courtyard. Room 7, to its east, is slightly larger. It is rectangular, measuring 5.40 m^2 and accessed from the courtyard through a doorway set in the middle of its south wall. The floor was particularly ashy, probably resulting from frequent cleaning and sweeping. Two hearths were uncovered along the west wall, one at the southwest corner of the west and south walls and the other at the northwest corner. There was also a large storage vessel set in the northeast corner. The features and installations uncovered in room 7 tend to indicate its use as a kitchen. Room

8, to the east, is a tiny cell-like 3.20 m² space, with walls painted red. As with room 5, this room may have been used as a sleeping space for a single individual. Room 9, attached to the east wall, is situated virtually at its middle. It is a trapezoidal space, slightly larger than the other sleeping rooms, but still quite small. It covers a surface of 4.62 m². Its walls are painted red and two shallow hearths are located along the north wall, as well as a set of three *in-situ* hearthstones. The position of the doorway is not clear, but the hearths, found at the bottom of shallow holes, were probably used for heating and pest control. The triangular hearthstones may have been used for hot beverage-making. Room 9 appears to have been a sleeping space that may have been used for reception from time to time. Room 10, at the south end of the row, is slightly trapezoidal, covering 4.8 m², and accessed through a doorway located at the eastern end of its north wall. It contained a shallow hearth located at the corner of the west and north walls. This room was very likely used for sleeping by one or two individuals.

In summary, during BS-5, unit HU-F had some architectural characteristics that set it apart. It was likely a building used for a special purpose of some sort. The unit has cell-like sleeping rooms, three of which are painted red. All the rooms along the east wall are attached to patios (between rooms 8 and 9, and 9 and 10), providing some private space for thinking and meditation. The southern courtyard, with its stone benches along the west and south walls, was probably used as a lecture room or auditorium. All these characteristics together suggest that the unit may have been used as a kind of boarding school—a *madrasa*—for advanced students in Koranic studies, or perhaps a community of traveling scholars. There may have been some additional rooms on the roof, accessed through the staircase in room 1.

Habitation Complex V

Habitation Complex V witnessed the most dramatic growth during this building sequence, when it was turned into a very large single household unit built according to an elaborate architectural design. The shift in design was so radical that the link with the previous BS-4 installation becomes problematic. The new design includes a maze of courtyards, patios, and rooms of different shapes and orientations. The complex, then, appears to have been settled by a new group of owners who may have purchased the land lot from the previous owners. There is also a clear indication of the rapid "gentrification" of Awdaghost Acropolis during the tenth century AD.

Household Unit A

HC-IV/HU-A is an extensive and impressive construction comprising ten rooms with a very large courtyard. It is a rough trapezoid in shape, covering 319.81 m², with sides measuring 19 m in the west and south, 17 m in the north, and 23 m in the east. It is accessed through a doorway set in the south wall leading to room 1, from a narrow east-west street. Room 1 was very likely the reception/living room that controlled the access to the whole habitation complex. It is an elongated 35.38 m² rectangular room, approximately four times as long as wide, and leads to two directions, to the west and to the north. Room

2, west of room 1, is roughly rectangular, covering 11.70 m², and was very likely used as a sleeping room. The corridor (room) 3 starts from the northeast of room 1, running north-south, 7 m by 1.5 m, and provides access to the inner sanctum of the household unit. Corridor 3 opens in the northwest at a right angle with another but shorter corridor, combined with a small vestibule. The additional corridor and vestibule cover a surface of 10.88 m². This area controlled the access to both west (HU-A) and east (HU-B) units of the habitation complex.

From the corridor and the vestibule, HU-A is accessed through room 4. It is a long 29.04 m² gallery leading to the courtyard in the north, and the living area in the south. In its west half is a hearth and a pit. The east half of the north wall contains a succession of three doorways leading to the courtyard. The central part of the south wall opens on two contiguous and parallel short corridors. The western half of the gallery (room 4) was in fact a virtual room walled on the north, west and south sides. It may have been used as a reception room where household members and visitors may have enjoyed drinking hot beverages.

The living space of HU-A, the "main house," consists of two almost symmetrical halves articulated on a central north-south wall. The east half is composed of two distinct spaces, the corridor (room) 5 and the large room 6. The west half includes the corridor (room) 7, room 8, and room 9.

In the east half, corridor 5 is the hallway to room 6, a pillared area that may have been used for the reception of prestigious guests, and accessed through a doorway set at the southern end of the west wall. It was an exceptionally spacious room, almost square in shape, and covering 22.54 m². The roof was laid over two large intersecting beams supported by a system of five pillars or buttresses. The central pillar, square in cross-section, was relatively well preserved with sides measuring 0.60 m. The buttresses set in the middle of the east, north, and west walls were rectangular in cross-section, 0.60 long and protruding some 0.40 m into the room (Robert-Chaleix 1989:65-66).

The west half is divided into three rooms. Room 7, a rectangular hallway, runs north-south, covering 11.50 m², and leading to two parallel east-west sleeping rooms (rooms 8 and 9). Room 8 covers 12.40 m². Room 9 is much larger, covering 16.4 m². A large storage vessel was found in the floor at the northwest corner of room 9. The room may have served a dual purpose, as sleeping and storage space.

The north half of HU-A is accessed through a series of three doorways across the gallery (room) 4 north wall, and consists of an extensive courtyard, a northern gallery and two rooms. The unit's well was dug in the southeast of the courtyard near the gallery 4 doorways. Details are not given in the original report but the well's mouth appears to be surrounded by a stone-paved margin. The courtyard is trapezoidal and covers 104 m². Beside the well is a pit of unknown function. Room 11, situated along the north wall, is a gallery with the roof supported by a series of five pillars 1 to 2 m apart. Four are part of the south flank and one, set against the north wall, was used as a buttress. A clay bench made of two courses of mud-brick was built along the west wall, and two storage bins in unfired clay were found leaning against the gallery's east wall. Besides the storage function suggested by the presence of unfired clay bins, the gallery may have been used as a stable for horses, as an informal meeting place, or even as a sleeping space during the hot nights of the dry season.

Rooms 12 and 13 were built along the west side of the courtyard and oriented north-south. Room 12, the southernmost, is trapezoidal and covers 8.93 m². It is accessed from the courtyard through a doorway set in the middle segment of the east wall. The west wall is thicker than average and appears to have been buttressed with an extra stone wall course. It was very likely used as a sleeping space. Room 13 is a slightly smaller rectangle, measuring 7.8 m². It has a doorway opening on the courtyard set at the south end of the east wall. The northwest corner of unit HU-A was reinforced with thick pillarlike buttresses, rectangular in cross-section, designed to enhance the stability of the whole construction.

In architectural terms, HC-V/HU-A is so far the most elaborate household unit exposed in the Awdaghost Acropolis area. It can be partitioned into three distinct sub-units that may have hosted different categories of people. Sub-unit 1 consists of the reception room 1 and sleeping room 2; it may have been used by a servant-guard or slave whose assignment was to control the access to the household private space. Sub-unit 2 is the main house, inhabited by the household head and family and comprising gallery 4, corridors 5 and 7, and rooms 6, 8, and 9, accessed through corridor 3. The west end of the gallery may have been used as a kitchen or storage space for household belongings. And finally, sub-unit 3, where most of the domestic chores may have been taken care of, accessed through the three doorways in gallery 4, includes the courtyard with a well, a probable storage pit, the gallery 11, and sleeping rooms 12 and 13. The smaller sleeping rooms 12 and 13 may have been used by domestic servants or slaves.

Household Unit B

Household unit B does not seem to be a self-contained and coherent household unit. It was more likely a special-purpose component of the Habitation Complex V under the control of HU-A. It covers 210.96 m², of which 167.24 m² was a courtyard. The remaining space is partitioned into five rooms, all located in the northern half of the unit.

The unit is accessed through room 14 (via the corridor 3 in the south) and has two doorways: one set in the south wall and the other in the east wall. The rectangular space covers 10.12 m². Two small sleeping rooms, rooms 15 and 16, are found on the north flank of the previous one. The southernmost, a rectangular room of 5.28 m², had a red-painted wall. Trapezoidal room 16 covers 5.72 m². These two rooms may have belonged to the household's servants or slaves.

The courtyard is oriented north, stretched on 22.6 m with a width varying from 4.6 to 7.4 m, and composed of two parts. The northern portion measures 12 m in length and 4.6 to 7.4 m in width. The southern one is narrower on the average, 4.6 to 5.5 m in width, with, however, an almost similar length of 11.4 m. A series of features of archaeological interest were exposed in the southern part of the courtyard, including pits, storage vessels, and an enclosure.

There were three pits and three large vessels in the southern part of the courtyard. Two of the pits and two of the vessels were clustered in the southeast corner near an enclosure. The enclosure was made of two 2 m lines of stone and a third line which was truncated on the south end, suggesting an entrance. The enclosure superstructure may have consisted of thorny tree branches and twigs demarcating a sheep/goat pen. The large clay vessels found nearby may have been used for the watering of the penned small livestock.

The northern courtyard portion had a series of additional constructions along its east side. A latrine, built within the confines of a small rectangular 4.6 m^2 room (room 17), was accessed through a doorway at the south end of the west wall. Shelter (room) 18 occupied the trapezoidal space north of the latrine (2.2 to 3 m wide). The roof, very likely made of light material like straw mat or hide, was supported by a stone pillar built at the midpoint. Shelter 18 may have been a versatile working and possible resting area used by the house servants.

In summary, HC-V units A and B were complementary components belonging to one family, and the elaborate architecture suggests it was a wealthy one. The eastern part of the complex was devoted to small livestock pens, food storage, servants' working space and sleeping facilities. The western one, with its own large courtyard, was inhabited by the owner's household with possibly some rooms for servants or slaves.

Summary

During Building Sequence 5, the whole Acropolis is filled with more elaborate build-ings separated by narrow winding streets. Stone was then the dominant material used in the construction of habitation facilities. Each of the habitation complexes discussed so far presents some specificity of its own. Habitation Complex III in the east is characterized by relatively large household units in an architectural blueprint singled out by straight lines and acute angles, with the internal arrangement of rooms derived from the North African "*Maghribi*" template. Habitation Complex IV, in the center, consists of smaller household units likely inhabited by elite members from local origins. "Household unit" F departs significantly from the spatial syntax currently in use in all the other units, suggesting that it may have had a special function: a school, for example. Habitation Complex V was entirely inhabited by one household and divided into two functionally distinct areas. That a wealthy household of that era could have had separate living quarters for domestic servants or slaves is suggested by this example from Egypt:

> of male servants, the master of a family keeps, if he can afford to do so, one or more to wait upon him and his male guests; another, who is called "sakka," or water-carrier, . . . a "bow-wab," or doorkeeper, who constantly sits at the door of the house; and a "sais," or groom, for the horse, mule, or ass. [Hunwick and Troutt Powell 2002:109]

On average, household units from BS-5 are larger, varying from a minimum of 102.24 m^2 (HC-IV/HU-B) to a maximum of 319.81 m^2 (HC-V/HU-A) (Table 8). The number of rooms per unit ranges from 5 in HC-V/HU-B to 12 in HC-V/HU-A, with units of 5 to 8 rooms more frequent. The size of courtyard presents an interesting patterning. Habitation Complex IV units appear to have been built with relatively small courtyards ranging in size from 34.72 m^2 (HU-A) to 70 m^2 (HU-D). Habitation Complex III, with three household units, is composed of middle-size courtyards varying in size from 67.5 m^2 (HU-C) to 74.48 m^2 (HU-A). And finally, the large courtyards in HC-V range from 104 m^2 (HU-A) to 167.24 m^2 (HU-B).

Class 1* to 4 rooms with 18 to 12 occurrences are widely distributed and the most frequent (Table 8). Class 2 has 18 occurrences, recorded in all but two units (HC-III/HU-B and HC-V/HU-A) with frequency varying from 1 (six cases) to 5 (HU-IV/HU-F). The distribution of 19 class 3 rooms is more even; absent from HC-V/HU-A, its frequency varies from 1 (two cases) to 4 (HC-IV/HU-A), with 2 as the most frequent situation. There are 12 recorded class 4 rooms, found in eight household units out of eleven. The frequency distribution ranges from 1 (four occurrences) to 3 (two occurrences), 4 (one occurrence), and 5 (one occurrence). The larger rooms, from classes 5 to 8, are rare in general. They are found in two household units, HC-III/HU-C and HC-V/HU-A, for class 5; in five units for class 6; in two units for class 7; and finally, in one unit for class 8.

The room mean sizes (Table 9) also indicate a tripartite patterning. In Habitation Complex III, mean room size ranges from 12.47 to 14.95 m^2, a very narrow difference of 2.48 m^2 which situates these units in the middle of the room-size spectrum. In Habitation Complex IV, the difference in mean room size is still surprisingly small, amounting to 3.58 m^2, with a minimum of 7.98 m^2 in HU-B and a maximum of 11.56 m^2 in HU-D.

Habitation Complex V presents a totally different situation. It can be viewed either as a two-household unit, or as a single-household unit with two complementary components. In the two-household option, HC-V/HU-A has the highest mean room size (17.40 m^2). HC-V/HU-B on the other hand, with a mean room size of 8.40 m^2, is one of the lowest figures compiled so far. The difference of 9 m^2 is important and can be explained by differences in wealth and social status. If it represents a single household of 17 rooms, the mean room size drops significantly, from 17.40 (HU-A) to 15.28 m^2. Despite this decrease, however, it is still the highest recorded mean room size.

Fluctuations in the coefficients of variation of room size are minimal in Habitation Complex V, varying from 0.48 to 0.66; moderate in Habitation Complex III, 0.47 to 0.72; and important in Habitation Complex IV, ranging from 0.48 to 1.06. These figures probably reflect the coherence and coordination—or lack of—in the building of each of the complexes. From this perspective, the construction of Habitation Complex V followed a masterplan that divided the unit into two complementary parts. Habitation Complex III was built with houses based on very similar blueprint, with a main habitation block, a large courtyard, and a narrow, elongated rectilinear side-room. And finally, Habitation Complex IV was the product of diverse architectural options implemented independently by each household.

Building Sequence 6 (Fig. 13)

Building Sequence 6 deposits were exposed at depths varying from 1.30 to 1.50 m. They date from the eleventh century AD and correspond to the peak in building intensity on Awdaghost Acropolis, and very likely the whole town. Almost all of the excavated household units went through extensive remodeling process. Stone is largely predominant as building material but mud-brick was still used, as will be shown later.

---

*Class 1: < 5 m^2; class 2: >5-10 m^2; class 3: >10-15 m^2; and so forth in 5 m^2 increments.

Habitation Complex III

Habitation Complex III was still made of three household units. However, a short stone wall was added in the northeast, delineating a three-wall structure that may have been a room of an adjacent but unexcavated household unit.

Household Unit A

HC-III/HU-A was extensively remodeled and its layout radically simplified. The BS-6 unit consisted of a 190 m² walled space divided into a large 160.60 m² courtyard and a 29.4 m² room. The unit entrance was set in the south half of the west wall facing the room's doorway. The courtyard is shaped like an upside-down L with six sides. The unique trapezoidal room 5 of the new unit is located in the southeast. The roof was supported by a series of four stone pillars, almost equidistant and built along the central longitudinal axis of the room. The northern and southern pillars are inserted in the walls and protruded into the room's internal space.

No specific features or activity areas were uncovered from the unit's extensive courtyard. It is very likely that the whole unit's function changed, becoming a caravansérail for example, with room 5 providing a shelter, cooking and sleeping space for caravan crews. The caravansérail hypothesis is particularly appealing even if slightly handicapped by the absence of a well with drinking troughs. One would expect dromedaries to be penned during the nights in a protected place with low humidity, which this would have been.

Household Unit B

The remodeling of HC-III/HU-B resulted in increased architectural elaborateness, with a shift from six to eight rooms. The small doorway connecting HU-B with HU-A was sealed, suggesting a change in relationship between these two households. The northern half of the unit was unchanged from BS-5. The unit's entrance was still in the same position, set in the west half of the north wall, allowing access to the house from the narrow street outside. As in BS-5, corridor (room) 1 controlled the access to the private block of sleeping rooms 3, 4, and 5. The block was accessed through a doorway leading to the middle room 4. Both lateral rooms 3 and 5 were accessed from room 4. The central and southern part of the unit were accessed through corridor 2. A rainwater drain channel was dug along the corridor. The courtyard is pentagonal, covering 54.40 m². A new well was dug at the center of the courtyard, approximately 5 m north of the previous BS-5 well. Its mouth was surrounded by a stone platform raised 0.80 m above the courtyard floor (Devisse 1983:192).

Two new rooms were added to the unit, and a third completed with a short extension on its south end. Room 6 was completed with a series of short stone walls at its southern end, oriented northeast-southwest for one and northwest-southeast for the other, thus demarcating a corner and a doorway. The doorway opened in the courtyard and the completed room measured 30.68 m². It is a narrow and elongated trapezoidal space, oriented northwest-southeast and may have been used as a stable for horses, a warehouse for storing merchandise, or as storage space for household goods. Room 7 is not strictly speaking a room but a small trapezoid (1.44 m^2) of three stone walls with the northwest side left open. It could have been used to store household equipment. Finally, room 8, located at the south tip of the unit, is almost rectangular and covers 3.08 m^2. A small hearth was recorded during the excavation (Devisse 1983:193) and the presence of ash deposits suggests that room 8 may have been used as a kitchen.

In summary, household unit B consists of two main parts, each characterized by a series of functions. The northern half was devoted to the reception of visitors, kin, and friends and also included sleeping rooms for household members. The southern half, with the courtyard, a well, a kitchen, and a stable/warehouse/storage space, was devoted to domestic maintenance activities and probably to the trade in which the household head may have been involved.

Household Unit C

Household unit C preserved the same degree of elaborateness with nonetheless some significant alterations. It is divided into three sub-units that seem to have been relatively autonomous.

They consist of the south sub-unit with rooms 6, and 7; the north sub-unit with rooms 1, 2, 3, 4, and 5; and finally, the east sub-unit with the courtyard and room 9. It was accessed from the southern half of the building through an entrance in the west wall, leading to rectangular room 6 (12.48 m^2) with a door to room 7 directly opposite the entrance. Its floor is carefully paved with stone slabs and may have been kept clean most of the time. The pillared room 7, on the eastern flank of the hallway, measures 36.96 m^2 in area. It is an exceptionally large room by local contemporary standards, suggesting that it may have been built for a special purpose. It is trapezoidal, with a roof supported by a series of four pillars: three set along the central longitudinal axis and one inserted in the east wall. The occupation floor consisted of a thick layer of ash, with a few ordinary artifacts. Devisse (1983:195-97) discusses two options for the use of this space. In one scenario, room 7 was a sort of "market place," with the thick layer of ash brought from elsewhere and accumulated on the room's floor to create an absorbent deposit. In the other scenario the ash layer is considered to have resulted from the burnt roof due to an accidental fire, though this option does not point to any particular room function. The area did not provide evidence for ordinary household activities. For Devisse (1983:195), "without any doubt, we are dealing with a carefully arranged space, with a skillful re-use of the remains of [occupation 3], constituting, very likely, *a public space*. Neither habitation, nor collective workshop, this well organized space makes one think of a selling place, a small market." The "small market" may have been in fact a household shop, attached to the owner's house, selling an array of local and imported goods to customers.

The north sub-unit was, very likely, the dwelling component of the household's core members. Surprisingly, it was accessed from the neighboring HC-III/HU-A unit in the north, through a staircase built against the room 5 west wall (Devisse 1983:199). From there, one turned west and entered the north sub-unit through the roofed corridor (room) 5, a 17.2 m^2 rectilinear space oriented east-west. Room 4, also a roofed corridor, starts at the west end of room 5, and runs perpendicular to it. It covers 18.48 m². The south end of corridor 4 could have been used as a sleeping area for the "door-keeper" or the storage of the household's belongings. In the east wall of corridor 4 is a doorway leading to a secluded courtyard (room 1), trapezoidal, covering 19.32 m². Half of the courtyard may have been sheltered by trees or tent material and used for reception and meals. The secluded courtyard is flanked by two rooms in the south and east. Room 2, in the south, is particularly narrow, measuring 1.4 to 1.6 m. It could have been used for sleeping, or storing household goods, or both. Room 3, in the east, was clearly a sleeping space. It is a rectangular space measuring 15.32 m² and oriented north-south.

The east sub-unit, with the main courtyard and room 9, was not excavated in its entirety. The courtyard covers 67.50 m² and may have been the main area for domestic maintenance activities. Room 9 found along the northeast side of the unit measures 18 m². The excavated portion is trapezoidal, oriented northwest-southeast. Its function is unknown, but based on its location, it may have been used as a storage annex for both the household domestic needs and the likely shop of the south sub-unit.

In summary, household unit HC-III/HU-C was segmented into distinct areas organized around the main central courtyard. Based on the new interconnection between HU-A and HU-C, and the radical remodeling of HU-A, it is likely, even if untestable, that both units belonged to same household. The northern unit may have been used for penning caravans involved in the Trans-Saharan trade transiting at Awdaghost. Part of the southern unit was used for local commerce, and the remaining portion used as dwelling facilities by the household's members. In fact, it appears that during this building sequence, the dominant activities performed in Habitation Complex III shifted significantly toward mercantile-related functions.

Habitation Complex IV

Habitation Complex IV presents a radically contrasted situation during Building Sequence 6. The northern half of the complex was remodeled in a more elaborate architectural design, while the southern half became simpler and more open.

Household Unit A

Stone is the exclusive building material used in the construction of HU-A. A new pattern of circulation was devised with a series of additional doorways. The unit's west wall is now a single-course stone wall with two entrances; the main and larger one is in the middle of the wall, and a secondary one was created at the very south end next to the unit's south wall. Both doorways provided access to room 1 which was turned into a sort of corridor, open at both ends. In the north, it leads to room 4 in the east and the upper floor on the roof. In the south, it communicates through a new doorway with unit HC-IV/HU-F. Three small hearths were exposed in the north half of room 1. They seem to have been used for light, hot beverage-making, or heating. The ash produced was disposed of in the pit located between rooms 1 and 4. The primary function of the pit had probably been the storage of foodstuffs.

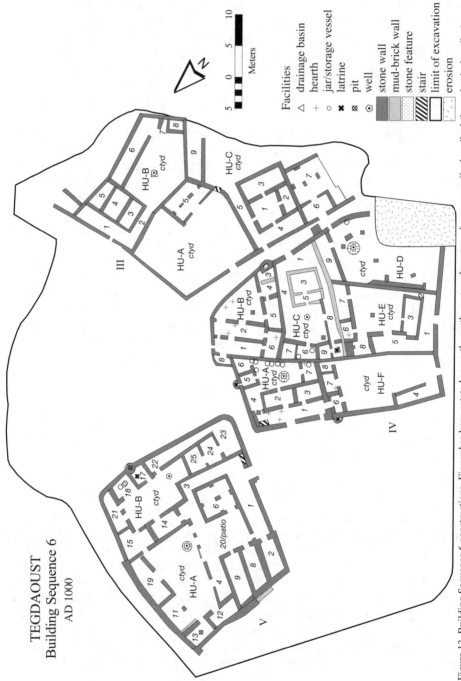

Figure 13. Building Sequence 6 constructions. Figure has been rotated so north, south, east, and west can be more easily described (i.e., what is described as "north" in text is actually closer to north by northeast).

Table 10: Building Sequence 6 constructions

Habitation Unit	Total Size (m²)	Courtyard (m²)	1	2	3	4	5	6	7	8	9	10	11	12	13	Shape
Habitation Complex III																
HU-III-A	190	160.60					29.4									H
HU-III-B	151.96	54.40	27.04	7.56	8.4	10.56	8.8	30.68	1.44	3.08						P
HU-III-C	217.08	67.50	19.32	6.72	15.32	18.48	17.2	12.48	36.96		18					H
Habitation Complex IV																
HU-IV-A	112.36	44.80	25.52	8.8	8	8.36	3.52	5.94	7.42							T
HU-IV-B	93.54	38.4	15.8	13.02	4.32	4	10	8		4.5						R
HU-IV-C	132.20	38.4	22.4		13.2	13.68	5.72	6	4.8	20.88	7.08					R
HU-IV-D	131.19	118.08									13.11					R
HU-IV-E	139.97	66.60	16.8	3.9	12.96		19.76	4.25	10.07	12.24						R
HU-IV-F	119.44	96				11.84		3.36	5.04	3.2						R
Habitation Complex V																
HU-V-A+B	500.87	190	37.12	11.7	21.38	29.04		22.54		12.4	17.52		13	8.93	7.8	R

HU-V/A+B Rooms [continued]

14	15	16	17	18	19	20	21	22	23	24	25
12.48	21		4.6	7.2	17.5	33	12	20.9	12.96	7.65	7.59

Key: H = Hexagonal; P = Pentagonal; R = Rectangular; T = Trapezoidal

Table 11: Variations in BS-6 room sizes (m²)

Habitation Unit	n	Minimum	Maximum	Mean	Range	Standard Deviation	Coefficient of Variation
Habitation Complex III							
HU-III-A	1	29.4	29.4	29.4	0	—	—
HU-III-B	8	1.44	30.68	12.19	29.24	10.06	0.82
HU-III-C	8	6.72	36.96	18.06	30.24	8.67	0.48
Habitation Complex IV							
HU-IV-A	7	3.52	25.52	9.65	22	6.68	0.69
HU-IV-B	8	4	15.80	9.19	11.80	4.30	0.46
HU-IV-C	8	4.8	22.40	11.72	17.60	6.99	0.59
HU-IV-D	1	13.11	13.11	13.11	0	—	—
HU-IV-E	7	4.25	19.76	12.99	15.51	5.29	0.40
HU-IV-F	4	3.20	11.84	5.86	8.64	3.52	0.60
Habitation Complex V							
HU-V-A+B	21	7.59	37.12	15.51	29.53	7.71	0.49

Ash disposal was the secondary function that ended up with the pit filled and sealed with a thick layer of clayey sediment (Polet 1985:202).

Room 2 had the same size and orientation but now had two doorways; the larger was in the southern half of the room's west wall and the smaller was in the middle of the room's east wall. In the new configuration, one could walk directly from the outside public sphere to the unit courtyard almost in a straight line, through room 1 and room 2. Room 2 therefore functioned as a vestibule, controlling the access to and from the courtyard, and as such may have departed from its previous function of sleeping room. It probably took over the function of reception room that was previously the purview of room 1. Room 3, in the south, was unmodified and very likely remained a sleeping room. Room 4 in the north was now entirely a sleeping room as the main courtyard could be accessed through room 2. Room 5, the unit's bathing/showering space, is slightly smaller, 3.52 m^2. It is accessed from the courtyard through a narrow doorway set in its south wall. Its floor is entirely paved with stone slabs and it provided access to the latrine. Room 6, the third room along the north wall, is located at the northeastern corner of the unit. It is a trapezoidal space, 5.94 m^2. The doorway set in the east half of the south wall opened in the main courtyard. Other than ashy sediment found on otherwise clean sand, there are no clear diagnostic elements. The location of some of the nearby storage vessels suggests it may have been a kitchen and storage space. Room 7, in the southeast of the unit, is a newly built walled space of 7.42 m^2. It is trapezoidal in shape, with the doorway set at the middle of the north wall and opening in the courtyard. In it were one large storage vessel leaning against the east wall, and a small hearth in the northeast corner. This room may well have served multiple functions; it could have been a sleeping room, with a water-storage facility, and a small "heating" hearth. Due to the reduction in size of the new room 7 in comparison to the previous BS-5 pillared version, the main courtyard is significantly larger, covering 44.80 m^2. It is trapezoidal, oriented north-south, with sides measuring 6.2 to 8 m in length and 3.4 to 5.6 m in width, with a well located more or less at the center. The courtyard is accessed through five doorways: in the south from room 7, in the west from room 2, and in the north from rooms 4, 5, and 6. Seven large storage vessels were recorded in the courtyard. They are all leaning against walls: one in the north against the south wall of rooms 5 and 6, and the remaining six arranged in distinct pairs along the unit's east wall.

Household Unit B

During BS-6, the remodeling of household unit HU-B occurred almost exclusively in the northern half. All the walls but one have now been built with stone. The unit perimeter wall has become a simple one-course stone wall and the main entrance has remained on the same spot in the north wall of room 1. In fact, room 1 has become a hallway providing access to a number of rooms. It is rectangular, oriented north-south and covers 15.8 m^2. Three other rooms were accessed from hallway (room) 1: the small 4.5 m^2 storage space (room 8) located in the northwest corner of the unit, room 2 in the east and finally, room 6 in the south. Room 2 was serviced by no less than five doorways: two in the northern half of the west wall, one in the south, and two in the east wall. It is a rectangular space oriented north-south, measuring 13.02 m². Two hearths were recorded in the north-central portion of the room, each set against the wall. This room was very likely a reception/meal-taking area that may have been used intermittently for cooking purposes. Room 6 in the southwestern part of the unit is rectangular and oriented east-west, covering 8 m². It was clearly a sleeping room with a small hearth used for heating purposes.

The shape and size of the main courtyard remained unchanged. The unit has no well; there is instead one storage pit in the southwest and a series of two hearths in the north. The hearth zone was probably the principal cooking area and may well have been sheltered with easily renewable material. A set of three rooms is found along the courtyard's south flank. Room 5 is the largest, measuring some 10 m², trapezoidal, and accessed from the courtyard through a doorway set at the middle of its north wall. It was also connected to the neighboring room 4 through a small doorway set in its east wall. Room 5 was very likely a sleeping room and its small 4 m² neighbor, a storage space. Room 3, in the southeastern corner of the unit, was a bathing/showering space attached to a latrine. It is a small trapezoidal room of 4.32 m², with the floor entirely paved with stone slabs. The used water was forced into a drain basin through a stone-paved drainage channel (Polet 1985:206).

Household Unit C

The remodeling of household unit HC-IV/HU-C was extensive during BS-6. The pattern of intra-unit circulation was completely overhauled. The position of the main entrance remained unchanged, still located in the northern half of the eastern perimeter wall. The household unit consists this time of two distinct room blocks situated west and east of the main courtyard, connected by two long and parallel corridors. The main entrance leads to what was very likely an unroofed space, labeled room 1 and situated in the east of the unit. It is trapezoidal, measuring 22.4 m². It connects in both the northwest and the southwest to parallel corridors. The northern corridor, termed room 4, was very likely under the same roof as the eastern room block. It measures 7 to 7.6 m in length and 1.8 m in width. The northern corridor also served as a drainage channel evacuating rain and used water from the main courtyard to the eastern street. The southern corridor, room 8, is much longer and narrower, 11.2 to 11.6 m long and 0.4 to 1.8 m wide, leading to the bathing/showering and latrine block in the west end. It is accessed from room 1 in the east and the main courtyard in the center through a doorway set in its north wall. The latrine is found in the small 3.52 m² trapezoidal room at the very end of corridor 5 and is attached to the 3.6 m² bathing/showering room 9.

The east room block, built in mud-bricks, includes rooms 5 and 3, accessed from the courtyard side. Room 5 is a narrow space that was very likely a vestibule to the main pillared room 3. It is a rectangular-shaped 5.72 m² space, oriented north-south, with two doorways, one in the east and the other in the west. Room 3, by far the largest room of the unit, measures 4.4 m in length and 3 m in width. The roof was supported by a central stone pillar. It was probably the sleeping room of the household head's family.

The latrine and bathing/showering room 9, room 6, and room 7 are the main components of the west room block. Room 6, in the middle, is trapezoidal and covers 6 m², with a doorway set in the middle of the east wall. The room contained two large clay storage vessels in diagonal southeast-northwest corners. The room's walls appears to have been painted red (Polet 1985:209); the room may have served the dual function of kitchen and storage space. Room 7, at the northwest corner of the unit, is relatively small but of a convenient size for a simple sleeping room. It is trapezoidal, 4.8 m², with a doorway that probably leads to the courtyard. Like room 6, its walls were also painted red.

The main and central courtyard has a well and a storage pit. The well is located virtually at the center and the storage pit is in the southwest corner. The courtyard is pentagonal, covering 38.4 m², with sides measuring 6.4 m in the east, 6 m in the south, 2 m in the southwest, 5 m in the west, and 4.4 m in the north.

Household Unit D

During BS-6, the HU-D layout was completely altered and simplified. It is doubtful that it was still used as a household unit (Polet 1985:209-11). The destruction by erosion of a significant portion of the east and southeast of the unit makes this assessment reasonably tentative, but it is nonetheless certain that the remodeled HU-D unit was divided into two parts: room 9 along the north side and the open but very likely walled space covering 118.08 m².

Room 9 is an elongated trapezoid measuring 13.11 m². Its north wall is built with mud-bricks and the remaining three with stone. It is accessed from the open space through a doorway set in the eastern segment of the south wall. A drain channel was built under the east wall leading to a drain pit located in the east street, suggesting the activities performed in the room were related to the use of water pulled from the well. It may have been used for laundry, livestock watering, or both.

The open space south of room 9 is pentagonal and was accessed from the east street through a narrow entrance set at the north end of the eastern perimeter wall. The west wall was strengthened by another 9 m long stone wall stabilized by two rectangular buttresses. The inner part of the open space included three rectangular pillar bases set 5 m apart. The northeast pillar is at some 3 m from the wall. The southern one is found at 4 m from the wall. These distinct installations were very likely part of a light roofing system. Accordingly, HU-D became a public space with an extensive sheltered verandah-like component that could have been used by laundry-washers, livestock, or both. The well, which according to Polet (1985:210) was one of the few still in operation, was particularly elaborate. It measured 7.05 m in depth, its sides lined with well-quarried stones with the margins raised at some 0.80 m above the occupation floor surface. The well's margin measured 1.80 m in diameter. The well was square in section, with sides measuring 0.93 m at the top and 0.90 m at the bottom.

A handful of additional features were recorded in the open space. They consist of one large clay vessel that may have been used for water storage, and two pits located in the immediate proximity of the well. The size and shape of the pits are unfortunately not presented in detail. Polet (1985:210), however, says that the southern pit contained "but ash and pot-sherds with water-stain"; the northern one had in addition "a large amount of bones."

Household Unit E

During BS-6, household unit HC-IV/HU-E was remodeled into five rooms, with the north perimeter wall built of mud-brick. The unit was still accessed through the south entrance, leading to room 1. This was more likely a roofed corridor oriented east-west and open at both ends. It is roughly rectangular, covers 16.8 m², and may have been used as a reception space. The presence of a short stone wall oriented north-south in its northeast side suggests the L-shaped portion of room 1 could have been used by a guard, servant, or slave as a sleeping space.

The disjunction between room 1 and room 5 east walls may indicate the presence of a mud-wall or an unpreserved feature separating these spaces. If that were the case, the internal part of the unit would have been accessed through the narrow corridor (room) 2 located in the northeast of room 1. It is a rectangular space, 2.6 m in length and 1.5 m in width, oriented north-south and leading to the main courtyard. The corridor was also used as a water drain that ran from the southeast of the courtyard southward under the south perimeter wall to the south street (Polet 1985:211). The courtyard is surrounded on three sides, the south, west, and north, by a series of rooms. It is a trapezoidal space covering 66.60 m², with the sides measuring 9 m in length in the east, 7.4 m in the north, 7.6 m in the west, and 6.4 m in the south. A pit filled with domestic refuse was recorded virtually at the center of the courtyard. Its shape, size, and diversity of content are unfortunately not available in print. It is however very likely that it was not originally designed to collect trash.

Room 3, along the south flank and oriented east-west, is slightly trapezoidal in shape, and covers 12.96 m². It was accessed from the courtyard through a doorway set in the west half of the north wall, and was likely one of the unit's main sleeping rooms.

Room 5, along the west flank, is oriented north-south and is roughly rectangular, covering 19.76 m². It is accessed from the courtyard through a wide doorway. Poor preservation had severely affected the features of this room, but it appears to have been the unit's largest sleeping room.

Three rooms were built along the northern side of the unit. Room 8, on the west end, is almost rectangular and measures some 12.24 m². The latrine from the previous occupation was filled with sediment and a rectilinear installation of "unknown use" (Polet 1985:214) was built across the northern third of the available space. In fact, the newly built installation consists of hard, beaten and compacted sediment that may suggest a connection with bathing/showering. Room 6, to the east, is a small 4.25 m² rectangular space. A large hearth was recorded at the northwest corner of the room, indicating its use as a kitchen. Room 7, the easternmost of this set, is trapezoidal, oriented east-west, and relatively narrow. It measures 5 to 5.6 m in length and 1.8 to 2 m in width. Two iron artifacts, a saw and an elongated axe blade, were recorded from the room floor, suggesting the space was used for the safe-keeping of household tool kits and belongings.

In summary, household unit E was still partitioned into seven distinct space blocks. One entered the reception room 1 from the main entrance on the south street. From the reception room 1, one walked along corridor 2 to access the courtyard that was the hub of the domestic unit. Sleeping rooms 3 and 5, bathing/showering room 8, kitchen room 6, and finally, the storage room 7, opened on the courtyard. In its basic elements, even if the architectural details were different, HC-IV/HU-E shares strong structural similarities with its northern neighbor HU-C.

Household Unit F

As with neighboring household units D and E, HU-F was extensively remodeled with its layout simplified. The northern portion was altered only slightly but the southern half was radically modified. The unit entrance was still set on the same spot, at the middle of the south wall. One could access room 4, located in the southwest corner, from the south street, and from the courtyard through a doorway set at the south end of the east wall. This elongated and narrow trapezoidal room, oriented north-south, covers 11.84 m^2 and appears to have been the only sleeping room of the remodeled unit.

The new courtyard covers 96 m^2 out of a total of 119.44 m^2 for the whole household unit. It is an irregular space with sides measuring 16 m in length in the east, 4 m in the south, 8 m in the southwest, 1.8 m for room 4's north wall in the middle west, 7.4 m in the west, and 8 m in the north. No feature of archaeological interest has been recorded in the excavated courtyard. Drainage channels directing the flow of excess water to the south and west streets were found below the south wall, west of the entrance, and the middle of the west wall (Polet 1985:215). The extensive courtyard could easily be used to corral animals, livestock or caravans calling at Awdaghost, as will be suggested later.

A series of three rooms are located along the unit's north side. Room 6 at the west end has an attached latrine. It was entirely paved with stone slabs with a set of three steps leading to the latrine. It was small and rectangular, measuring 3.36 m^2, and probably used for bathing/showering. A new doorway was created through room 6's north wall, connecting household units A and F, suggesting the establishment of a new relationship between these neighboring units. The northern neighbor may have appropriated the southern unit, remodeling it to be used as a sort of caravansérail for the visiting caravans and their crews. Room 7, in the middle, was used as a kitchen with a hearth located at the southwest corner. It was a rectangular 5.04 m^2 space, accessed from the courtyard through a doorway set in the middle of the room's south wall. Finally, room 8, at the east end, was much smaller, measuring 3.2 m^2, and very likely used for the storage of visitors' or caravan crews' belongings. It was accessed from the courtyard through a doorway set at the east end of the room's south wall.

In summary, during BS-6, HU-F was remodeled with each of its four rooms devoted to a specific function. Room 4 was the sleeping room. Room 6 was the bathing/showering room with an attached latrine. Room 7 was the kitchen. And room 8 was the storage space. The connection with the north unit and the enlarged courtyard tend to indicate that the southern unit was turned into a "specialized" dependence, a dependence that may have been used to provide shelter and protected space to visiting caravans and crews.

Summary

There are significant shifts in architectural characteristics and patterns of space allocation in Habitation Complex IV during Building Sequence 6. The habitation is split into two parts consisting of three household units each, showing opposite trends. The northern part, with units A, B, and C, are remodeled with greater elaborateness and architectural complexity. In general, the internal pattern of circulation is seriously altered and many alternative paths are created. There is more than one way of accessing the main courtyard. There are two options in HU-A and HU-C and three in HU-B.

The southern part, on the other hand, shifted toward architectural simplification. HU-D in the east was turned into a public space with an extensive open space anchored on the use of a well. The central unit, HU-E, was minimally altered and still used for habitation purposes. Finally, HU-F in the west was radically modified and turned into a caravansérail. As was the case for units A and C in Habitation Complex III, HC-IV/HU-A and HC-IV/HU-F may have belonged to the same household.

Habitation Complex V

During BS-6, Habitation Complex V appears to have witnessed a significant increase in the number of household members. The remodeling documented archaeologically attests to the construction of additional rooms leading to the emergence of a second household unit. The whole habitation was still serviced by a unique entrance located in the eastern half of the south perimeter wall.

Household Unit A

The architectural modifications of unit HU-A did not alter the overall building blueprint from BS-5. The unit was accessed from the south. Room 1 was slightly altered but its size and shape remained the same. The west side of the main entrance was buttressed with a short north-south stone wall. Room 1 is a hallway or vestibule leading to four different directions, to room 2 in the west, patio 20 in the northwest, corridor 3 in the east-northeast, and finally, to the roof through the new staircase built in the southeastern corner.

Corridor room 3 and the elongated gallery room 4 were largely unchanged. There was nonetheless a new and additional doorway set in the western part of the gallery north wall, providing a fourth access to the main courtyard. The prestigious reception and sleeping room 6 with its system of five roof-supporting pillars, as well as sleeping rooms 8 and 9, were rebuilt on the same BS-5 template. Patio 20, on the other hand, was a new space that provided access to all four cardinal directions. The doorway from the south wall connects with the vestibule (room) 1. The door in the east allowed access to the pillared room 6. The doors on the west flank lead to sleeping rooms 8 and 9. The patio was an unroofed space that may have had multiple functions: as a reception area for visitors, for meals and refreshments, or for discussion among household members. It is a 33 m^2 rectangular-shaped area, 6 m in length and 5.5 m in width.

The courtyard side of the unit had witnessed some architectural alteration along the north side, while rooms 12 and 13 in the northwest remained virtually unchanged. The same well was still in use, its margin now rectangular instead of circular. A new door was set in the northeast of the courtyard. A pit was recorded at the center of room 13, suggesting that this room may have been used for the storage of foodstuffs. Room 11 had an open south side, the roof being supported by a stone pillar. It is a rectangular space oriented east-west, and

13 m² in surface area. Room 19 was built in the northeast of the unit. It was accessed from
the courtyard through a wide doorway set in the middle of the room's south wall. It is trapezoidal, oriented east-west and occupies 17.5 m². No function-specific diagnostic features
or artifacts have been recorded from room 19's floor, making it difficult to determine its
use. It may have been used to store household belongings.

In summary, HU-A is partitioned into two complementary halves. Most, if not all, of the
domestic maintenance activities were performed in the northern half which included the
courtyard and surrounding rooms. Accordingly, room 12 may have been a servant or slave
sleeping room, as was suggested for BS-5. The southern half can be called the main house.
It includes a number of sleeping and reception rooms, what looks like a "door-keeper" room
(room 2), a patio, a vestibule, a gallery, and a corridor.

Household Unit B

Household unit B witnessed an extensive remodeling, shifting from a service area for
unit A to a complex habitation building. It was accessed from the south street through the
long corridor 3 in HU-A, which branched northward, leading to room 14 which acted as a
vestibule.

Controlling the access to the whole unit, Room 14 is rectangular with an area of 12.48
m². It has two doorways: the entrance in the south, and the other in the east. The southern
doorway opens from a small recess. The eastern doorway, built at the northern end of the
east wall, leads to the main courtyard. Room 14, in addition to its role as vestibule, may
have been used as a reception space.

Room 15, at the northwestern corner of the household unit, is an L-shaped space of a
relatively large 21 m² with two doorways. One, almost at the middle of the west wall, connects HU-B with the HU-A main courtyard. The other, at the south end of the east wall,
opens in the unit's courtyard. It was very likely used as a sleeping room.

Room 21 is stretched all along the north side of the unit. It is roughly trapezoidal in
shape, oriented east-west, and covers 12 m². It is accessed from the courtyard through a
twin doorway in the west half of the south wall. Iron slag and broken crucible fragments are
particularly numerous among the cultural remains recorded from room 21's floor. According
to Robert-Chaleix (1989:91), it may have been a blacksmith's or jeweler's workshop. Since
no traces of hearth or furnace were found on an otherwise well-preserved room floor, this
seems unlikely. The room was more likely used as a mixed sleeping and storage space.

Room 18 is found in the northeast of the unit. It is an open but roofed space of 7.2 m²,
trapezoidal and oriented north-south. Most of the room's west side is without a wall, suggesting an easy access to the products that may have been stored in the three large clay
vessels found in the center. The area may have sheltered water coolers that may have been
filled with water pulled from the unit's new well.

The latrine room 17, on the south flank of room 18, is a small rectangular space of 4.6
m². The latrine installation is in the northeast corner of the room, with the remaining space
devoted to bathing and showering.

The central courtyard is irregular in shape. Its south appendage, the junction of which
contains the new well, is a trapezoid of 9.6 m². The larger component of the central court-

yard is roughly rectangular and covers 53.2 m^2. The entire courtyard measures 62.8 m^2. Unfortunately, the characteristics of the newly dug well were not spelled out in detail (Robert-Chaleix 1989:79-85).

The southern part of HU-B is composed of a long corridor and three rooms. Room 22, the elongated corridor, is oriented north-south and is 11 m long, with a width ranging from 1.9 m in the north to 1.1 m in the south. It is accessed from the courtyard through a doorway set at the northern end of the west wall and leads to room 23 in the south.

Room 23, at the southern end of the sub-unit, has a rounded southeast corner and is roughly rectangular, oriented west-east and 12.96 m^2. It may have been used as a reception and living room, and perhaps because of this, had two doorways, both in the north wall. The eastern doorway connects room 23 with the long corridor 22, and the other provides access to the sub-unit's sleeping rooms.

Room 24 is accessed from the south side but has another doorway set in the west half of the north wall. The location of both doorways in the west half of the room suggests the east half may have been used as a sleeping area. The room is trapezoidal and oriented east-west, with an area of 7.65 m^2.

Room 25, the last in the sequence, is located north of room 24. It was probably the principal sleeping room of the southern part of the household unit. It is trapezoidal, oriented east-west, and covers 7.59 m^2. Remarkably, both sleeping rooms from the southern sub-unit are almost exactly the same size.

In summary, HU-B appears to have been inhabited by two distinct families, each with a suite of three rooms: rooms 14, 15, and 21 in the north and rooms 23, 24, and 25 in the south. They have common use of the storage room 18, the bathing/showering and latrine in room 17, and the courtyard and well. These two families were, very likely, founded by the grown-up children from the HU-A household.

During BS-6, Habitation Complex V appears to be the archetype of a wealthy household estate. It can be partitioned into four distinct sub-units, two for each household unit.

The senior household unit (HU-A) comprises the main house that can be called the "mansion" and a service component. The mansion with long corridors, a central patio, a long gallery, a prestigious pillared room, and a series of three contiguous sleeping rooms are located in the south and controlled the access to the unit's spaces. The service component spread over the northern half consists of a large courtyard and well, with a series of somewhat large rooms set along the west and north perimeters.

The junior household (HU-B) consists of two virtually similar sub-units with three rooms each, one in the north and the other in the south. They shared a common service space that included a well, a courtyard, a storage room, and a bathing/showering/latrine room. In fact, the bathing/showering and latrine installations appear to have been used by all the members of both senior and junior households.

Conclusion

During BS-6, very likely during the late tenth or early eleventh century AD, the residential area of the Acropolis went through extensive architectural remodeling. Large open but walled spaces were made available in Habitation Complexes III and IV. The northern half of Habitation Complex IV and the whole Habitation Complex V witnessed a significant increase in the number of rooms. The size of household units ranged from a minimum of 93.54 m^2 for HC-IV/HU-B to a maximum of 500.87 m^2 for HC-V/HU-A and HU-B. The number of rooms varies from 1 for units HC-III/HU-A and HC-IV/HU-D to 21 for HC-V/HU-A and HU-B (combined). The size of the courtyard or open space changed dramatically for three household units, HC-III/HU-A, HC-IV/HU-D, and HC-IV/HU-F, signaling a significant shift in use. It has been suggested such open spaces may have been used as caravansérail or public laundry and livestock watering installations, or both.

The distribution of room class-sizes indicates a higher representation of the small size end of the spectrum. Class 1* is represented by eleven occurrences, recorded with frequencies varying from 1 to 2 in seven household units out of a total of eleven (Table 10). Class 2 rooms are the most frequent, represented by twenty occurrences, also recorded in seven household units with frequencies ranging from 1 (two cases) to 6. Class 3 rooms with fifteen occurrences are the most widespread, recorded in 8 household units out of a total of 11. Its frequency varies from 1 to 6. Class 4 to 8 rooms are predominantly clustered in Habitation Complexes III and V. Nine class 4 to 8 rooms are found in Habitation Complex III, with frequency ranging from 1 to 6. Eight such rooms are recorded in Habitation Complex V, with frequency varying from 1 to 4.

As can be seen in Table 11, room size variation is large in Habitation Complexes III (29.24 m^2 and 30.24 m^2) and V (29.53 m^2), and moderate to small in Habitation Complex IV. The same pattern, with a certain amount of overlap, is seen in the distribution of room mean size, with a mean value of 12.19 and 18.06 m^2 in Habitation Complex III and 15.51 m^2 in Habitation Complex V in comparison to 5.86 to 13.11 m^2 for Habitation Complex IV household units. A careful examination of the distribution of coefficient of variation reveals no general trend. Room size appears to have been the result of each household's needs and possibilities and not the product of an architectural norm.

Finally, Building Sequences 5 and 6 appear to have been the peak of the mushrooming growth of Awdaghost economy and urban development. The observation of Ibn Hawqal and the description of Al-Bakri in 1068 provide a strong support to the discussion conducted in this chapter. Ibn Hawqal traveled in the Maghrib and in Spain in AD 947-951. He gave a detailed description of Sijilmasa and its trade with the Sudan (Levtzion and Hopkins 1981:43) and was the eyewitness of an impressive transaction: "Merchants in the countries of Islam seldom approach them in affluence. I have seen a warrant written concerning a debt owed by Muhammad b. Abi Sa'dun in Awdaghust [Awdaghost], and witnessed by assessors, for 42,000 dinars" (Ibn Hawqal in Levtzion and Hopkins 1981:45). As for Al-Bakri, his extensive description of Awdaghost wealth, religious practices, and political culture is very revealing. He asserted that most of the "inhabitants of Awdaghust are natives of Ifriqiya, members of [such tribes as] Barqajana, Nafusa, Lawata, Zanata, and Nafzawa, but there are also a few people from other countries" (Al-Bakri in Levtzion and Hopkins 1981:68). On religious practices, he remarked that "in Awdaghust there is one cathedral mosque and

---

*Class 1: < 5 m^2; class 2: >5-10 m^2; class 3: >10-15 m^2; and so forth in 5 m^2 increments.

many smaller ones, all well attended. In all the mosques there are teachers of the Koran" (Al-Bakri in Levtzion and Hopkins 1981:68). He then described the bustling economic activity of the town: "The people of Awdaghust enjoy extensive benefits and huge wealth. The market there is at all times full of people. . . . Their transactions are in gold, and they have no silver" (Al-Bakri in Levtzion and Hopkins 1981:68). Building Sequences 5 and 6 are the material manifestation of the climax in wealth and appeal of the Medieval town of Awdaghost.

—6—

The Unsteady Post-Climax
(AD 1000–1200)

The unsteady post-climax period lasted some two hundred years, from ca. AD 1000 to AD 1200. In the Awdaghost Acropolis archaeological record, this time segment is represented by three building sequences, BS-7, BS-8, and BS-9, part of level IV. The deposit was exposed at depths varying from 1.50 m to 0.75 m and is characterized by two distinct trends. On the one hand, there is a rough stability in the architectural design of some habitation complexes and household units. On the other hand, there is a significant decrease in architectural elaborateness, if not total abandonment, of some household units.

The eleventh century had witnessed a number of crucial events that impacted the fate of western Sudan towns and commercial places. The rise of the Almoravid revivalism created a powerful ripple that shook the entire western Dar al-Islam, from Spain in the north, to Morocco and the Ghana Kingdom in the south (Levtzion and Hopkins 1981). Al-Bakri wrote his *Kitab al-masalik wa-'l-mamalik* ("The Book of Routes and Realms") in 1068. He provides information on "the origins of the Almoravid movement in southwestern Sahara, the conversion of the King of Takrur in 432/1040, the conquest of Awdaghost by the Almoravids in 446/1054, and the accession of a new king to the throne of Ghana in 455/1063" (Levtzion and Hopkins 1981:63). Al-Bakri's rendering of the Almoravid saga at Awdaghost is worth a long quote:

> In the year 446/1054-5 'Abd Allah b. Yasin invaded the town of Awdaghost, flourishing locality (*balad*), a large town (*madina*) containing markets, numerous palms, and henna trees resembling olive trees with their large size. . . . This city was inhabited by the Zanata with Arabs who were always at loggerhead with each other. They owned great riches and slaves so numerous that one person from among them might possess a thousand servants or more. The Almoravids violated its women (*harimaha*) and declared everything that they took there to be the booty of the community. 'Abd Allah b. Yasin killed there a man called Zibaqara, a half-caste Arab from Qayrawan who was known for his piety and virtue, his diligence in reciting the Koran, and for having performed the Pilgrimage. The Almoravids persecuted the people of Awdaghust only because they recognized the authority of the ruler of Ghana. [Al-Bakri in Levtzion and Hopkins 1981:73-74]

Awdaghost went through a series of difficult years. Its appeal and economic prosperity dwindled. In the second half of the twelfth century AD, Al-Idrissi presents the town in totally different terms in his *Nuzhat al-mushtaq fi ikhtiraq al-afaq* ("The Pleasure of Him Who Longs to Cross the Horizons") completed in 1154 and offered to King Roger of Sicily (Levtzion and Hopkins 1981:104). Awdaghost was then "a small town in the desert, with little water. The town itself is situated between two mountains, like Mecca. Its population is not numerous, and there is no large trade. The inhabitants own camels from which they derived their livelihood" (Al-Idrissi, in Levtzion and Hopkins 1981:118). The latter assertion is particularly interesting since it asserts that camel husbandry became the dominant source of people's livelihood in Awdaghost in the late twelfth or early thirteenth century. It will be shown in the discussion later how this fact helps explain some characteristics of the Acropolis spatial layout.

Building Sequence 7 (Fig. 14)

Building Sequence 7 deposits were exposed at depths varying from 1.15 to 1.50 m. All three habitation complexes are still present and each follows a specific trajectory. Habitation Complex III was unchanged. Household units HC-III/HU-A, HC-III/HU-B, and HC-III/HU-C kept the same spatial layout and an identical number of rooms. Habitation Complex IV witnessed a significant reduction in both size and architectural elaborateness, while Habitation Complex V was still on the path of increasing architectural elaboration, with the addition of new rooms.

Habitation Complex IV

During BS-7, Habitation Complex IV comprised five distinct units, two of them still used as household units, and the remaining three remodeled into mostly walled open spaces.

Household Unit A

Household unit HU-A in the northwest of the complex was extensively remodeled, but preserved its original size and trapezoidal shape. The number and size of rooms was reduced. As was the case during BS-6, the unit was still accessed from the west street through two entrances in the west wall. Room 1, in the southwest, was serviced by the narrower south entrance. It is a L-shaped space, the northern segment covering 22 m² and the southern segment (running east-west) covering 11.2 m². The southern part of this new, large 33.2 m² space was very likely a small unroofed courtyard, while the northern part was an elongated corridor. A small hearth was uncovered in the middle part of the corridor, positioned against the corridor east wall next to the doorway into room 2. The area was probably used for hot beverage-making and heating but not cooking.

A set of two small rooms, 2a and 2b, was built at the center of the unit, with 2b possibly a vestibule. The set of rooms was accessible from both the west and east through doorways

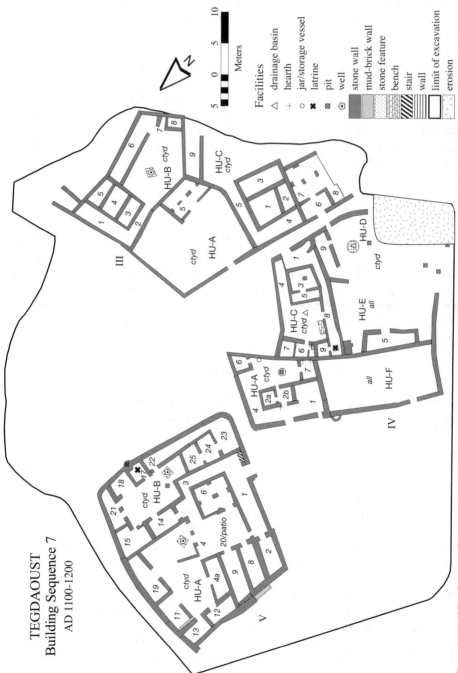

Figure 14. Building Sequence 7 constructions. Figure has been rotated so north, south, east, and west can be more easily described (i.e., what is described as "north" in text is actually closer to north by northeast).

Table 12: Building Sequence 7 constructions

Habitation Unit	Total Size (m²)	Courtyard (m²)	1	2	3	4	5	6	7	8	9	10	11	12	13	Shape
Habitation Complex III																
HU-III-A	190	160.60					29.4									H
HU-III-B	151.96	54.40	27.04	7.56	8.4	10.56	8.8	30.68	1.44	3.08						P
HU-III-C	217.08	60.12	19.32	6.72	15.32	18.48	17.2	12.48	36.96	4.48	18					H
Habitation Complex IV																
HU-IV-A	115.16	44.8	33.2	4+3.6		16.2		5.96	7.42							T
HU-IV-C	199.12	38.4	22.4		13.2	13.68	5.72	6	4.8	20.88						R
HU-IV-D	131.19	115.99									3.2					R
HU-IV-E	143.81	120.01					20.8				15.2					
HU-IV-F	145.6															R
Habitation Complex V																
HU-V/A+B	496.39	192.88	37.12	11.9	21.38	12	13.2 [4a]	22.54		12.4	17.52		12	8.93	7.8	R

HU-V/A+B Rooms [continued]

14	15	16	17	18	19	20	21	22	23	24	25
12.48	20		4.6	7.2	17.5	33	12	27.6	12.96	7.65	7.59

Key: H = Hexagonal; P = Pentagonal; R = Rectangular; T = Trapezoidal

Table 13: Variations in BS-7 room size (m²)

Habitation Unit	n	Minimum	Maximum	Mean	Range	Standard Deviation	Coefficient of Variation
Habitation Complex III							
HU-III-A	1	29.4	29.4	29.4	0	–	–
HU-III-B	8	1.44	30.68	12.19	29.24	10.06	0.82
HU-III-C	9	4.48	36.96	18.21	32.48	19.18	0.55
Habitation Complex IV							
HU-IV-A	5	3.60	33.2	10.83	29.60	11.26	1.04
HU-IV-C	8	3.20	22.4	10.37	19.20	7.02	0.67
HU-IV-D	1	15.2	15.2	15.2	0	–	–
HU-IV-E	1	20.8	20.8	20.8	0	–	–
Habitation Complex V							
HU-V/A+B	21	7.2	37.12	15.73	29.92	7.77	0.49

leading to room 2b. Room 2b is rectangular, covering 3.6 m². The west doorway was wider and positioned immediately facing the unit's entrance. The eastern doorway leading to the courtyard was narrow and set in the room's northeast corner. Despite these two doorways, room 2b could have been used as an additional sleeping space. Room 2a was a more secluded space accessed through a doorway in the west end of its south wall. Square in shape, covering 4 m², it may have been used for sleeping

The north corridor (room) 4 is a trapezoid, oriented east-west and measuring 16.2 m². It leads to the courtyard, which is slightly elongated and trapeze-shaped. It covers 44.8 m², with its sides measuring 6.8 m in the west, 8 m in the east, 3.4 m in the south, and 5.6 m in the north. The central well was then out of use, filled with trash, and sealed with stone slabs at 1.5 m below the surface. The remaining "void" was filled with dark soil rich in rootlets. According to Polet (1985:219), the old well may have been "recycled" into a tree-bearing installation. If that was the case, the central part of the courtyard may have been an inviting cool and shaded place. One specimen of a clay storage vessel was found in the northeastern part of the courtyard, leaning against the east wall.

Room 6 is located at the northeast corner of the unit. It is a trapeze-shaped 5.96 m² space. It is accessed from the courtyard through a relatively narrow doorway set in the south wall. The floor was slightly ashy (Polet 1985:219), but no function-specific evidence was recorded. The room may have continued to be used for the storage of household belongings. Room 7, located in the southeast corner of the unit, is a 7.42 m² trapezoidal-shaped space accessed from the courtyard. Its doorway is set at the middle of the north wall and the room contained two hearths, both against the east wall.

In summary, the pattern of intra-unit circulation was set up with different alternatives. The unit could be entered through two entrances from the west street. Once inside, the courtyard could be accessed through the west and east doorways of room 2b or through the north-south corridor, then the west-east corridor (room 4). Room 1 was probably not roofed and may have been used as a reception space and "chat-room." The small size and the small number of rooms tend to indicate that HC-IV/HU-A was no longer a standard household unit. It may have had a narrower range of use. It could have been used for housing dromedary herders, as will be discussed later.

Household Unit C

During BS-7, all of the HU-C walls were built with stone. The south perimeter wall, some 20 m long and previously built with mud-brick, was entirely reshaped and constructed with stone, as were the walls of the east room set. There were minor alterations of the unit's architectural blueprint. The layout still consisted of two room sets located to the east and west of the central courtyard. The unit was still accessed from the east street, through room 1, a relatively large 22.4 m² space that seems to have been unroofed and may consequently have been a small courtyard. An installation involving a U-shaped wall was built in the southeastern corner. Its function is still unknown. A line of stone slabs runs along the northern side of the small courtyard and may have served to control the flow of rain and used water (Polet 1985:221).

The core of the household unit, the central courtyard, could be accessed from room 1 north to corridor 4, and then west to the central courtyard. Corridor 4 measures 7 to 7.6 m in length and 1.8 m in width. A relatively large water drain made of large stone slabs was built in the north half of the corridor, under the north segment of the unit's east perimeter wall. The courtyard could also be accessed from room 1 via the narrow and elongated corridor 8, a route that also provided access to the bathing/showering room 9 in the west end.

The size and shape of the central courtyard remained unchanged. The well, then out of use, had been recycled into a water drain. A low bench made of stone and clay, 2 m long and 0.9 m wide and 0.4 m high, was built along the wall in the southwest. The set of east rooms, with the pillared room 3 and the vestibule room 5, were preserved in the new construction. There were however some alterations in the west room set, specifically in room 6, a 6 m^2 trapezoid where a relatively thin partition wall oriented east-west was built, demarcating the south third of the room. The delineated space was clearly used for cooking, suggested by the presence of a relatively large hearth set in the southeast corner. The remaining part of room 6 may thus have been used for food preparation activities and possibly some storage.

In summary, HU-C appears to have been the only relatively coherent general-purpose household unit left in Habitation Complex IV during BS-7.

Household Units D, E and F: A Radical Shift

During BS-7, units D, E, and F across the southern half of Habitation Complex IV were remodeled radically for a very different use. The remodeling left HU-D and HU-E with a large open courtyard and one room each, and HU-F with an open and empty but walled space.

Despite the destruction by erosion of the southeastern part of HU-D, it is very likely that no archaeological feature of interest, beside the perimeter wall, was located in that part of the unit. The remaining features thus include room 9 along the north wall, a former well recycled into a water drain, and four pits of unknown function. The unit is accessed from the northeast through an entrance in the perimeter wall. Room 9 is oriented east-west and accessed from the courtyard, through two openings: one, a standard doorway located in the eastern side of the south wall, and the other a larger gap at the west end that does not appear to have ever been closed. The room is a trapezoid, covering 15.20 m^2. No function-specific artifacts or features have been recorded from room 9, making the assessment of its function difficult. However, in view of its architectural characteristics, room 9 could have been used for the storage of fodder and other equipment used in livestock husbandry. The pits are found along the central north-south axis of the unit. One is found near the water drain and the remaining three are clustered in the south.

HU-E, with room 5 along its west side, was a large livestock penning space. Room 5 is trapezoidal and oriented north-south, covering 20.8 m^2. It is accessed from the courtyard through a doorway set near the middle of the east wall. Room 5 may have housed shepherds who were in charge of the livestock. In the social and economic context of the eleventh/twelfth-century AD, these shepherds may have been servants or of slave status.

The new penning space measured 275 m^2 (131.19 m^2 for HU-D and 143.81 m^2 for HU-E), and may have been one small camel-rearing complex located in the northeast of the town.

HU-F at the west of the block was a walled empty space of some 145.6 m². It is roughly rectangular and oriented north-south, measuring 18 to 18.2 m in length and 8 m in width. It was accessed from the west street through a doorway in the south half of the west wall. It was clearly a livestock penning space, a small caravansérail probably belonging to another household unit.

In summary, using the "nearest-neighbor" rationale, and even if it is practically untestable at this stage, some "ownership" link can be suggested. Accordingly, the large HU-D/HU-E caravansérail may have belonged to household unit HU-C, with which it shares a long common perimeter wall. The smaller HU-F caravansérail may have been owned by those living in household unit HU-A, with which it equally shares a common transversal wall. The information provided by Al-Idrissi in 1174 (in Levtzion and Hopkins 1981), and according to which camel rearing was the main occupation of Awdaghust inhabitants, is supported by the architectural transformation that took place in Habitation Complex IV during BS-7.

Habitation Complex V

The extent of remodeling was scaled back in Habitation Complex V. Unit HC-V/HU-A was barely modified. It had the same layout with an identical number of rooms. The doorway in the west wall of room 15 in HU-B present during BS-6 and allowing for the smooth circulation between A and B was removed. During BS-7 then, HU-B was accessed exclusively from the south, through corridor (room) 3 and room 14. In the central courtyard, a new square margin was built around the well, and a pit of unknown function was dug in the immediate proximity.

More important but still minor transformations were implemented in HU-A. The overall pattern of rooms, doorways, corridors, and patios designed during BS-6 was preserved. The unit was still accessed from the south street, the path branching into two directions, in room 1 westward and in corridor 3 north and westward. The remodeling was chiefly in the gallery (room) 4, the patio, room 11, and the unit's courtyard. The western end of gallery 4 was transformed into a room, here termed 4a, reducing the surface area of the gallery to 12 m², 6 m in length and 2 m in width. The gallery was then an extension of the patio from which it was separated by a rectangular stone pillar that may have supported the north side of the gallery's roof. The new room 4a was trapezoidal, covering 13.2 m². It was accessed from the central courtyard through a doorway set in the middle of the room's north wall.

A system of two perpendicular low walls made of two superimposed stone courses (forming an L shape), measuring 3.6 m (north-south) and 2 m (east-west), was built along the south and west sides of the well. The margin of the well was raised and remodeled into a rectangular platform. A drain channel was dug across room 19, its bottom lined with flat stone slabs. According to Robert-Chaleix (1989:95), all these installations were engineered to control the flow of excess rain, to protect the well from the rushing rainwater and channel the flow outside, somewhere along the north street.

Room 11 was the fourth element of the unit's remodeling program during BS-7. The transformation consists of a new 3 m long wall built along the south side of the room, oriented east-west, leaving the eastern side open, presumably a doorway. The new room then measures

12 m²; its use is unclear. No function-specific installations, features, or even artifacts were recorded. It may have been used as a sleeping space, a storage area, or both.

In summary, unit HU-A witnessed the addition of two new rooms during BS-7; the well area was also explicitly separated from the rest of the main courtyard. Robert-Chaleix's (1989:95) suggestion that these installations acted to mitigate the consequences of heavy rains is very likely. Comparable stone-lined drain channels are documented in Habitation Complex IV units. The increase in the number of rooms may have been triggered by the growth in household membership. Whatever the case, Habitation Complex V, with its maze-like spatial layout, stands apart among the units exposed in the excavated probes.

Summary

During BS-7, four household units out of a total of ten have been allocated to different sets of activities, possibly livestock husbandry, and in this case, more likely dromedary husbandry, since Al-Idrissi has specifically described this in Awdaghust in the eleventh/twelfth century. The total number of rooms dropped significantly from 72 during the previous BS-6 to 54 in BS-7, with the frequency per household unit ranging from 1 (Units HC-III/HU-A, HC-IV/HU-D, HC-IV/HU-E, and HC-IV/HU-F) to 13 (HC-V/HU-A) (Table 12).

On average, small rooms are predominant, with 32 out of 51 rooms belonging to room classes 1 to 3.* They are also among the most "evenly" distributed rooms with frequency varying from 1 (class 1) to 6 (class 3) (Table 12). Very large rooms, belonging to room classes 6 to 8, are found exclusively in Habitation Complexes III and V, with frequencies of 1 or 2. Room mean size is on average on the rise when compared to the previous BS-6 situation. It ranges from a minimum of 10.37 m² for the eight-room HC-IV/HU-C to a maximum of 29.4 m² for the single-room HC-III/HU-A (Table 13). The range in room size is, however, significant in all the units, varying from a minimum of 19.20 in HC-IV/HU-C to a maximum of 32.48 for the nine-room unit HC-III/HU-C. Coefficient of variation ranges from 0.49 for the combined units of Habitation Complex V to 1.04 for the five-room unit HC-IV/HU-A, and suggests each situation to be particular. There is no evidence of any widely shared template for room size beside the technical constraints on roof beams.

Building Sequence 8 (Fig. 15)

Building sequence 8 deposits were exposed at depths varying from 1.10 to 1.50 m. Construction activities were concentrated on Habitation Complex V in the northwest. Habitation Complex III and IV layouts were unaltered for BS-8.

Habitation Complexes III and IV

Habitation Complex III still consisted of three household units. HU-A in the north remained an extensive enclosed space with one large pillared room in the southeast. HU-B

---

*Class 1: < 5 m²; class 2: >5-10 m²; class 3: >10-15 m²; and so forth in 5 m² increments.

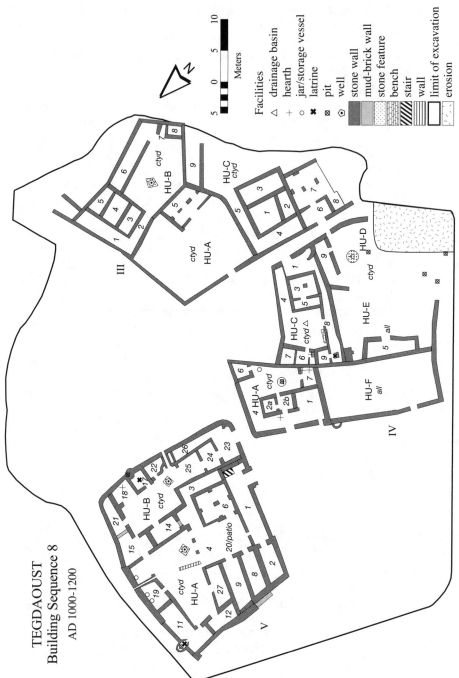

Figure 15. Building Sequence 8 constructions. Figure has been rotated so north, south, east, and west can be more easily described (i.e., what is described as "north" in text is actually closer to north by northeast).

Table 14: Building Sequence 8 constructions

Habitation Unit	Total Size (m²)	Courtyard (m²)	1	2	3	4	5	6	7	8	9	10	11	12	13	Shape
Habitation Complex III																
HU-III-A	190	160.60					29.4									H
HU-III-B	151.96	54.40	27.04	7.56	8.4	10.56	8.8	30.68	1.44	3.08						P
HU-III-C	217.08	60.12	19.32	6.72	15.32	18.48	17.2	12.48	36.96	4.48						H
Habitation Complex IV																
HU-IV-A	115.16	44.8	33.2	4+3.6		16.2		5.96	7.42		18					T
HU-IV-C	199.12	38.4	22.4		13.2	13.68	5.72	6	4.8	20.88	3.2					R
HU-IV-D	131.19	115.99									15.2					R
HU-IV-E	143.81	120.01					20.8									
HU-IV-F	190	190														R
Habitation Complex V																
HU-V-A	361.35	143.16	37.12	11.9	21.38	12.6		22.54		12.4	17.52		30.4	8.93		R

HU-V-A Rooms [continued]

19	20	27
10.4	33	13.2

Habitation Unit	Total Size (m²)	Courtyard (m²)
HU-V-B	148.68	56

HU-V-B Rooms [continued]

14	15	17	18	21	22	23	24	25	26
12.48	20	4.6	7.2	12	7.8	11.96	12.96	7.56	19.8

Key: H = Hexagonal; P = Pentagonal; R = Rectangular; T = Trapezoidal

Table 15: Variations in BS-8 room size (m²)

Habitation Unit	n	Minimum	Maximum	Mean	Range	Standard Deviation	Coefficient of Variation
Habitation Complex III							
HU-III-A	1	29.4	29.4	29.4	0	–	–
HU-III-B	8	1.44	30.68	12.19	29.24	10.06	0.82
HU-III-C	9	4.48	36.96	18.21	32.48	19.18	0.55
Habitation Complex IV							
HU-IV-A	5	5.96	33.2	14.07	27.24	11.42	0.81
HU-IV-C	8	3.20	22.4	10.37	19.20	7.02	0.67
HU-IV-D	1	15.2	15.2	15.2	0	–	–
HU-IV-E	1	20.8	20.8	20.8	0	–	–
Habitation Complex V							
HU-V-A	12	8.93	37.12	18.18	28.19	8.25	0.45
HU-V-B	10	4.6	20	11.63	15.4	5.15	0.44

in the northeast still had a functioning well in the central courtyard with a series of eight rooms and corridors. HU-C in the south still preserved its tripartite organization, with three distinct sub-units: one in the south with the pillared room 7, the vestibule 6, and the small side room 8; another in the north articulated around the small courtyard (room) 1; and finally, a last one in the east with the main courtyard and the elongated room 9.

Habitation Complex IV in the south also preserved its dual organization with inhabited buildings in the north and livestock penning structures or caravansérails in the south. Surprisingly, the whole Habitation Complex did not have any operating well, suggesting that HC-IV/HU-A and HC-IV/HU-C household members relied on their neighbors for their access to water.

Habitation Complex V

In Habitation Complex V, both HU-A and HU-B witnessed important remodeling projects. HU-A was still accessed from the south street. But this time, there was only one route to the central courtyard: from the main entrance through vestibule (room) 1 and the patio. The doorway between the vestibule and corridor (room) 3 was closed with a short stone wall. The new walled space preserved the same size and shape, a 10.5 m^2 rectangular surface. The eastern end of the vestibule was altered to fit a "staircase" providing access to the roof. The main house was not altered; the patio, the prestigious pillared room 6, and sleeping rooms 2, 8, and 9, as well as gallery 4, were still part of the main house built in the southern half of the unit. More alterations were executed in the northern half of the unit, in the courtyard as well as surrounding rooms. In the courtyard, a narrow wall of two courses, 3.6 m long, was built some two meters along the west flank of the well. It was probably built to deflect rainwater from the main house roof to flow in the well. The deflected rushing rainwater was directed to a heavy-duty drainage channel engineered through room 19 and the unit's north wall. In fact, room 19 was split into two distinct spaces by a stone-paved drainage channel that poured the excess rainwater in the north street. Room 19, west of the drainage channel, measured some 10.4 m^2. The doorway to room 19 was found at the eastern end of the room's south wall. The space east of the channel was roughly rectangular in shape, 7.8 m^2. Both parts of the new room 19 appear to have been used for storage, as suggested by the presence of three large clay vessels found against the north wall.

Room 11 was an L-shaped space measuring 30.4 m^2 accessed through a doorway located in the southeast corner of the western portion. The larger portion was oriented east-west and measured 8 m by 2.4 to 2.8 m. The smaller part was oriented north-south, and measured 3.6 to 4 m by 1.8 to 2 m. A latrine associated with a drain pit was part of the installation found in the larger new room 11. It is unlikely that the whole 30.4 m^2 of room 11 was used for bathing/showering and the latrine. The eastern part of the room may have been used for the storage of household belongings. A new doorway connecting household units HU-A and HU-B was set in the east wall, in the northeast of the unit.

In summary, during BS-8, HU-A had one room less in the northern half, the area of the courtyard likely devoted to the service of the main house members. The main southern part of the house gained an additional room 3 along its eastern flank where there was previously a circulation corridor. As suggested already, room 2, at the west end of vestibule (room) 1, may have been for the use of the guard, who could have been a servant or a slave.

Household unit HU-B gained its autonomy during BS-8, but kept a communication link with the west neighbors in HU-A. It was accessed from the south street through an entrance set in the middle of the south wall. The entrance provided access to a small courtyard (room) 23. One could then either go through corridor 26 to an impasse, or pass through rooms 24 and 25 to the well and the central courtyard. There was no significant alteration of room size and shape. A drainage channel paved with flat stone slabs, running east-west, was dug in the north tier of corridor 26. It was composed of a series of low stone walls to collect and force running water from around the well to the drainage channel and under the unit east wall, to pour it outside in the east street. A small room measuring 7.8 m^2, 3 m in length and 2.6 m in width, was added at the north end of corridor 26, as a consequence of the building of the drainage channel. It could also have been used as a secondary entrance to the household unit. During BS-8 then, the southern half of HU-B appears to have been devoted to the reception of visitors. It can be argued that the space available in rooms 24 and 25 could have been used for a multiplicity of purposes, including reception, meal taking, sleeping, or a combination.

In the northern half of the unit, the central courtyard and the well were unaltered. Room 14, previously a vestibule with two doorways, was turned into an effective room, very likely devoted to sleeping. This was achieved through the construction of a mud-brick wall in the south wall doorway. The space's shape and size were not modified; it was still 12.48 m^2. It was accessed from the central courtyard through a doorway in the north half of the room's east wall. Room 15, in the northwest corner, got another doorway, allowing circulation between HU-A and HU-B. The room's south appendage may have been large enough for sleeping, or storage, or both. The east wall, shared with room 21, was built of mud-bricks.

Room 21 in the northeast had its south wall remodeled. The second doorway of the BS-7 occupation was obliterated. The remaining door made a walled, relatively elongated and narrow 12 m^2 space that could have been used for sleeping or storage.

Room 18 to the south was unchanged. It was more of a sheltered space than a room. The presence of a hearth suggests that this space was used as a kitchen during BS-8. Finally, the latrine, bathing and showering space in the east-central part of the unit was unaltered.

In summary, household unit HU-B became independent and autonomous, with its own entrance during BS-8. It maintained strong relationships with HU-A, suggested by a communication doorway in room 15. The unit structure and building layout was clearly divided into two complementary parts. The southern part with the small courtyard 23, rooms 24 and 25, and corridor 26, was made of reception and circulation spaces that controlled and monitored the access to the household unit's inner sanctum. The core of the household unit was the northern part of the building. It included the central courtyard with its well, surrounded by the bathing/showering and latrine room, the kitchen room 18, and very likely the sleeping/storage rooms 14, 15, and 21.

Summary

During BS-8, the remodeling work was carried out almost exclusively in Habitation Complex V in the northwest of the excavated Acropolis probe. As a result, there were six household units inhabited by a substantial number of individuals, if not coherent family groups. Four of the units, one in Habitation Complex III and three in Habitation Complex IV, were partially or entirely devoted to livestock husbandry activities. The total of recorded rooms amounted to 55, varying from a maximum of 12 in HC-V/HU-A, to 1 in HC-III/HU-A and HC-IV/HU-D (Table 14). But the distribution is skewed as the frequency of rooms per unit effectively fluctuates between 5 and 12. With 33 rooms out of a total of 55 belonging to classes 1 to 3,* the small-size end of the spectrum is largely predominant. Class 1 is represented by 10 rooms, found in six household units with frequency varying from 1 to 3. Classes 2 (11 occurrences) and 3 (12 occurrences) are the most frequent, found in five to six households units, with frequency ranging from 1 to 5. Large rooms (classes 4 to 8) occurred 20 times with frequency per class varying from a minimum of 2 (class 8) to a maximum of 7 (class 4). On average, large rooms tend to be found in Habitation Complexes III and V: the former with 9 rooms out of a total of 20, and the latter with 7. Habitation Complex IV, in the center-south, had three relatively large rooms in units C and D, all confined to classes 3 and 5. If single-room units are not taken into consideration, the mean room size varies from 10.37 to 18.21 m² (Table 15), a relatively narrow range. The coefficient of variation suggests that both units from the Habitation Complex V come closest to having developed a standard for rooms. This development may be explained by the fact that HU-B was clearly a descendant and an extension of HU-A.

Building Sequence 9 (Fig. 16)

Building sequence 9 deposits were recorded at depths varying from 0.75 to 1.50 m. Habitation Complexes III and IV in the center and east of the excavated portion of the Acropolis were still inhabited but without any visible architectural modification. Habitation Complex V, in the northwest, did witness some remodeling. It is this remodeling that is outlined and discussed here.

Habitation Complex V

Habitation Complex V still comprised two household units. The larger one, HU-A, was remodeled in its central north-south axis and vestibule. The main entrance providing access to the vestibule (room) 1 was rearranged and reconstructed more elaborately with a series of large flat stone slabs set on a compacted clay sediment. A new circular and spiraling staircase leading to the roof was built in the southeastern corner of room 1. A doorway leading directly to the pillared room 6 was set in the east segment of the room's south wall. And finally, the wall between room 1 and the patio was removed. A new installation was built

---

*Class 1: < 5 m²; class 2: >5-10 m²; class 3: >10-15 m²; and so forth in 5 m² increments.

in the northwest corner of the vestibule; it consists of a shallow, circular dry stone-lined pit filled with clean sand. It may have been used as a "water-cooler," as it was under the roof shade, with the wet sand enhancing the stability of the water containers (Robert-Chaleix 1898:130). The vestibule during BS-9 was a hub allowing access to the unit's roof, the prestigious pillared room 6, room 2, and the patio. Room 2 may still have been used as the door-guard's sleeping space. The position of the water cooler is interesting and revealing; in Sub-Saharan Africa, and particularly in the drier parts of the Savanna, Sahel, and Sahara, visitors once seated were generally offered a bowl of cool water. In wealthy and prestigious households, this service was performed by a servant or slave. The location of the water cooler installation virtually at the door of room 2 suggests the existence of such a practice at Awdaghost at the very end of the twelfth century AD.

The patio, previously confined within three walls, was open on both north and south sides during BS-9. It still provided the access to three rooms of the main house, the prestigious pillared room 6 on the east flank, and rooms 8 and 9 on the west side. The patio was very likely turned into the main reception space. Room 6 size, shape, and general configuration remained unchanged but it was given a second, narrower 0.90 m wide doorway in the southeast.

As was the case during BS-8, the eastern half of gallery (room) 4 and the former corridor (room) 3 may have been used as storage areas. The stone bench built in the northeastern corner of gallery (room) 4 may have been devised to protect supplies from the humidity of the floor. Two new installations were then constructed in the main courtyard. A circular dry well, engineered to drain the excess water from the rain or activities performed around the well, was dug in the west half of the courtyard. It was relatively shallow, measuring some 1.1 m in depth but entirely lined with stones without mortar (Robert-Chaleix 1989:129). A large circular hearth with a stone perimeter was built in the north-northeast. It measures approximately two meters in diameter and appears to have been used for roasting entire carcasses (*mechoui* in Arabic) of butchered animals of sheep/goat size. Such cooking methods are generally used in festive contexts, to feed a large number of guests. The evidence thus suggests that the HU-A household had organized feasts and banquets, and may have been of high status. This possibility was already suggested by architectural characteristics.

Room 27, on the south flank of the courtyard, contains an unspecified amount of iron slag and one copper ingot, which Robert-Chaleix (1989:119) interpreted as an indication of a jeweler-smith workshop, despite the crucial absence of key working installations such as furnaces, or tuyere (blow-pipe) fragments, or bellow bases.

Finally, room 19 appears to have been used this time as a kitchen. A hearth was built in the northwest corner and a pit, originally used to store foodstuffs, was dug at a few meters east, against the north wall. HU-A communicated with the neighboring HU-B by a doorway into room 15.

In BS-8, a doorway set in the west wall of room 15 allowed people to move from HU-A to HU-B, and this remained in BS-9. The main entrance to HU-B was still found in the south, where the unit was accessed through a doorway leading to the small courtyard (room 23). The general pattern of intra-unit circulation and the room distributions, shape, size, and functions were unaltered.

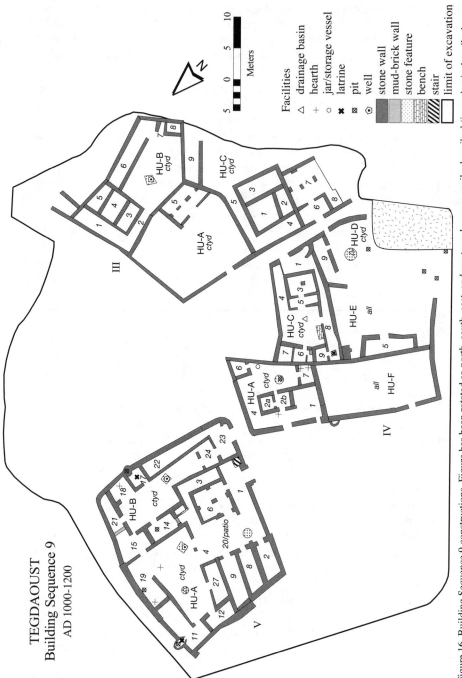

Figure 16. Building Sequence 9 constructions. Figure has been rotated so north, south, east, and west can be more easily described (i.e., what is described as "north" in text is actually closer to north by northeast).

Table 16: Building Sequence 9 constructions

Habitation Unit	Total Size (m²)	Courtyard (m²)	Rooms (m²)													Shape
			1	2	3	4	5	6	7	8	9	10	11	12	13	
Habitation Complex III																
HU-III-A	190	160.60					29.4									H
HU-III-B	151.96	54.40	27.04	7.56	8.4	10.56	8.8	30.68	1.44	3.08						P
HU-III-C	217.08	53.13	19.32	6.72	15.31	18.48	17.2	12.48	36.96	4.48	18					H
Habitation Complex IV																
HU-IV-A	115.16	44.8	33.2	4+3.6		16.2		5.96	7.42							T
HU-IV-C	199.12	38.4	22.4		13.2	13.68	5.72	6	4.8	20.88	3.2					R
HU-IV-D	131.19	115.99									15.2					R
HU-IV-E	143.81	120.01					20.8									
HU-IV-F	190	190														R
Habitation Complex V																
HU-V-A	361.35	143.16	37.12	11.7	21.38	12.6		22.54		12.4	17.52		30.4	8.93		R
HU-V-B	148.68	63.72														

HU-V-A Rooms [continued]

19	20	27
17.5	33	13.2

HU-V-B Rooms [continued]

14	15		17	18		21	22		23	24
12.48	20		4.6	7.2		12	27.6		11.96	9.12

Key: H = Hexagonal; P = Pentagonal; R = Rectangular; T = Trapezoidal

Table 17: Variations in BS-9 room size (m²)

Habitation Unit	n	Minimum	Maximum	Mean	Range	Standard Deviation	Coefficient of Variation
Habitation Complex III							
HU-III-A	1	29.4	29.4	29.4	0	—	—
HU-III-B	8	1.44	30.68	12.19	29.24	10.06	0.82
HU-III-C	9	4.48	36.96	18.21	32.48	19.18	0.55
Habitation Complex IV							
HU-IV-A	5	3.60	33.2	10.83	29.60	11.26	1.04
HU-IV-C	8	3.20	22.4	10.37	19.20	7.02	0.67
HU-IV-D	1	15.2	15.2	15.2	0	—	—
HU-IV-E	1	20.8	20.8	20.8	0	—	—
Habitation Complex V							
HU-V-A	12	8.93	17.50	19.85	8.57	9.24	0.46
HU-V-B	8	4.6	27.6	12.13	23	6.86	0.56

The courtyard was extended in the south and included the space formerly part of what had been room 25. It became an L-shaped space with the well located at the junction. The northern part was oriented north-south and extended over 44 m^2, 8.8 m by 5 m. The southern part was slightly trapezoidal; it covered 19.72 m^2, with sides measuring 5.8 to 5.4 m long and 3.4 to 2.6 m wide. The new and larger courtyard now had a total area of 63.72 m^2 and was accessed from room 24 in the south. It was surrounded by the latrine (room 17) and the kitchen room 18 in the east, room 21 in the north, room 15 in the northwest, and room 14 in the west.

The west side of the floor of room 14 was entirely "plastered" with a reddish material. The new layer, 5 cm thick, topped a beaten clay surface (Robert-Chaleix 1989:130). The walls were also resurfaced with alternating white and red ochre material. Shallow round depressions, apparently built-in vessel stands, were part of the room's remodeling. Two such pottery stands were found in the south side of the room, and a third one was located opposite the doorway against the west wall. A significant accumulation of refuse was exposed in the northern part of room 14, indicating the possibility of a planned abandonment of the feature, a suggestion elaborated further by Stevenson (1982):

> [F]ew artifacts and features will be found in processes of manufacture, use, or maintenance on sites abandoned under normal and planned conditions. Most materials on sites undergoing this type of abandonment are expected to be characteristic of discard since there would be sufficient time to plan for departure (which would result in the decreased manufacture and maintenance of most items not intended for future use at the next site) and to clean most sites of all valuable and required supplies and materials. [Stevenson 1982:241]

The record then suggests that the members of HU-B anticipated leaving, and started throwing domestic refuse in one of their most elaborate rooms.

Summary

During BS-9, at the end of the twelfth or beginning of the thirteenth century, the excavated portion of the Acropolis still had ten distinct partially or completely walled architectural units. Four were partly or totally devoted to livestock. The remaining six were household units, inhabited by social groups of different size and composition.

The pattern of unit size already discussed in previous chapters still holds during BS-9 (Tables 16 and 17). There were, however, slight variations in the number and size of rooms within and between household units. The number of rooms per unit varies from 5 in HC-IV/HU-A to 12 in HC-V/HU-A. Small rooms (classes 1 to 3*) are represented by 32 occurrences. Frequency per class varies from 10 for class 1 to 11 for classes 2 and 3. Medium-size rooms (classes 4 and 5) are found in three household units, with frequency ranging from 2 to 4. Larger rooms (classes 6 to 8) are found in five out of a total of six household units, with 1 to 2 occurrences in each. With 7 out of 12 rooms belonging to classes 4 to 8, HC-V/HU-A shows a trend toward large room size, giving additional support to its characterization as a high-status residence.

---

*Class 1: < 5 m^2; class 2: >5-10 m^2; class 3: >10-15 m^2; and so forth in 5 m^2 increments.

Conclusion

The unsteady post-climax period is documented in Awdaghost's Acropolis archaeological record by the three Building Sequences 7, 8, and 9. They appear to range from AD 1000 to 1200. A number of walled units were devoted to livestock husbandry, which may have involved the rearing of not only camels, but also sheep, goats, and possibly cattle. The others were classic household units with different arrangements of courtyards, rooms, corridors, and other living facilities. Habitation Complex V, located in the northwest of the excavated probe, was architecturally the most elaborate set of buildings exposed so far. It indicates important wealth differentials between the household units of Awdaghost's Acropolis in the eleventh through thirteenth centuries.

Each of the habitation complexes has a unique look that may have been linked to the ethnic background of its builders/owners. One must, however, keep in mind that house construction was very likely a highly specialized activity, requiring well-trained and skilled specialists. A wealthy individual or group could have had a house built by experts following specifications connected to the ethnicity of its future owners. Habitation Complex III consists of relatively long straight walls intersecting at right to obtuse angles. It belongs to a general *Maghribi* building style, suggesting that its builders or owners originated from North Africa. Habitation Complex IV in the center consists of relatively narrow and elongated buildings with smaller rooms. It is very likely the local oasis architectural style; their builders or owners were probably of local extraction. Finally, Habitation Complex V, in the northwest, was an hybrid. The wealthy owners or builders may have belonged to any of the settled Saharan Berber tribes.

Interestingly enough, all the courtyards of all inhabited household units are located at some distance from the unit's main entrance. One had to walk through a vestibule and a corridor or patio to finally access the courtyard, which was very likely the core of the domestic sphere of activities. The movement from the public sphere of the city streets to the inner sanctum of the courtyard, which is in the Arabo-Moslem world the women's domain, appears to have been tightly constrained and controlled.

—7—
The Decline and Demise
(AD 1200–1500)

As seen from the archaeological record of Awdaghost Acropolis, the decline and demise of the previously thriving trade town started at the very beginning of the thirteenth century, in AD 1200. Not surprisingly, it coincided with the shift of regional primacy to the south-western rival state of Mali. It is not unlikely that later habitations were built in other still unexplored parts of the town. As alluded to in Chapter 2, and according to Ibn Saïd (AD 1214-1287), who wrote that "there is no town worthy of mention in this section except for Awdaghost. It is inhabited by a mixture of Berbers but authority rests with the Sanhadja" (Levtzion and Hopkins 1981:192; Levtzion and Spaulding 2003:45), the town may still have had some importance. The reliability of Ibn Saïd's testimony depends on the source of information he relied on to write his *Kitab al-jughrafiya* ("Book of Geography") published in 1269. Levtzion and Hopkins (1981:181) assert that some of Ibn Saïd's accounts of the Western Soudan appear outdated, very likely because he used older material from Al-Bakri and Al-Idrisi.

This having been said, the period of decline and demise of Awdaghost spans some 300 years, from AD 1200 to 1500, documented in the topmost deposit of the tell, in levels V and VI. The uncovered archaeological record is distributed into six building sequences, BS-10 to BS-15. Four of the building sequences, BS-10 to BS-13, are found in level V at depths ranging from 1.20 m below to 0.10 m above datum. BS-14 and BS-15 belong to level VI, both exposed at 0.90 m below to 0.80 m above datum. In general, the maintenance of buildings seems to have been minimal, triggering an attritional process that ended with the collapse of the constructions and an opportunistic use of the "freed" space.

The Decline

Building Sequence 10 (Fig. 17)

The Building Sequence 10 deposit was exposed in level V at a depth ranging from 1.20 m to 0.60 m. It reveals a dramatic transformation of a previously densely built area of the

Acropolis. HC III in the east was still relatively well maintained and consisted of two household units. HC III/HU-AC, built exclusively with stone, measures 407.08 m² and resulted from the conflation of previously independent HU-A and HU-C. One of the units may have been purchased to expand the living space of a household, or, if both buildings belonged to close relatives, they finally decided to allow for unimpeded movements from one sub-unit to the other. Whatever the case, the new unit comprises two distinct courtyards measuring 283.08 m² (Table 18) with eight rooms and corridors.

The north sub-unit, hexagonal in shape with a large courtyard and two rooms, is accessed from the west street through two entranceways about 1 m in width and set 3 m apart in the south half of the west wall. The west wall oriented roughly north-south measures 20 m in length. The north wall is 11 m long, the northeast one 6 m, the east one 6.6 m, the southeast one 5 m, and the south one 8 m. Three hearths and a staircase were recorded in the courtyard. Surprisingly, the distance from each hearth to the next is identical, 7 m. The northern hearth is found next to the unit's west wall at two meters north of the entrance. The southern hearth is set at the west end of the south wall. And the eastern hearth is located at the foot of the staircase at the junction of the southeast and south walls.

Room 4c was built at the southwest corner of the sub-unit with its north side left open. It is a rectangular 12 m² space, 6.0 m long and 2.0 m wide, oriented north-south, and accessible from three directions: from the west street through the south main entrance; from the courtyard in the north; and from the east through corridor 5c. A hearth was uncovered in the central part of room 4c, suggesting that this space may have been used for refreshment and reception.

Room 5a is trapezoidal and located in the southeast corner of the sub-unit. It is a relatively large 29.40 m² room, with four stone pillars along the central axis. The doorway, unusually wide and set in the middle of the room's west wall, measures 2.0 m. Room 5a may have been used for a range of activities that could have included: the reception of guests, friends and relatives; meal taking and food sharing; hot-drink parties; and sleeping. The staircase abutting the southwest angle of the room is a clear indication that the roof was used; there may even have been an additional room-set above. A plain flat roof could have been used for a broad range of domestic activities involving sun exposure, but also simply for sleeping during the peak of the dry-season heat. If the upper level contained rooms, they may have been used as sleeping quarters by the household head and his spouse(s).

The south sub-unit has an irregular shape and consists of a three distinct courtyards, one corridor, and three rooms. It was accessed from the north and the west. The west entrance, in the west wall, was very likely the main one. It provided access to the south courtyard, a rectangular 130 m² space, measuring 13 m east-west and 10 m north-south. From the south courtyard, and proceeding northeastward, one entered the more secluded central courtyard. It is smaller in size, triangular, and covers 67.5 m². It was very likely the hub of domestic activities where household chores were performed. Room 9 is located along the northeast flank of the sub-unit. It is a trapezoidal 20.88 m² space. The doorway, opening in the courtyard, was set at the southeast end of the room's wall. The room could have been used for storage, sleeping, or a combination of both. A short and massive stone wall was built at the apex of the courtyard. It was built to strengthen the wall and buttress the staircase on 5's other side.

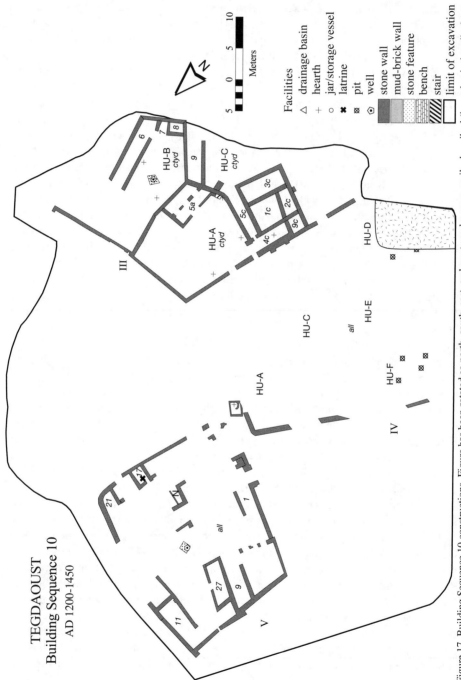

Figure 17. Building Sequence 10 constructions. Figure has been rotated so north, south, east, and west can be more easily described (i.e., what is described as "north" in text is actually closer to north by northeast).

Table 18: Building Sequence 10 constructions

Habitation Unit	Total Size (m²)	Courtyard (m²)	Rooms (m²)											Shape
			1c	2c	3c	4c	5a	5c	6	7	8	9	9c	
Habitation Complex III														
HU-III-AC	407.08	283.08	19.32	6.72	15.36	12	29.4	16				20.88	3.52	P
HU-III-B	95.2	60							30.68	1.44	3.08			P
Habitation Complex IV														
HU-IV-A	2.88													T
Habitation Complex V														
HU-V-A+B	572	510.2	9	11	21	27	17	N						R
			14	24	6	12	3.3	2.5						

Key: H = Hexagonal; P = Pentagonal; R = Rectangular; T = Trapezoidal

Table 19: Variations in BS-10 room size (m²)

Habitation Unit	n	Minimum	Maximum	Mean	Range	Standard Deviation	Coefficient of Variation
Habitation Complex III							
HU-III-A/C	8	3.52	29.40	15.38	25.88	7.65	0.49
HU-III-B	3	1.44	30.68	11.71	29.24	13.41	1.14
Habitation Complex IV							
HU-IV-A	1	2.88	2.88	2.88	0	—	—
Habitation Complex V							
HU-V-A+B	6	2.50	24	10.30	21.50	7.44	0.72

The main habitation block, composed of a small more private courtyard and three rooms, is found in the west of the sub-unit. It was accessed from three sides: from the east via corridor 5c, from the north, and from the west. Corridor 5c, along the north flank of the habitation block, is an elongated rectangle running east-west. The doorway providing access to the small secluded courtyard 1c was probably in the corridor's south wall. The pattern of circulation within the habitation block is still unclear; there was no evidence of doorways in the preserved wall portion. The small secluded courtyard 1c, the rectangular room 3c, and the trapezoidal space 2c were unchanged and were rebuilt using the BS-9 "blueprint." A small room 9c was added and built in the southwest corner of the block. It was a 3.52 m^2 rectangular space that may have been used for the storage of household supplies.

The remodeling of HC-III/HU-AC resulted in the construction of a large building complex with complementary components. The large courtyard from the north sub-unit may have been used as an animal pen for dromedaries, sheep, goats, and possibly cattle. Room 5a, with its relatively elaborate architecture, may have been the household head's reception hall for visitors, friends, and relatives. It may have had an upper extension, an upper room, or simply a flat roof surface, made accessible by a solid and well-built staircase. With the exception of milking the livestock, an activity that could be performed by male or female, the north sub-unit appears to have been a predominantly male space at the interface between the outside and the inner sanctum of the domestic life.

Room 4c appears to have serviced both sub-units. It is a hallway that could have been used for the reception of visitors, for conversation, and for hot beverage parties. Two of the rooms, 2c and 3c, were predominantly used for sleeping. Room 9c was used for the storage of household supplies, while room 9 could have been used for cooking, storage, and even sleeping. The small secluded courtyard 1c could have been the main meal-taking area and the large central courtyard the main hub of domestic maintenance and cooking activities.

HC-III/HU-B on the east flank of the habitation was remodeled by the leveling of the northern end of its northern portion. This previously densely built portion was turned into an open space that could have been used for fencing livestock or caravans. The newly available open space is rectangular and measures 65 m^2, 10 m in length and 6.5 m in width. The area does not appear to have been in sustained use as it was left to rubble (Devisse 1983:198-99). The occupation of the habitation was confined to the south half of the building, contained within a pentagon measuring 25 m along the NW-SE axis and 20 m on the SW-NE axis.

The remodeled household unit included a relatively large courtyard, two rooms, and one partially walled space. It was accessed from the northwest, through a long and narrow 12 m by 2 m corridor that was oriented roughly north-south. The courtyard is also pentagonal, slightly elongated along the north-south axis. Three features of archaeological interest, two hearths and a well all located in the north half, were recorded in the courtyard. The well dug during BS-6 was still in use without major alteration. Surprisingly, the recorded hearths are equidistant (both 2 m) from the well. The main room 6 was rebuilt on top of the previous BS-9 walls with a minor shift in orientation in the south end of the west wall, which is slightly tilted west. As in the previous BS-9, room 6 is an elongated trapezoidal 30.68 m^2 space. It was accessed from the courtyard through a doorway in the south half of the west wall, and may have been used for several functions. In fact, as the only significant room of the remodeled habitation, it was by definition a multifunctional space, used principally for storage and sleeping. The small partially walled 1.44 m² space 7 and the 3.08 m² room 8, along the southeast wall, could have been used for the storage of household belongings.

In summary, HC-III/HU-B appears to have experienced a significant reduction in the size of its owner's household, and probably a decline in wealth and prestige. In fact, during BS-10, it became "a single room" household unit that maintained the well servicing the whole habitation complex. The attritional process documented in the HC-III BS-10 deposit seems to have been triggered by the trend toward the reduction in size of individual households. Such a process, which involves a split and relocation of family members to adjust to changing patterns of regional and long-distance exchange systems, is congruent with the dynamics of trade diasporas. The other habitation complexes, HC-IV and HC-V, see an even more dramatic shift in occupation during the BS-10.

HC-IV, in the south-central part of the excavated probe, has been literally abandoned. There are still a few indications of occupation, however intermittent they may have been. These indications are a series of pits, portions of the west wall, and a small room.

The documented pit series is divided into two distinct clusters located along the south flank of the complex. The western cluster consists of four pits in a lozenge-shaped arrangement 3 to 5 m apart. The eastern cluster comprises two pits 3 m apart along a north-south axis. Three portions of the west wall are preserved with gaps ranging from 5 to 10 m. The south and middle portions of the wall are approximately 4 m in length. The north portion consists of two perpendicular walls, the south-north part 6 m long and the east-west part 3 m. The east-west wall is attached to a small 2.88 m² room with a built-in hearth. All of these features seem to indicate a shift from permanent to intermittent occupation.

The three free-standing wall portions were very likely part of the camping "infrastructure"; each may have been combined with movable tent material to delineate a caravan crew or visitors' living quarters on their way in and out of Awdaghost. If this were the case, the general maintenance of the area would have been at best intermittent. A small cooking area, protected from wind and dust and open to all the campers, was adjacent to the camping ground. The pit clusters found in the south are more difficult to interpret; key characteristics like depth, width, and shape were not published in detail (Polet 1985:228-29). The published feature plan (Polet 1985:229) suggests the predominance of circular to potato-shaped pits, with the largest one located in the southeast corner. Unlike the previous occupation, all the pits contained a relatively large amount of potsherds, a fact interpreted by the excavator as evidence of refuse pits (Polet 1985:228). According to this scenario, HC-IV was completely abandoned, the unclaimed space used for the disposal of trash in pits dug explicitly for that purpose. It is more an assumption than a well-argued proposition; the fact that pits are filled with refuse when exposed during an archaeological excavation does not necessarily mean that they were designed originally to fulfill such a function. Very likely, these pits were dug for other purposes. After abandonment, they were filled with cultural remains, purposely or through erosional accumulation. The pits in the southwest could have been used as water-cooling devices: large clay vessels may have been set in the ground, filled with water, and stored in shaded spots. The southeast pits, and most likely the largest southeastern-most specimen, may have been used for garbage dumping. Finally, the open space between the west wall and the eastern HC-III may have been used to tether the pack animals for the night.

HC-V was extensively remodeled. The aim appears to have been the creation of a simpler and more coherent habitation articulated around a large central courtyard. The emphasis was clearly on the organization of a large courtyard that measures 510.2 m^2 during BS-10, with the well at its center. The remodeled HC-V was accessible from three sides: a 10 m wide opening in the north wall; two 1 to 3 m wide entrances along the east wall; and the main entrance in the south wall along with an additional 5 m wide gap.

Rooms 9, 11, and 27 of HC-V are all east-west oriented rectangles. Their sizes changed little, ranging from 12 m^2 (room 27) to 24 m^2 (room 11), with room 9 measuring 14 m^2 (Table 18). The secluded courtyard south of room 9 was a new addition to the complex. It is a trapeze-shaped 30 m^2 space. Most of the east wall consisted of four equidistant pillars set at approximately 1 m apart, allowing for unimpeded access to the rest of the complex. The corridor 1, on the south side, was reshaped to be open-ended with the construction of a middle wall portion measuring 4 m in length and 0.5 m in width. The newly reconfigured space, entered from the south street through the main entrance, was 14 m long and 3 m wide and provided access to the secluded courtyard in the southwest and the main courtyard in the north and east. The extensive central courtyard area was subdivided into two subcomponents, the southern one measuring 20 m by 7 m, the northern one 25 m by 7 m. The central well, a short L-shaped stone wall, and a small rectangular room separate the north and the south part of HC-V's spacious courtyard. The latrine and shower/bath area (room 17) rebuilt along the east wall was smaller in size.

The function of open-ended rooms located along the north wall is more difficult to decipher. Robert-Chaleix (1989:143), without supporting evidence, suggests the northeast corner of the complex was used for camping purposes. In general however, and within the context of the decreasing and relocating population, the whole Habitation Complex was reorganized to increase livestock space. This may have been part of the new economic strategy linked to livestock husbandry, or more likely geared to offer adequate facilities to dromedary caravans and their crews.

During BS-10, there appears to have been a significant architectural shift toward a simplification of the building structures. Architectural devolution was sharp and radical in HC-IV; it was extensive with far-ranging consequences in HC-V, and more gradual in HC-III. This reconfiguration of Awdaghost settlement evidence took place within the context of shifting balance of power between the two previously competing West African kingdoms of Ghana and Mali. The former was declining and the latter, rising. Awdaghost, the hub of the interregional and "international" trade between North Africa and the Sahara, the Tekrur kingdom along the Middle Senegal valley in the southwest, and the hinterland and the capital of Ghana at Kumby Saleh, declined in importance. Merchants who had been part of the trade diaspora that contributed to the prosperity of Awdaghost would have left the town and relocated to take advantage of emerging new economic opportunities. Those who stayed appear to have been involved in a fierce competition to provide the dwindling number of caravans with adequate caravansérail-like facilities and amenities. It is such a combination of processes that may have triggered the architectural remodeling visible in the Awdaghost BS-10 archaeological record.

Building Sequence 11 (Fig. 18)

The BS-11 deposit measures 0.30 m thick, and was exposed at depths below datum ranging from 0.90 to 1.20 m in the east and 0.60 to 0.30 m in the west. HC-III and HC-IV were unaltered during BS-11. Most of the architectural alterations occurred in HC-V.

HC-III was inhabited without architectural modification. The western combined household unit had an additional hearth built in the very south of the courtyard (Fig. 18), with possibly a new entrance set at the south end of the west wall. The general layout of the recorded habitation units, as evidenced by the size, positioning, shape, and orientation of rooms, corridors, and courtyards, remained unchanged (Table 20). HC-IV was still in use as an open camping area with a small 2.88 m² kitchen attached which still contained a built-in hearth.

HC-V in the west was literally left to degrade. The constructions located in the eastern half of the complex were left to collapse, and the space was more or less leveled. The western part of the unit was still relatively well-maintained. One could almost draw a diagonal line from the southeast buttress, to the well, and finally to the mid-north wall separating the degraded eastern area from the maintained western area. The reconfigured complex covers 250 m², with sides measuring 27 m for the diagonal line, 25 m for the south wall, 19 m for the west one, and finally, 13 m for the north wall. The space was subdivided into seven mostly walled compartments. The same well was still in use and the presence of only one complete room was a clear indication of the shift in the use of the building. The complete room 27 was an exact replica of the BS-10 room 27. It was located in the central part of the new complex, surrounded in the north, west, and south by spaces that could have been used for the intermittent storage of caravan crew members' belongings. The south corridor and the small courtyard in the southwest were part of a larger open space. Room 9, an open-ended room, measured approximately 7 m by 2 m. An elongated and narrow space ending in a

Table 20: Building Sequence 11 constructions

Habitation Unit	Total Size (m²)	Courtyard (m²)	Rooms (m²)								Shape
			1c	2c	3c	4c	5a	5c	9	9c	
Habitation Complex III											
HU-III-AC	407.08	283.08	19.32	6.72	15.36	12	29.4	16	20.88	3.52	P
								6	7	8	
HU-III-B	95.2	60						30.68	1.44	3.08	P
Habitation Complex IV											
HU-IV-A	2.88										T
Habitation Complex V											
HU-V-A+B	250	200	9	11	27						R
			14	21	12						

Key: H = Hexagonal; P = Pentagonal; R = Rectangular; T = Trapezoidal

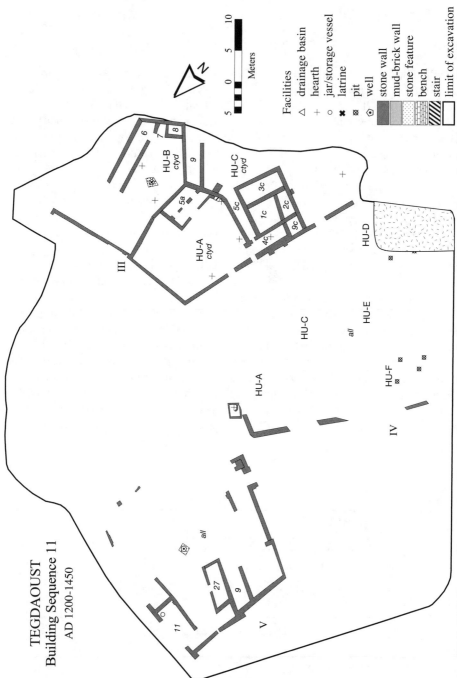

Figure 18. Building Sequence 11 constructions. Figure has been rotated so north, south, east, and west can be more easily described (i.e., what is described as "north" in text is actually closer to north by northeast).

cul-de-sac, delimited by the west wall and the room 27 west wall, and oriented north-south, was probably used as a corridor. It measured 18 m², 9 m in length and 2 m in width. The walled space along the north wall called room 11 was not strictly speaking a room; it was a verandah measuring 7 m by 3 m. It was open on the north street and provided access to the corridor and ultimately to the main room 27. A large clay vessel, probably used as a water cooler, was found in the northeast corner of the verandah. Finally, the eastern appendage of the verandah was delimited by three walls with the east left open.

During BS-11, the remodeling of HC-V resulted in the creation of a large open and leveled space which could have been used to host large caravans, and had direct access to water. The process of space reallocation to activities other than household habitation that started during BS-10 was amplified. The remodeled features were, very likely, used intermittently by some special purpose groups, such as caravan crews, merchants, or even traveling scholars.

The Demise

Building Sequence 12 (Fig. 19)

The incremental attrition of household-type facilities documented in BS-10 and BS-11 deposits was characteristic of the decline phase of the Awdaghost Acropolis settlement. In chronological terms, this phase is assigned tentatively to the thirteenth and fourteenth centuries. The "Demise" phase that followed probably lasted from the fifteenth to the very beginning of the sixteenth century AD.

During BS-12, HC-III and HC-IV were left to collapse and were virtually abandoned. The north wall of HC-III was used to delineate the southeastern limit of the space still in use. A water drain basin was built in the small space formerly used as a storage room and located in the southeast of the excavated probe. The small 2.88 m² kitchen with a built-in hearth located at the northern end of the HC-IV west wall was still in use. HC-V in the west was segmented and subdivided into distinct spaces by a number of stone walls. None of the delineated space was roofed, making the use of the term "room" misleading. A roughly rectangular 6 by 5 m space, walled on three sides, was delineated in the southwest of the complex. A segment of the south corridor serviced by the main entrance was situated 5-6 m east of this space, with all the remaining walled spaces to be found in the north. A relatively short rectangular space oriented east-west was attached to the north side of the rectangular courtyard, now with a slight gap in it. The courtyard shares a wall with an elongated rect-angular space that was accessed from three sides (the west street through a narrow gap, the north, and the east). Another rectangular space oriented east-west was built in the northwest, connecting the complex to the north street through its open north flank (room 11). A new pit was dug 2-3 m southwest of the well. Both features are located in the central part of the complex and appear to have been two key elements of the architectural reconfiguration.

During BS-12, an extensive and relatively coherent caravansérail appears to have finally emerged. The excavation of the north-central part of the Acropolis is unfortunately not yet published. Despite this limitation, it is very likely that the general process of decline documented in all three habitation complexes under consideration also operated in the north-central quarter. From this perspective, the remodeled extensive space was delimited by the HC-V west wall in the west; the HC-V south wall and the HC-IV kitchen with a built-in hearth in the south; and finally, the HC-III north wall in the southeast, with a well. The subdivision of the architectonic features into HC-III, HC-IV, and HC-V, which has been used so far, becomes irrelevant during BS-12 and the later periods.

The exposed south portion of the newly developed caravansérail was probably part of a much larger construction extending northward. The excavated portion is roughly oval-shaped, measuring 70 m along the west-east axis and 37 m north-south.

Building Sequence 13 (Fig. 20)

Once the caravansérail was designed and built during BS-12, it became the focus of considerable remodeling during the following BS-13. All the remodeling effort was focused on the west installations. The main entrance/exit from the south street was rebuilt with a simple east "bastion." A new room was built attached to the west wall. The new addition was oriented north-south and measured 12 m², 6 m in length and 2 m in width. It was accessed from both west and east; the west entrance was but a narrow gap in the wall while the eastern one was a more standard doorway. No additional features or installations were recorded in the new room, suggesting that it may have been used for resting and sleeping by caravan crew members. Additional walled spaces were built along the south flank of the new room, superimposed on the previous BS-12 walls.

During BS-13, there appears to have been a sustained architectural effort to improve the comfort of the "living" component of the caravansérail. The well was no longer in use, however. At some point, it was filled and its margins leveled. The filling and leveling of the well may indicate the relocation of caravansérail activities somewhere else. If that was the case, the BS-13 remodeling may have resulted in the construction of room space to provide travelers with "guest rooms."

Building Sequence 14 (Fig. 21)

The BS-14 archaeological deposit is confined to the northwestern part of the excavated probe. It measures 0.25 m in thickness and was exposed at depths ranging from 0.20 to 0.45 m above datum, and dated tentatively to AD 1500. The remodeling effort focused on the HC-V west wall which was used as the central axis of the new building. Most of the eastern part of HC-V went out of use. The new construction consists of three main elements: a courtyard, a small walled but open-ended space, and finally, an elaborate room.

The courtyard is located at the south end of the building. It is rectangular in shape, spread over 30 m², 6 m in length and 5 m in width, open on the east, and surrounded by stone walls on three sides. It would have been large enough to contain a small number of riding and pack animals: for instance, a few horses and a handful of dromedaries. A small 4 m² space is found along the north flank of the courtyard. It is open in the east. It is not known if this small "room" was roofed. Whatever the case, it was accessed from the east and could have been used for the storage of travelers' or caravan crew members' belongings. Room

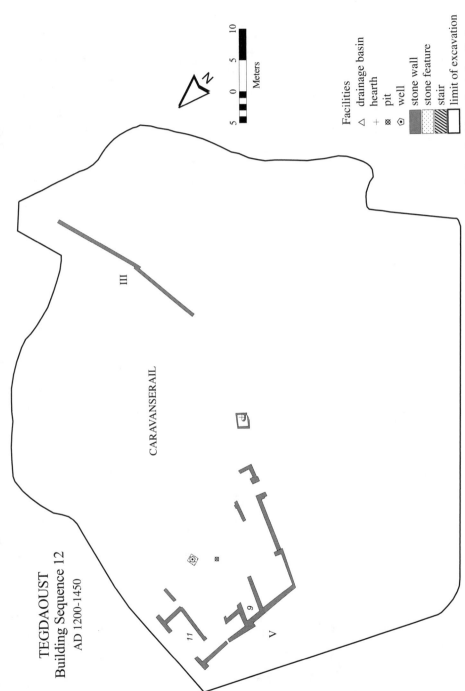

Figure 19. Building Sequence 12 constructions. Figure has been rotated so north, south, east, and west can be more easily described (i.e., what is described as "north" in text is actually closer to north by northeast).

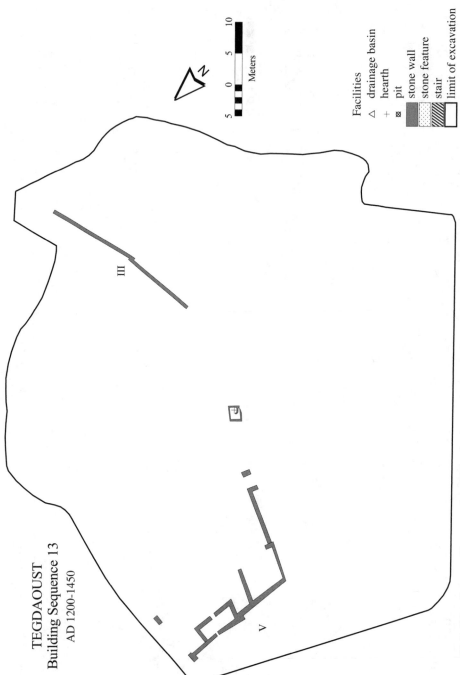

TEGDAOUST
Building Sequence 13
AD 1200-1450

Facilities
△ drainage basin
+ hearth
⊠ pit
   stone wall
   stone feature
   stair
   limit of excavation

Meters
0   5   10

Figure 20. Building Sequence 13 constructions. Figure has been rotated so north, south, east, and west can be more easily described (i.e., what is described as "north" in text is actually closer to north by northeast).

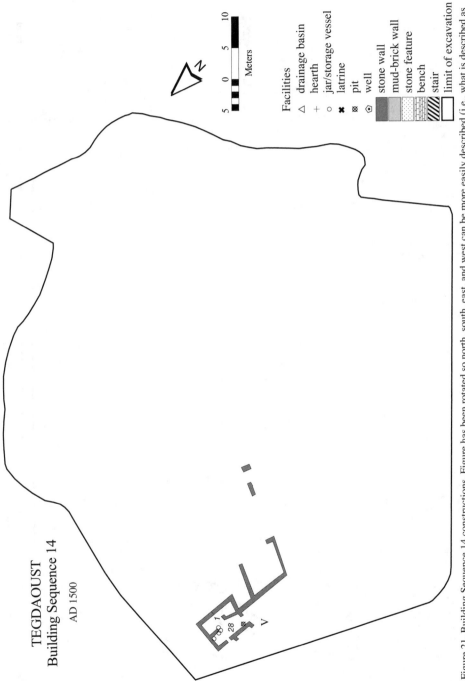

Figure 21. Building Sequence 14 constructions. Figure has been rotated so north, south, east, and west can be more easily described (i.e., what is described as "north" in text is actually closer to north by northeast).

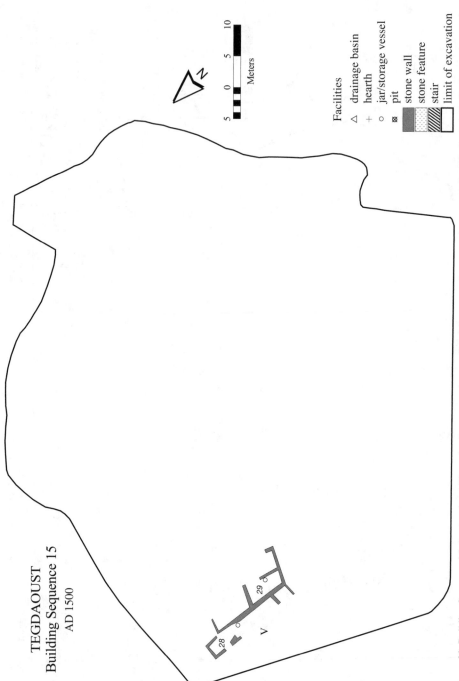

TEGDAOUST
Building Sequence 15
AD 1500

Facilities

△   drainage basin
+   hearth
○   jar/storage vessel
⊠   pit
▨   stone wall
▦   stone feature
▧   stair
□   limit of excavation

Figure 22. Building Sequence 15 constructions. Figure has been rotated so north, south, east, and west can be more easily described (i.e., what is described as "north" in text is actually closer to north by northeast).

28, built at the north end of the building, is particularly elaborate. It is trapezoidal in shape and divided along its north-south axis. It had two entrances, the wider in the south and the narrower in the west, and is divided into three distinct spaces.

The entrance hall is trapezoidal. Its west wall was strengthened by two buttresses, and the east wall tilted northeast. The space delineated in the southwest of room 28 measures some 4.5 m², and contains an empty clay-lined pit dug against the wall, suggested to have been a storage bin (Robert-Chaleix 1989:165). However, it could have been used as a supporting device for a large water container, thus functioning as a water-cooling device. The entrance area was very likely devoted to food-processing and meal-taking and provided access to three smaller rooms. A small 3 m² storage space is found in the northwest. Four storage jars were exposed, all leaning against the room's east wall. The eastern half of room 28, accessed through a doorway set in the middle of the partition wall, was subdivided into what can be considered two small "sleeping" rooms. The southern one is a trapezoid, with a doorway set in the east half of the north wall. The north room is much larger; it is a rectilinear 6 m² space oriented north-south.

The new shift toward the construction of habitation facilities initiated during the previous BS-13 was amplified during BS-14. A relatively compact but coherent house, differentiated internally, was built and may have been inhabited by a small family unit. There was therefore a shift back to the use of the area by household units, but of significantly smaller size if compared to those of the rapid growth and climax periods. In architectural terms, the blueprint materialized by the construction exposed in the BS-14 archaeological deposit is very distinctive. It has no equivalent in all the building sequences discussed so far. It seems to indicate the installation in the area of smaller and less wealthy households.

Building Sequence 15 (Fig. 22)

BS-15, the topmost and the last major occupation event to occur in the Awdaghost Acropolis, probably accumulated around AD 1500 or during the very early part of the sixteenth century. As was the case with the BS-14 deposit, BS-15 is also confined to the northwestern part of the excavated probe. It measures 0.35 m in thickness and was exposed at depths varying from 0.45 to 0.80 above datum.

The reconstruction carried out during BS-15 was more extensive. The new building complex measures 16 m in length along its central north-south axis, and 9 m in maximum width in the south. It is made up of two roughly symmetrical units that may have been inhabited by related but distinct households. The western unit consists of three spaces arranged linearly along the north-south axis. The southern space is delineated by three short walls and is open in the west. It is rectangular, covers approximately 4 m² and may have been used for storing the household's belongings. A courtyard separates the south storage space from the main north room; it is 8 m north-south and probably extended westward. If we use the 2 m width of the unit, the size of the courtyard was a minimum of 16 m². A relatively large storage container was found in the courtyard's northeast corner. The north room is rectangular, oriented north-south, and measures approximately 12 m², 6 m by 2 m. It was accessed from three sides; the south entrance, measuring 1.5 m in width, is narrowed by a buttressing wall tilted slightly southeast. The west doorway, set in the middle of the west wall, is 1 m wide. The east entrance in the middle of the east wall is relatively narrow. The north room offered a sizable living and sleeping space. Relying exclusively on the extent of the building exposed in the archaeological record, the newly built west unit measured some 32 m^2.

The east unit was a variation on the same theme: a courtyard, a storage space, and a living/sleeping room. In this case, the building is constructed following an L-shaped plan. The main living and sleeping room (room 29) is located at the southwest corner of the construction; it is a trapezoid oriented north-south, measuring 5.6 m in length and 2 to 3 m in width, approximately 14 m^2 in surface area. It is accessed through a large 2 m wide doorway set in the northeast. One large storage vessel, probably used as a water container, was found set against the room's east wall, next to the entrance. A small space walled on three sides with the north left open was built along the east flank of the main room 29. It is irregular in shape and measures 3 m on both west and south sides, and 1 m on the east. Its walled space is therefore trapezoidal in shape and measures approximately 4.5 m^2 in surface area. Finally, the unit's courtyard, located along the north side of the main room 29, measures 6 m north-south, and 2 to 3 m in width, depending on the length of the demarcating walls. This trapezoid covers approximately 15 m^2. With its three constituent parts combined, the total size of the east unit is 33.5 m^2.

Despite variation in shape and space arrangement, the housing units built during BS-15 are virtually of the same size, 32 m^2 for the west unit and 33.5 m^2 for the east unit. New housing standards consisting of three-space components appear to have emerged during BS-14 and amplified during BS-15. This architectural shift probably resulted from the combined effects of a general decrease in wealth, the relocation on the Acropolis of different social groups, and the smaller size in membership of the incoming households. According to Robert-Chaleix (1989:167), wall construction is in general much less careful. She adds that "the imported items are certainly older objects brought to the surface, without any doubt by new construction work, archaeological excavation, or the digging of refuse pits" (ibid.). The abandonment and collapse of the BS-15 building complex marks the closure of more than one thousand years of occupation of the Awdaghost Acropolis.

Conclusion

The decline and demise of Awdaghost Acropolis was a long and protracted process that probably mirrored the shifts in the regional balance of wealth and power. The first sign is the halting of any new construction after BS-9, at the very end of the twelfth century. This halt triggered the first phase of architectural remodeling of the whole area, with a trend toward architectural simplicity combined with the creation of large open spaces for livestock. HC-IV area is the first to be transformed into an intermittent camping area during BS-10, while more extensive courtyards develop in HC-III and HC-V. This trend is sustained and amplified during BS-11 when it is accelerated in HC-V in the west of the excavated probe.

The second phase of remodeling is kicked off during BS-12 and lasted to the end of BS-13. HC-III in the east and HC-IV in the south and center are definitely abandoned, and either left to collapse or actively leveled. The north wall of HC-III and the small kitchen from HC-IV are included in a new and larger feature, a caravansérail. It included a relatively large open space used to corral the visiting caravans, a well for both humans and animals, and built facilities for caravan crew members.

The third and final phase documented in BS-14 and BS-15, around AD 1500, is a new shift toward domestic architecture, with a simpler blueprint for smaller household units. Surprisingly, the evidence from BS-15 seems to indicate the emergence of some housing standards. Such standards could have been enhanced by close relationships between the two household units, their similarity in size or wealth, or a combination of all three factors. Whatever the case, it is an interesting finding.

Awdgahost was not deserted after demise of the Acropolis settlement. The town appears to have been settled with a sparse population up to the seventeenth century (Devisse 1983; Mauny 1961:482). A new but smaller town was built in the seventeenth century by the Moorish tribe of Tegdaoust in the southwest, on top of the old town's archaeological accumulation. According to Mauny (1961:482), even if it is not known how he reached these conclusions, "the population of the medieval town may have reached 5-6,000 inhabitants at its peak, approximately 200 inhabitants per hectare, and that of the seventeenth-century town, with less densely packed buildings, hardly 1000."

—8—

Awdaghost in the Historical Record

Introduction

The early history of West African cities has fascinated colonial officers from the beginning of the colonial administration. Many of the towns and cities mentioned in the Arabic historical sources were difficult to identify on the ground, leading to a mushrooming scholarship on the best exegesis of medieval authors. This discussion on the allusions to Awdaghost in Arabic historical sources is therefore divided into two distinct components. The first one deals with the medieval Arab writers from different parts of the Dar al-Islam; the second focuses on the Colonial period, a period during which a number of individuals and scholars, as well as civil servants and military officers, were involved in an intensive search for all the prominent Sahara and Sahelian medieval towns.

Awdaghost in the Arabic Historical Sources

All the testimonies of the Medieval period must be evaluated on their own merits. Some of the authors never left their country of birth; others traveled extensively across the Dar-al-Islam, from Spain to India. In any case, with the notable exception of Ibn Battuta (fourteenth century AD) who visited many places in West and East Africa, most if not all the authors and scholars wrote their accounts from informants' interviews or references to earlier works. Accordingly, the information conveyed by the authors varies from anecdotal to factually accurate, with the accuracy generally increasing as international trade links intensified.

The approach to the historical record followed in this book has been articulated by Moses Finley and is a key element in the critical analysis of historical documents. Following Finley (1998:266),

> the first question that must be asked before trying to discover what an author is saying is: What were the traditions and the social and intellectual context in which he was writing? The second is: What questions was he addressing himself to, and what were his interests in the subject under consideration.

Elements of the biographies of the relevant authors are therefore a crucial ingredient in the assessment of the plausibility and reliability of their works.

Awdaghust in the Ninth- and Tenth-Century Historical Record

The earliest written allusion to the town of Awdaghust/Awdaghost is found in *Kitab al-Buldan* by Al-Ya'qubi, a book he completed in Cairo in 889-890 AD. Al Ya'qubi, originally from the eastern province of Khurasasn, belonged to a family with pro-Alid leaning. His occupation is not well known. He may have been a functionary, "perhaps in the Post and Intelligence service," (Levtzion and Hopkins 1981:19) a fact that may partly explain his extensive geographic knowledge. He traveled to India and the Maghrib, and later settled in Egypt at the court of the Tulunids where he died in 897.

The *Kitab al-Buldan* is a description of places, itineraries, and cultural practices encountered in different lands. His allusion to Awdaghost consists of a few lines:

> Then the traveller will reach a town (*balad*) called Ghust which is an inhabited valley with dwellings. It is the residence of their king, who has no religion or law. He raids the land of the Sudan, who have many kingdoms. [Al-Ya'qubi in Levtzion and Hopkins 1981:22]

The concept of kingdom as used by Al Ya'qubi is far from clear. Awdaghost (or Ghust in this case) is claimed to be the residence of their king, but it is not known which group's king. It is probably not the king of the Anbiya of the Sanhaja, referred to in the same paragraph. The Anbija have "no permanent dwellings," "veil their faces with their turbans," "do not wear [sewn] clothes," "subsist on camels," and "have no crops" (in Levtzion and Hopkins 1981:22).

The absence of Islam is emphasized by the fact that the king "has no religion or law." However, that king raids the Sudan, "who have many kingdoms"; it is not clear if Awdaghost is one of the Sudan kingdoms or not.

The allusion to Awdaghost is interesting mostly for chronological reasons. It indicates that a significant town was known to exist in the southwestern part of the Sahara during the ninth century AD. All other information is clouded in vagueness and uncertainty.

In the tenth century, Ibn Hawqal provided a richer description of Awdaghost in his geographical book *Surat al-Ard* ("The Picture of the Earth") written in 967. He gathered his information on faraway lands from traders and travelers. In 947-951 he traveled in the Maghrib and Spain. It was in Sijilmasa and other commercial centers of the Maghrib that he collected information about the Sahara and the Sudan (Levtzion and Hopkins 1981:43). Ibn Hawqal described different itineraries followed by traders' caravans, some more dangerous than others. According to him, "Awdaghust is a pleasant town, and of all God's lands it most resembles Mecca and the town of Jurzuwan in the district of Juzjan in Khurasan, because it is situated between two mountains intersected by ravines" (Ibn Hawqal, in Levtzion and Hopkins 1981:46). He was also more specific about the slave trade that was particularly active in the western Sudan and Spain: "As for what is exported from the Maghrib to the East there are very comely slave girls (*muwalladat*) . . . and slaves (*khadam*) imported from the land of the Sudan and those imported from the land of the Slavs by way of al-Andalus" (ibid.:47). For Ibn Hawqal, Awdaghost was a Sanhaja town, ruled by Tinbarutan b. Usfay-shar, king of all the Sanhaja (ibid.:48). It is further specified that "this king of Awdaghust maintains relations with the ruler of Ghana. Ghana is the wealthiest king on the face of the earth" (ibid.:49).

One of the most famous assertions of Ibn Hawqal concerning the Sudan is an allusion to a financial transaction with an unusual amount of money. "I saw at Awdaghust a war-rant in which the statement of a debt owed to one of them [the people of Sijilmasa] by one of the merchants of Awdaghust, who was [himself] one of the people of Sijilmasa, in the sum of 42,000 dinars. I have never seen or heard anything comparable to this story in the East. When I told it to people in Iraq, Fars, and Khurasan it was considered remarkable" (ibid.:47). It is, however, suggested that Ibn Hawqal never crossed the Sahara nor set foot at Awdaghost but instead saw the 42,000 dinar promissory note at Sijilmasa (Levtzion 1968; Levtzion and Hopkins 1981:381).

Whatever the case, the impression that emerges from Ibn Hawqal's geography is that Awdaghost was a prosperous and wealthy town, ruled by an efficient and skilled "king," with excellent "international" connections. If Ibn Hawqal's reading of the political geography of the western Sudan is accurate, Awdaghost was an autonomous and independent polity during the tenth century AD, while Ghana was already a centralized state that would soon shift to an expansionist empire.

Al-Hassan b. Muhammad al-Misri al-Muhallabi (Al-Muhallabi) died at the end of the tenth century AD, in 990. He wrote a geography book, the *Kitab al-'Aziz* ("The Book of Aziz"), dedicated to the Fatimid Khaliph Al-'Aziz who reigned from AD 976 to 996. Unfortunately most of his work was lost. Some of its fragments were salvaged as quotations in the book Yaqut wrote a few centuries later, between 1212 and 1229 (Levtzion and Spaulding 2003:6). It is not known if Al-Muhallabi, who lived in Cairo for most of his life, visited the Maghrib and the western Sudan. In the tenth century however, the Fatimids controlled much of the trade of North Africa and the Sahara; information gathered all over these territories by mer-chants, traders, scholars, or simply travelers was easily accessible to Fatimid functionaries in Cairo. Al-Muhallabi attributed the conversion to Islam of Awdaghost to the founder of the Fatimid dynasty, Mahdi 'Ubayd Allah, who ruled from 909 to 934.

As far as the description of Awdaghost is concerned, the salvaged excerpt comprises three main components. The first described the location of the town: "Awdaghust is a town between two mountains deep inland, 40-odd stages to the south of Sijilmasa, through sands and arid wastes, with known water points" (Al-Muhallabi, in Levtzion and Spaulding 2003:7). He added that some of the known water points, located along the itinerary to Awdaghost, were surrounded by Berber tents. The second refers to the dynamic economy of the tenth-century town. Al-Muhallabi had but praises for Awdaghost: "There are excellent markets in Awdaghust," he wrote, adding that "it is one of the most important metropolises," with a "continual flow of traffic toward it from every land." The third focuses on religious matters: "its people are Muslims, who recite the Koran, study Islamic jurisprudence, and possess mosques and oratories." He goes on, ascertaining that "they have been converted to Islam by the Mahdi 'Ubayd Allah, for previously they were infidels who worshipped the sun, who used to eat carrion and blood" (ibid:7).

During the tenth century AD, Awdaghost was an economic hub in western Sudan, an active market place servicing an extensive territory. The trade in slaves was one of the key elements in the northbound side of the Trans-Saharan exchange system. In parallel to these developments, Islam became the institutional religion; learning and scholarship, articulated through oratories, mosques, and possibly Koranic schools, were widespread.

In summary, from the earliest allusion in Al-Ya'qubi's *Kitab al-Buldan* dating to the second half of the ninth century AD, to Al-Muhallabi's *Kitab al-'Aziz* at the end of the tenth century AD, the information from and on Awdaghost improved significantly. It is nonetheless clear that neither Al-Ya'qubi, Ibn Hawqal, nor Al-Muhallabi ever visited the southwestern Sahara metropolis. The impression that emerged from the review of these early sources is that of a dynamic, almost explosively expanding town in the context of a fast growing international economy and a tighter integration in the Dar al-Islam. It seems to have been an autonomous and independent polity ruled by a "princely" family of the Sanhaja Berbers. The remote and obscure origins of the town are not addressed, and in fact could not be addressed in these sources. It is not known if there was any native population that was later joined by Saharan Berbers, North Africans and other Sub-Saharan Africans.

Awdaghost in the Eleventh- and Twelfth-Century Historical Record

The eleventh and twelfth centuries AD witnessed the ascent of Awdaghost to wealth and fame, the takeover by the militant Almoravids, and within the same time frame, its conquest by the expansionist state of Ghana. During this period, the earliest allusion to Awdaghost is by Abu 'l-Rayhan Muhammad b. Ahmad al-Biruni (AD 973-1050) in *Al-Qanun al-masudi fi 'll-hay'a wa-'l-nujum* ("The Mas'udi Canon on Astronomy and the Stars"), written in 1030. Al-Biruni is famous for his independence of mind and impartiality. He is considered one of the greatest scholars of Islam (Levtzion and Hopkins 1981:56). He did not provide any description of Awdaghost but simply mentioned the town in one of his "tables of longitudes of towns from the shore of the Western Surrounding Sea and their Latitudes from the Equator." According to his geographic work, Awdaghost is located in the Second Clime, in the Maghrib at 15°00' longitude and 26°00' latitude (Al-Biruni, in Levtzion and Hopkins 1981:57).

In 1068, Al-Bakri, who died at an advanced age in 1094, completed one of his major works, the *Kitab al-masalik wa-'l-mamalik* ("The Book of Routes and Realms"). Abu 'Ubayd 'Abd Allah b. 'Abd al-'Aziz al-Bakri was born to a princely family in Spain. He lived most of his life in Cordova and Almeria, as a geographer, theologian, philologist, and botanist, or, in short, a genuine scholar. He is considered one of the most important sources of the history of western Sudan. According to Levtzion and Hopkins (1981:62), one of the principal sources of Al-Bakri was the lost geographic work of Muhammad b. Yusuf al-Warraq (AD 904-973) whose title he appropriated for his own work. "Some of the material borrowed from Al-Warraq is acknowledged, but occasionally al-Bakri omits reference to his source. In reading al-Bakri's text one has to watch carefully for evidence drawn from al-Warraq, which may refer to the middle of the tenth century" (Levtzion and Hopkins 1981:62).

Al-Bakri's account of Awdaghost is articulated around four related topics: (1) the road to Awdaghost; (2) the religious life and economic activities; (3) people and their manners; and finally, (4) the kingship.

In discussing the road to Awdaghost (Levtzion and Hopkins 1981:66-68), Al-Bakri provides a detailed account of the route between the town of Tamdult and the town of Awdaghost, with precise descriptions of the landscapes as well as information on the topography, the "road," the wells, and the places the caravans had to walk through. Awdaghost, at the end of a "40-stages" long road, is "a large town, populous and built on sandy ground, overlooked by a big mountain, completely barren and devoid of vegetation" (Al-Bakri, in Levtzion and Hopkins 1981:68). The town had "handsome buildings and fine houses" and "possesses wells with sweet water." He claims that Islam took root and was well infused in the fabric of Awdaghost society. The Mosques, both the cathedral and many smaller ones, were well attended. And all had teachers of the Koran. Subsistence and other economic activities included agriculture, livestock husbandry, craft activities, and trade. Date palm gardens were found around the town; wheat, consumed by the king and the wealthy, was cultivated in plots watered with buckets. Sorghum, cucumbers, fig trees, vines and henna were also grown. Livestock was abundant and affordable: "Cattle and sheep are so numerous there that for a *mithqal* one may buy ten rams or more" (ibid.:68). The market was permanently active, crowded with noisy buyers and sellers with the transactions conducted in gold. In general, "the people of Awdaghust enjoy extensive benefits and huge wealth" (ibid.:68). Over long distances, they imported from the domain of Islam objects of worked copper, ample robes dyed red on blue, wheat, dates, and raisins. His agricultural reporting is ambiguous. Wheat, dates and vines are said to have been grown locally: "around the town are gardens with date palms. Wheat is grown there . . . and there are . . . some vines" (ibid.:68). Apparently the local production was not large enough to satisfy the demand. Finally, he says (ibid.:69), "the gold of Awdaghost is better and purer than that of any other people on earth."

The majority of Awdaghost inhabitants were natives of North Africa; they belonged to "such tribes as Barqajana, Nafusa, Lawata, Zanata, and Nafzawa, but there are also a few people from other countries" (ibid.). But the Sudan women, referred to as good cooks, were bought as slaves, "one being sold for 100 mithqals or more" (ibid.). There were also "pretty slave girls" who were bought for the sexual enjoyment of their owners.

But Awdaghost inhabitants had an endemic health problem: "it is a country where the inhabitants have yellow complexions because they suffer from fever and splenitis. There is hardly one who does not complain of one or the other" (ibid.:68).

The Awdaghost king, Tin Yarutan b. Wisanu b. Nizar, was powerful, controlled an extensive territory, could muster an impressive mounted armed force, and extracted tribute from more than twenty kings of the Sudan. He was also a reliable ally, helping or backing those faced with difficulties. This description refers to the tenth century AD, precisely to the decades after 961-962, and appears to be an excerpt from Al-Warraq's lost *Kitab al-masalik wa-'l-mamalik* (Levtzion and Hopkins 1981:62). The events of the middle of the eleventh century took place during the active scholarly life of Al-Bakri. In the year 446/1054-5, 'Abd Allah b. Yasin with his Almoravid troops and followers invaded the town of Awdaghost, "a flourishing locality (*balad*), a large town (*madina*) containing markets, numerous palms, and henna trees resembling olive trees with their large size" (Al-Bakri, in Levtzion and Hopkins 1981:73). In the middle of the eleventh century AD, the political situation and demographic make-up appeared to have changed considerably. On the political side, Awdaghost is claimed to have been the residence of the "king of the Sudan who was called Ghana before the Arabs entered [the city of Ghana]" (ibid.), shifting from a previous Sanhaja kingship. On the demographic side, Awdaghost was "inhabited by Zanata together with Arabs who were always at loggerheads with each other." They were still very wealthy and "owned great riches and slaves so numerous that one person from among them might possess a thousand servants or more" (ibid.:74). The demographic make-up of the town's population was different; it consisted of the Zanata who supplanted the Sanhaja, North African Arabs, other Berbers, and thousands of slaves, very likely from Sub-Saharan Africa.

The Almoravid conquest of Awdaghost was particularly harsh and cruel. It included arbitrary and gratuitous murder: "'Abd Allah b. Yasin killed there a man called Zibaqara, a half-caste Arab from Qayrawan who was known for his piety and virtue, his diligence in reciting the Koran, and for having performed the Pilgrimage" (ibid.:74). People lost their property and belongings, as the Almoravids "declared everything that they took there to be the booty of the community. And violence and cruelty were exerted on women and the weak: The Almoravids violated its women . . ." (ibid.:74). For Al-Bakri, these harsh punishments were not the consequences of deep and serious religious and theological antagonism. "The Almoravids persecuted the people of Awdaghost only because they recognized the authority of the ruler of Ghana" (ibid.:74).

Awdaghost lost its autonomy and independence during the second half of the tenth century AD. The thriving economic metropolis was conquered by the emerging expansionist state of Ghana. The capital city of the dominant regional power was at Kumbi Saleh, a few hundred kilometers to the east of Awdaghost. The Almoravid expedition of the mid-eleventh century was a blow to the town's prosperity, wealth, and economy; major trade routes slowly shifted east toward the Niger River, leaving Awdaghost to sink into indifference and later oblivion.

Abu 'Abd Allah Muhammed al-sharif al-Idrisi (Al-Idrisi), probably a Moroccan, was a descendant of the Banu Hammud dynasty which ruled Malaga until 1055. He spent most of his life in Spain where he collected information from travelers on topics such as "trade patterns, as well as detailed descriptions of food, weapons, ornaments, dwellings, flora and fauna" (Levtzion and Hopkins 1981:105). His book, *Nuzhat al-Mushtag fi ikhtiraq al-afaq* ("The Pleasure of Him Who Longs to Cross the Horizons"), also called *Kitab Rujar* ("The Book of Roger"), was completed in January 1154. It is a geography book with maps and text written at the request of Roger II, the Norman king of Sicily (Levtzion and Hopkins 1981:104). Al-Idrisi mentions Awdaghost several times; he described the geographic position of Awdaghost in relation to the neighboring towns: "Likewise from the town of Barisa to Awdaghost is twelve stages. Awdaghost is north of Barisa" (Al-Idrisi, in Levtzion and Hopkins 1981:108). In his second reference to Awdaghost, Al-Idrisi alludes to "travellers going to Awdaghust, Ghana, and to other regions" (ibid:117-18).

The third allusion is the most substantial, asserting that Awdaghost is located in the northern part of the land of Ghana, and that it was no more an autonomous and independent polity.

It discusses the nature, topographic location, and general characteristics of the town: "This is a small town in the desert, with little water. The town itself is situated between two mountains, like Mecca. Its population is not numerous, and there is no large trade. The inhabitants own camels from which they derive their livelihood" (ibid.:118). All the qualifiers of Awdaghost in the second half of the twelfth century AD point to a downward spiral, a slow demise of its reputation, fame, and prestige. The town's size and population dwindled. The supply of water was uncertain. Economic activities were anemic. And the inhabitants relied almost exclusively on camel husbandry to make a living. In another passage, Al-Idrisi discusses the geographic location of Awdaghost in relation to other major towns. It is located at some 12 stages from Ghana, 31 stages from Warqalan, 25 stages from Jarma, and one month's travel from the salt mine of the island of Awlil. Finally, he refers to Awdaghost gastronomy. The information was obtained from a "trustworthy" itinerant merchant who knew the land of the Sudan: "truffles, each weighing three pounds or more, grow in the ground near the stagnant pools which adjoin the town of Awdaghust." These impressive truffles "are brought to Awdaghust and cooked with camel meat. They eat them and assert that there is nothing like these in the world, and they are right" (ibid:118).

Awdaghost also appears in the *Kitab al-Istibsar,* completed in 1191. Compiled by an unknown author who calls himself *al-nazir* ("The Reviser"), Al-Bakri's works provided the bulk of The Reviser's material on North Africa and the Sudan. The western Sudan section of the *Kitab al-Istibsar* is far from a literal quote from Al-Bakri; it is more of an interpretative adaptation with some new material (Levtzion and Hopkins 1981). It therefore refers to the eleventh century AD, when Awdaghost prestige and wealth were at their peak. For The Reviser (*Kitab al-Istibsar*, in Levtzion and Hopkins 1981:143), "the city of Awdaghust lies between the desert of the Lamtuna and the land of the Sudan." The city itself is big, densely populated and cosmopolitan, "with people of more nations than can be counted." It is rich in agricultural products, cucumbers, sorghum, wheat, and date palms, cultivated in gardens "irrigated" with buckets. People are wealthy; the market is noisy, dynamic, and very active, with transactions made exclusively with gold. In fact, the whole description of Awdaghost and its activities (Levtzion and Hopkins 1981:143-44) is an abbreviation of Al-Bakri's with an occasional word from The Reviser (Levtzion and Hopkins, notes 20-23, p. 394). The *Kitab al-Istibsar* does not report on the social, political, and economic situation of Awdaghost at the end of the twelfth century AD.

In summary, Al-Bakri and Al-Idrisi present two successive stages in the history of Awdaghost. The former had included the material from Al-Warraq, an earlier author. Most of his narrative deals with a town at the peak of its power and wealth, that shifted from an autonomous and independent entity to the status of a regional market town, part of the Ghana kingdom. Such a rich, dynamic and cosmopolitan town was the target of an Almoravid expedition in the middle of the eleventh century (AD 1054). The Almoravid conquest and ensuing occupation of Awdaghost were a serious blow to the "future" of the town, and probably triggered its downward spiral. This reversal in the fortune of the town and its inhabitants is echoed by Al-Idrisi when he completed the writing of his book in 1154, precisely one century after the Almoravid conquest.

Awdaghost in the Thirteenth- and Fourteenth-Century Historical Record

The references and allusions to Awdaghost are in general short notices in post-twelfth-century Arabic historical sources. They are found in the works of five authors: Yaqut, Ibn Said, Abu 'l-Fida, Al-Dimashqi, and Al-Umari.

Yaqut b. 'Abd Allah al-Hamawi al-Rumi was born in 1179 and died in Aleppo, Syria, in 1229. He was a Greek by origin, enslaved in Damascus. He wrote his geographical book *Mu'jam al-buldan* ("The Dictionary of Countries") from 1212 to 1229 in two main installments. The first draft was completed in 1224, but he kept working on the details in the following years up to his death in 1229 (Levtzion and Hopkins 1981). Yaqut's information on Awdaghost presents no originality or novelty. It does not refer to the political, social and economic situation of the Sub-Saharan metropolis at the beginning of the thirteenth century. He was a scrupulous scholar who cited the sources of his excerpts. He excerpted some material from Ibn Hawqal, Al-Bakri, and Al-Idrisi, with his most important source being the lost *Kitab al-'Aziz*, written in the tenth century by Al-Muhallabi. The topic he selected revolves around the location of Awdaghost within the network of Saharan and Sudan towns, and the description of the town and its inhabitants, as well as their economic activities and religious practices before and after their conversion to Islam (Yaqut, in Levtzion and Hopkins 1981:168-69).

Ali b. Musa Ibn Said belonged to a famous family of Andalusian scholars. He was born in 1214 at Granada and died at Tunis in 1286 or 1287. His work, *Kitab al-Jughrafiya*—"The Book of Geography"—divides the earth into seven climes, and each clime into sections. He relied heavily on Al-Bakri and Al-Idrisi for his information on the Sahara and the Sudan. His reference to Awdaghost asserts that it is the single town worthy of mention in the "second section of the second clime." Its inhabitants are a mixture of Berbers, with the rulership in the hand of the Sanhaja. This description points to the independent and autonomous ninth- or tenth-century Awdaghost, and provides no clue on the early thirteenth-century town.

The geographic work of Abu 'l-Fida (short for Al-Malik al-Mu'ayyad 'Imad al-Din Abu 'l-Fida Ismail b. al-Malik al-Afdal Nur al-Din), called *Taqwin al-buldan* ("The Survey of Lands"), was completed in 1321, but he kept working on this first draft until his death in 1331 at Hamah in Syria. He was born in 1273 at Damascus and belonged to the Ayyubid princely family. When writing of the Sudan, he relied heavily on Ibn Said. Though his work "does not add any original data on the Sudan, his text is important as an example of a scholarly treatment and interpretation of earlier sources" (Levtzion and Hopkins 1981:195). His reference to Awdaghost is written in a more or less tabular form, indicating its geographic coordinates:

AWDAGHUST *Atwal* 15°00', 6°00' *Qanum* [blank] 26°00'

followed by short excerpts from Ibn Said, the *Qanum*, and Al-Idrisi (Abu 'l-Fida, in Levtzion and Hopkins 1981:199).

Shama al-Din Abu 'Abd Allah Muhammad b. Abi Talib al-Ansari al-Dimashqi (Al-Dimashqi) lived all his life in Syria where he was born in 1256 and died in 1327. His book *Nukhbat al-dahr fi 'aja ib al-barr wa-'l-bahr*—"The Choice of the Age, on the Marvels of Land and Sea"—was published in the first quarter of the fourteenth century. According to Levtzion and Hopkins (1981:204), Al-Dimashqi used his sources uncritically, most of time without acknowledgment: "Corruption of names and his own interpretation of evidence from earlier sources ought to be watched carefully." His notes on Awdaghost have not raised any objection from Levtzion and Hopkins. At first glance, they appear to be the only genuine information on the post-twelfth-century Awdaghost that clearly refers to the situation of the town at the beginning of the fourteenth century. First, he describes Awdaghost as "a sandy town with palms," and "a very unhealthy place." That characterization points clearly to a metropolis in decline as was already indicated by Al-Idrisi in the mid-twelfth century. He goes on with a short sentence on the food habits that were articulated around two elements, sorghum (*dhura*) and meat. This assertion is particularly vague; one can but speculate on the kind(s) of meat Al-Dimashqi was referring to. The reference to the mine of excellent gold located in the neighborhood of Awdaghost is to be understood in the light of folk tales about gold in the Sudan that had spread all over the Dar al-Islam by the Medieval period. The information on the population and its ethnic composition as well as the sociopolitical situation is the most interesting part of Al-Dimashqi's Awdaghost notes. The Lamtuna, Tazzakkaght, Masufa, Kakdam and Juddala, all Berber, are the ethnic groups living at Awdaghost. He singled out the Masufa as the most handsome of the Berbers, and the Juddala as the most numerous. They all adopted the Almoravid way, "are [commonly referred to] as *al-mulaththamun* [the veiled] or *al-murabitun*, and all but the women veil the face" (Al-Dimashqi, in Levtzion and Hopkins 1981:209). It is not known if 'Abd al-Mu'min b. Ali was the actual ruler of Awdaghost in the beginning of the fourteenth century. All of the names of individuals and places, Yusuf b. Tashufin, Muhammad b. Tumart, and the foundation of Marrakech, refer to the second half of the eleventh century (Hrbek and Devisse 1990). After a closer examination, with the minor exception of the allusion to the widespread practices of Almoravid ways and manners, most of Al-Dimashqi's writings on Awdaghost consist of earlier but recycled material. Consequently, he does not provide any insight on the situation of the Saharan metropolis in the fourteenth century.

Ibn Fadl Allah al-Umari, born in Damscus, Syria, in 1301 is the last medieval Arab scholar to mention Awdaghost. He spent many years in Cairo and died in Damascus in 1349. His book, *Masalik al-Absar fi mamalik al-amsar* ("Pathways of Vision in the Realms of the Metropolises"), which is a sort of encyclopedia combining world geography and universal history, was never published entirely. Al-Umari simply made a casual reference to Awdaghost when describing the rivers of the western Maghrib. After a long description of the course of the Nile, he presented an unlikely river connecting the Mediterranean Sea along the Moroccan coast in the north to the town of Awdaghost deep in the Saharan desert in the south. "From here a side-channel branches off southwards to the town of Awdaghust. The main stream continues to Fez and empties itself into the Mediterranean" (Al-Umari, in Levtzion and Hopkins 1981:259).

In summary, after the middle of the twelfth century with the work of Al-Idrisi, Awdaghost seems to have vanished from the sights of Arab scholars. The authors of the thirteenth and fourteenth centuries, starting with al-nazir whose *Kitab al-Istibsar* was completed at the end of the twelfth century in 1191, integrated portions of previous works into their geography treatises. This absence from the mainstream of Arabic medieval scholarship may suggest a loss of momentum in the evolution of Awdaghost. The town was not totally abandoned but it became an ordinary and small caravan station in a oasis of palms and wells.

The Search for Awdaghost during the Colonial Period

The search for all major towns from the Medieval period in West Africa was launched at the very beginning of the twentieth century. It was carried out following two distinct but complementary strategies: One, implemented principally by the Gouverneur Général M. Delafosse, consisted of a thorough exegesis of the Early Arabic historical material and oral traditions. The other, which developed after 1920, involved exploration forays, field investigations and site surveys.

Maurice Delafosse, the Governeur Général of French West Africa at the beginning of the twentieth century, rekindled the scholarly interest on West African medieval towns, with a special emphasis on Awdaghost (Delafosse 1912, 1924; Mauny 1950, 1960). Delafosse graduated from the École des Langues Orientales and had a profound interest in the study of the Oriental world and its cultural impact on Sub-Saharan Africa. He was clearly a proponent of diffusionist theories and held the view that all major cultural achievements to be documented in the African past were more or less the result of influence of higher oriental civilizations. In his two-volume *Haut—Sénégal—Niger* published at the very beginning of the century in 1912, he deals with what Mauny (1950) later termed the "Question of Awdaghost" (Delafosse 1912: [vol. 1] 187, [vol. 2] 13). Without having ever visited the area, he suggested looking for Awdaghost in the Rkiz massif, in the Circus of Noudache in south-central Mauritania. The site was finally documented here, at 17°25' N and 10°27' W.

Four other authors, P. Amilhat (1937), Lieutenant Boery (1923), P. Laforgue (1940, 1943), and J. Vidal (1923), offered two versions of the succession of exploratory forays conducted in southwestern Mauritania. Vidal (1923) and Laforgue (1940, 1943) later thought they found the medieval town of Awdaghost in the Rkiz. They discovered impressive ruins of a relatively extensive stone town. It was not Awdaghost, however, but Togba, a more recently abandoned town located some kilometers southwest of Awdaghost (Mauny 1950:108). It was Lieutenant Boery (1923) who found the precise location of the medieval Awdaghost. He was sent on duty in the Hodh, and had detailed knowledge of the area and good contacts with informants. He relied heavily on oral sources and local informants to write his *Le Rkiss (Mauritanie): Essai de Monographie Locale* published in 1923, a work containing the precise location and an extensive description of the ruins of Awdaghost. The area was in fact inhabited by the Tegdaoust, a Moorish tribe that migrated south and settled on a portion of the medieval ruins in the seventeenth century. His access to local oral sources allowed him to equate Awdaghost with Tegdaoust. A later article by Amilhat (1937) relied on Lt. Boery's work but added the descriptions of many other smaller villages in the east of the Tagant, a region of the southwestern Mauritanian Sahara.

With the appointment of Raymond Mauny as director of the archaeological section of the Institut Français d'Afrique Noire (IFAN), archaeological research entered the scene. Mauny visited the ruins of Awdaghost and Togba in January of 1949 and was immediately convinced of the imperative need for an important archaeological project (Mauny 1950, 1961:71). His statement is well argued and worth quoting extensively:

> It would be of the highest interest for the history of the Medieval Period in west Africa to conduct archaeological excavation at Tegdaoust to enhance a comparison with the building style and the material record unearthed from Kumbi Saleh. Let's hope that, within the multiplicity of tasks to be dealt with in order to reconstruct the history of our immense French West Africa (A.O.F), this one can be carried out rapidly. The Ancient Awdaghost rightly deserves it. [Mauny 1950b:109]

However, despite his urgent call for an archaeological project, Mauny still appeared to have some doubts about the identification of Awdaghost. In a letter to Theodore Monod, the director of the IFAN, dated January 18, 1961, he wrote: "I think the identification of Awdaghost-Tegdaoust is plausible. To what experts in Berber studies [*berberisant*] refer to to know if the first (Awdaghost) could have generated the second (Tegdaoust] toponym." A query to which Monod replied in a handwritten note at the bottom of the page, suggesting the name of a "district commissioner" (Commandant de Cercle) Mohammed O. Daddah, the cousin of the President, whom he met at Aïoun: "a remarkable man, well read and erudite, with whom we had very interesting conversations" (IFAN Archives, File XV-5-MAU). In fact, one of the goals of the archaeological research program was to strengthen the identification of Awdaghost.

Conclusion

The Arabic sources portray some of the key steps in the development of the town of Awdaghost. The quality of the reporting varies depending on the location of the writers and their informants. In fact, the material contained in early works acquired its own peculiar "life" in the cascade of borrowings and nonattributed quotes that followed. Despite these limitations, the historical sources provide precious data that can put the archaeological record into a richer and more challenging cultural, social, political, and economic context.

—9—

Patterns of Space Allocation

Introduction

As discussed in this book, the settlement history documented from the excavation of Awdaghost Acropolis can be divided into four periods, each characterized by a dynamic trajectory. The Pioneer period lasted from the beginning of the settlement in the eastern part of Awdaghost that may have started in the sixth or seventh century AD to 900. It was followed by the Accelerated Growth period that lasted from approximately 900 to 1000. That was the peak of wealth and prosperity in the town history that led to the Unsteady Post-Climax period, from 1000 to 1200. This period is characterized by significant fluctuations in the town's fortunes. It ended with the collapse of the Ghana Kingdom and the rise to primacy of Mali. A period of decline and finally demise marks the end of Awdaghost Acropolis history. During the decline there was a radical shift in the use of the Acropolis space, leading to complete abandonment of the area at the beginning of the sixteenth century AD.

A note of caution should be introduced here. The Acropolis was part of much larger settlement system. Earlier occupations can still be documented in nonexcavated parts of the town, and a later seventeenth-century city located to the west is beyond the scope of this book. This having been said, it is still valuable to examine how the built space was allocated to activities throughout the Acropolis settlement history: how these patterns of space allocation changed through time; why did or didn't they change; and why these different pathways were followed. These are some of the issues that will considered in this chapter.

Structure of Public Space

What is referred to as "public space" in this context took shape through time following the evolution of habitation complexes. Public space consists essentially of that part of the urban space that can be used by anyone without restriction. It is part of the public arena, made up of the street network, open plazas, and worship facilities. Worship facilities include mosques and open-air prayer facilities. None of these features were recorded in the archaeological record from the Acropolis, where public space consists exclusively of narrow streets and open places.

The street system that started to take shape during the Pioneer period is difficult to delineate with accuracy. No street can be identified from the BS-1 occupation. There are two clearly identifiable and intersecting streets in BS-2 urban layout. The longest street found along the south wall of HC-IV runs east-west. It measures 27 m in length and 2 m in exposed width. It intersects in the southwest with a 20 m long and 2-3 m wide north-south street, set along the complex's west wall, leading to a central open plaza north of HC-IV and southeast of HC-V. During BS-3, the north-south street is extended 10 m northward intersecting with a new east-west street, measuring 20 m in length and 2 m in width. The open plaza is significantly smaller and confined to the northeast of HC-IV extending eastward. At the end of the Pioneer period, the street system in the BS-4 urban layout consisted of four axes surrounding HC-IV and was composed of an east-west street in the south, a north-south street in the west, an east-west street servicing HC-V, and a long curved north-south street in the east. The open plaza was then confined to the east of the excavated probe.

The Acropolis street network was completely set during the Accelerated Growth period. It comprised five intersecting axes articulated on the main east-west central street that ran all across the tested probe, along the north walls of HC-III and HC-IV, and the south wall of HC-V. It measured 70 m in length with width varying from 2 to 3 m. Two streets ran south along the HC-IV west and east walls, intersecting with an east-west street in the south. The eastern street branched in a small plaza in the southeast. And finally, one street ran north along the HC-V east wall.

The attrition of the architectural landscape that started slowly during the Unsteady Post-Climax period did not impact the street network very significantly. The open plaza that was "privatized" and built on from BS-4 to BS-6 was restored to the public in the northeast of HC-IV during BS-7. The structure of the public space remained unchanged from BS-7 to BS-9 during the entire Unsteady Post-Climax period.

The street system lost its utility during the Decline and Demise period with HC-IV transformed into a large open camping space. Some portions of streets were likely still maintained along the HC-III west wall and HC-V south and east walls. In general, the lack of maintenance, the collapse of walls, and finally, the leveling of collapsed features through shifting uses of space made the streets a less and less necessary component of the dwindling urban life.

Structure of Habitation Complexes

The habitation complex, a key concept in this book, is an architectural element of the built urban landscape delimited by streets and open places, and composed of contiguous household units. How did these structures ("structure" used in its most simple meaning, that of "constitutive element") change through time?

During the Pioneer period, the excavated area lacked solidly built features. The area, exposed on 2,936 m^2 (Table 21), was very likely settled by groups of pastoral-nomadic herders using tents or other light camping gear. The built space increased from 1,085 m^2 to

Table 21: The main parameters of the built space

Building Sequence	No. of Habitation Complexes	No. of Household Units	No. of Rooms	No. of Courtyards	Total Size (m²)
Pioneer (?AD 600 – 900)					
1	—	—	2	—	2,936
2	2	5	28	4	1,085.28
3	2	7	42	6	1,282.16
4	2	8	46	7	1,422.46
Accelerated Growth (AD 900 – 1000)					
5	3	11	81	11	1,870.72
6	3	10	72	11	1,958.60
Unsteady Post-Climax (AD 1000 – 1200)					
7	3	9	54	8	1,841.19
8	3	10	55	9	1,854.83
9	3	10	53	9	1,873.59
Decline and Demise (AD 1200 – 1500)					
10	2	4	18	4	1,095.78
11	2	4	14	4	773.78
12	2	2	3	?	40.88
13	2	1	3	?	44.88
14	1	1	3	?	56.08
15	1	2	3	?	26.88

1,422 m² from BS-1 to BS-4. Two habitation complexes were delineated and built during this period with the total number of household units increasing from 5 to 8, the frequency of such units per habitation complex shifting from 2-3 (BS-2) to 2-6 (BS-4). The number of rooms and courtyards followed a comparable trajectory. The distribution of rooms increased from 28 (BS-2) to 46 (BS-4), and courtyards from 4 to 7. All the architectural elements of the documented habitation complexes point to a sustained and steady growth. It is as if a new system of property allocation was being devised to satisfy a growing demand. Habitation Complexes IV and V attest to the existence of at least two standards during the Pioneer period. In HC-IV, household units of comparable size are architecturally elaborate and compact. In HC-V, they consist of diagonally opposed two-room units with an intervening extensive courtyard. HC-IV was very likely inhabited by merchants, traders, scholars, or town employees, while HC-V belonged to a group of craft specialists, working copper and iron and making local pottery.

During the Accelerated Growth period (AD 900-1000) that followed, the built space increased to 1,870.72 m² (BS-5) and 1,958.60 m² (BS-6). There was a significant influx of accessions to property in the Acropolis. The exposed probe was filled with constructions all built with stone and divided into three habitation complexes. Each has a unique layout and virtually each household unit has its well. The number of household units increased sharply from 8 (BS-4) to 11. A similar path was followed by the frequency distribution of courtyards, 11 for each building sequence of the period. The number of rooms on the other hand fluctuated from 81 (BS-5) to 72 (BS-6). There was a visible shift in the sociological profile of the Acropolis inhabitants. An increase in the average size of household units, as well as general wealth, resulted in a homogenization of the population. HC-V, previously owned by craftpeople, was very likely purchased by a wealthy incoming family, who built a unique, sophisticated and elaborate palacelike household unit. The adjustment of rooms, corridors and courtyards tends to indicate an adherence to strict Islamic standards:

> domestic space is referred to in the *Quran* and the *Hadith,* where the sacrality of the house is indicated, and strict rules to maintain domestic privacy are outlined. The primary and overriding concern is with privacy and the protection and seclusion of women, . . . and the sanctity of the family. . . . The private area is for family life, including the harem or women's quarters, which is the arena for domestic activities and from which all men except immediate male relatives (husbands, sons, brothers) are usually excluded. The second area forms a male communal sphere. [Insoll 2003:19]

At the end of the Accelerated Growth period, the architectural standards started to loosen in the southern half of HC-IV. The construction density had reached its peak and started to decrease, a trend amplified with minor fluctuations during the ensuing Unsteady Post-Climax period (AD 1000-1200).

The area of built space decreased after the Accelerated Growth period, then increased slightly from 1,841.19 m^2 (BS-7), to 1,854.83 m^2 (BS-8), and finally, 1.873.59 m^2 (BS-9). In fact, the range of variation is minimal. Rooms vary from 54 (BS-7) to 55 (BS-8) to 53 (BS-9), and courtyards, from 8 during BS-7 to 9 during BS-8 and BS-9.

In general, the Unsteady Post-Climax period is characterized by two parallel trends: a trend toward the simplification of architectural "blueprints" that started during BS-6; and a trend toward the creation of large enclosed spaces for the management of livestock, particularly dromedary caravans.

The first trend is manifest in the northern half of HC-IV where BS-7 to BS-9 household units are less crowded with rooms and partition walls. HC-III and HC-V remained relatively stable with nonetheless some architectural simplification starting in BS-9 HC-V. The second trend, the creation of large enclosed unimpeded spaces, is documented in one of the household units from HC-III, and in all the southern half of HC-IV, for the whole period.

The last period, Decline and Demise, presents three successive shifts in the structuration of the used space. The first shift, documented in BS-10 and BS-11 feature layout, is marked by the opening of a relatively large camping ground in the central and southern part of the Acropolis. Household units were confined to both east and west ends of the excavated probe—HC-III and HC-V—with some significant remodeling. Large open but enclosed spaces were created in both habitation complexes, with the number of rooms reduced drastically. The second shift, recorded in BS-12 and BS-13 occupations, resulted in the construction of a "caravansérail," a combination of housing facilities with a large central livestock-corralling space. And finally, the third and final shift in BS-14 and BS-15 deposits marks a move back to ordinary habitation, but this time with smaller constructions probably inhabited by modest nuclear families. This third shift closed the settlement history of Awdaghost Acropolis.

Interestingly enough, the population that settled on the Acropolis and decided to build houses there was diverse and sociologically heterogeneous all through the Pioneer period. A "gentrification" movement characterized the onset of the Accelerated Growth period. Wealth and access to imported goods homogenized the population and decreased the diversity of the inhabitants of the Acropolis. These social, economic, and political profiles of the Acropolis population persisted for approximately two centuries, from AD 1000 to 1200, up to the collapse of the Ghana Kingdom. Wealthy merchants or caravan operators seem to have taken over during BS-10 and remodeled the Acropolis space according to their economic needs. Habitation space is combined with the livestock space, with livestock space taking more and more precedence. This dynamic is amplified during BS-12 and BS-13, with the construction of installations devoted exclusively to the management caravans and their crews. And at the end, when caravan roads were diverted from Awdaghost, the Acropolis was sparsely populated and inhabited by less wealthy, small (nuclear) family groups living in small one- or two-room houses.

Structure of Household Units

The number of independent housing units per habitation complex varies from 2 to 6 during the major part of the Acropolis settlement history. The built space delineated by each household unit can be partitioned into two principal components: rooms and courtyards. What constitutes a "room" is somewhat ambiguous as the catagory includes corridors and hallways, but courtyards are straightforward and obvious. Shifts in space allocation of rooms and courtyards, as well as their locations in the house "blueprint," are good indicators of changes occurring in the composition of the household and its internal organization.

During the Pioneer period (excluding BS-1 occupation), the built space shifted in size from 1,085.28 m² during BS-2 to 1,422.46 m² during BS-4. Courtyards were allocated the biggest share of the domestic space with their sizes ranging from 810 m² (BS-2) to 944.16 m² (BS-4); 74.63% to 66.37% of the household space was therefore devoted to courtyards and their implied activities (Table 22). The room component, which shifted from 275 m² (BS-2) to 478 m² (BS-4), represented 25.33% to 33.62% of the household space. The rough figures presented above indicate an interesting trend in the space allocation pattern: the decreasing share of the courtyard space was compensated by an increase in the proportion of room space.

Habitation Complex V was a special case with direct access to the large courtyard that was used for most of the craft production. In HC-IV, however, the courtyard was generally the core of the household's private domain, strongly secluded and located away from the building's main entrance. With one exception, HC-IV/HU-B which had direct access from the street to the courtyard, a number of hallways, rooms, and corridors had to be walked through to reach the family inner sanctum. Small rooms were largely predominant during the Pioneer period, with almost all of them belonging to classes 1 to 4 (see Table 22). There were nonetheless a handful of large (class 5 and 6) to very large (class 7 and 8) rooms built progressively through time.

With the onset of the Accelerated Growth period, the size of the built space increased to 1,870.72 m² (BS-5) and 1,958 m² (BS-6). The space allocated to courtyard ranged from 794.46 m² (BS-5) to 874.78 m² (BS-6), 42.46% to 52.77% of the available household domain. The space devoted to rooms emerged as predominant in the space allocation system. The proportion of the rooms' share varied from 57.53% (BS-5) to 47.22% (BS-6) (Table 22).

Table 22: Structures of the built space

Building Sequence	No. of Units	Courtyard (m²)	%	Rooms (m²)	%	Room Classes*							
						1	2	3	4	5	6	7	8
Pioneer (?AD 600 – 900)													
BS-1	–	–	–	–	–	–	–	–	–	–	–	–	–
BS-2	5	810	74.63	275	25.33	8	6	7	4	–	–	–	–
BS-3	7	879.16	68.00	433.04	33.00	10	9	14	6	1	1	1	–
BS-4	8	944.16	66.37	478.30	33.62	10	9	14	6	–	2	–	1
Accelerated Growth (AD 900 – 1000)													
BS-5	11	794.46	42.46	1,076.26	57.53	18	18	19	12	2	5	2	1
BS-6	10	874.78	52.77	782.63	47.22	11	20	15	9	6	4	2	2
Unsteady Post-Climax (AD 1000 –1200)													
BS-7	9	787.20	44.03	1000.30	55.96	9	13	11	7	5	3	3	2
BS-8	10	991.20	54.10	840.95	45.89	10	11	12	7	4	3	5	2
BS-9	10	984.21	53.71	847.94	46.28	10	11	11	7	4	3	5	2
Decline and Demise (AD 1200 – 1500)													
BS-10	4	853.08	79.19	224.08	20.80	6	1	3	3	2	1	1	–
BS-11	4	513.08	67.94	242.08	32.05	4	1	4	3	2	1	–	–
BS-12	2	–	–	40.88	??	1	–	1	–	1	–	–	–
BS-13	1	–	–	44.88	??	1	–	1	–	–	1	–	–
BS-14	1	30	49	31.20	51	1	–	–	–	1	1	–	–
BS-15	2	32	53.33	28	41.66	1	1	–	1	–	–	–	–

* class 1: < 5 m²; class 2: >5-10 m²; class 3: >10-15 m²; class 4: >15-20 m²; class 5: >20-25 m²; class 6: >25-30 m²; class 7: >30-35 m²; class 8: >35-40 m².

The normative pattern of Muslim architecture (Insoll 2003:17-19) with its strong emphasis on family privacy seems to have been strictly implemented here. None of the courtyards were immediately accessible from the street. Small rooms, from classes 1 to 4, were still numerous and represented the majority of cases. Large (class 5 and 6) and very large (class 7 and 8) rooms were however represented in higher frequency throughout the Accelerated Growth period.

The shift to the Unsteady Post-Climax period amplified most of the characteristics put in place during the previous period. Large to very large rooms were a normative part of any household unit, with frequency varying from 2 to 5. Small rooms were nonetheless still largely predominant. The size of the built space, ranging from 1,841.19 m^2 (BS-7) to 1,873.59 m^2 (BS-9), was stable for the whole period. There was an important shift in the ratio of courtyard to rooms. The BS-7 layout amplified the trend put in motion during the previous Accelerated Growth period; the share of the household space allocated to rooms was 1000.3 m^2, 55.96% of the household unit space, with only 44.03% (787.20 m^2) left to courtyards. During BS-8 and BS-9, there was a shift back to the predominance of courtyards, with a more balanced distribution. Courtyards occupied 54.10% (BS-8) to 53.71% (BS-9) of built space, and rooms from 45.89% to 46.28%.

Finally, during most of the Decline and Demise period, the use of enclosed space shifted toward the creation of large open spaces, much of which was used for corraling livestock, making the courtyard/room dichotomy less useful. At the end of the Acropolis settlement history, there was another shift toward small one room/courtyard household units. With the courtyard left open to the outside, the concern about family privacy was cleared from the actual inhabitants' social landscape.

The long-term patterns that emerge from the analysis of the space allocation system are particularly interesting and unsuspected. During the Pioneer period and excluding BS-1, approximately one-third of the household built space was allocated to rooms. The remaining two-thirds was devoted to courtyards, with significant variation between HC-IV and HC-V.

The pattern of space allocation shifted during the Accelerated Growth and early part of the Unsteady Post-Climax periods. The largest share of the domestic space was devoted to rooms, which occupied more than half to almost two-thirds of the surface. Courtyards were smaller on average and were situated in the inner sanctum of the household units. A virtually identical structure of the domestic space is evident in all the excavated household units. It was characterized by a higher number of rooms surrounding secluded courtyards located on the opposite side of the main entrance and reached through a maze of hallways and corridors.

Such a development could have resulted from two distinct processes. One of the processes may have involved an increased specialization in the purpose of rooms. Series of rooms may have been assigned to specific and precise activities: reception of guests, meals; hot-drink parties; cooking; storage; guard, servant, or slave quarters; living; and sleeping. In this scenario the multiplication of rooms is related to a comfort standard. Alternatively, the increase in rooms may have involved demography. Larger and wealthier households build larger habitations with more rooms. Arabic sources (Levtzion and Hopkins 1981) unfortunately give us few, and vague, glimpses of the composition and size of a typical wealthy

Awdaghost merchant household. In this Afro-Muslim context, there were three main options for the emergence of large family units: (1) the polygamous option with several wives and many children; (2) the extended family option, with the grown-up and married children, with their children, staying in the same household unit; and (3) the polygamous and extended family option, combining 1 and 2.

During most of the Unsteady Post-Climax period, there was a sort of balanced allocation of space to both rooms and courtyards. The courtyard component was generally larger but the difference amounted to less than 10% (see Table 22). The system shifted away from equilibrium during the early part (1200-1300) of the Decline and Demise period. The proportion of room space that still existed in HC-III and HC-V declined to somewhere between one-third and one-fifth. The move toward the creation of the caravansérail took place during BS-12 and BS-13 in the middle (1300-1400) of the Decline and Demise period. There was a handful of rooms left but they were very likely part of a public facility.

The end of the period (ca. 1400-1500) witnessed another shift toward smaller dwelling units with a balanced distribution of space allocated to rooms and courtyards. The architecture is different as is the case for the structure of domestic space. The small houses from BS-14 and BS-15 were inhabited by small, very likely modest, nuclear family units.

Variations in Household Unit Size

The number of household units increased slowly from 5 to 8 during the Pioneer period and sharply during the Accelerated Growth period when it rose to 11 and 10. It fluctuated from 9 to 10 during the Unsteady Post-Climax period and dropped sharply to 4 and finally 2 during the Decline and Demise period. The mean size of household units varies considerably from one habitation complex to another. It is the long-term trend in the size of the built household units that is taken into consideration in this part of the discussion.

In general, the mean size of household units shifted from 271.32 m^2 during BS-2 to 13.44 m^2 during BS-15 (Table 23) with significant fluctuations in between. During the Pioneer period, the mean size dropped from 271.32 m^2 (BS-2) to 203.20 m^2 (BS-4). There appeared to be a trend toward the reduction in size of the household units as indicated by the recorded minimum which varied from 129.02 to 97.76 m^2. The coefficients of variation (0.80 to 0.85) suggest the variations in house size were random.

The situation changed during the Accelerated Growth period. The mean household unit size dropped sharply to 170.01 m^2 from the 203.20 m^2 in the previous BS-4, and rose to 178.86 m^2 during BS-6. Interestingly, the coefficients of variation ranged from 0.39 (BS-5) to 0.66 (BS-6), suggesting the development of house standards, at least in size. Concomitantly however, such a development may be linked to the "scramble" for urban space that may have peaked with very high demand. The system of space allocation that would have developed from such a situation would result not only in homogenization but also in the reduction in size of plots attributed or sold to applicants.

The situation remained unchanged during the Unsteady Post-Climax period, despite important fluctuations in household unit mean size, which varied from 198.61 m^2 during BS-7 to 184.83 m^2 (BS-8 and BS-9). The maximum size fluctuated from 496.39 m^2 (BS-7)

Table 23: Variation in household unit size

Building Sequence	No. of Household Units	Min.	Max.	Mean	Range	Standard Deviation	Coefficient of Variation
Pioneer (?AD 600 – 900)							
BS-1	—	—	—	—	—	—	—
BS-2	5	129.02	646.34	271.32	517.32	217.28	0.80
BS-3	7	110.06	627	218.70	516.94	184.21	0.84
BS-4	8	97.76	627	203.20	529.24	174.55	0.85
Accelerated Growth (AD 900 – 1000)							
BS-5	11	102.24	319.81	170.01	227.69	67.86	0.39
BS-6	10	93.54	500.87	178.86	407.33	118.91	0.66
Unsteady Post-Climax (AD 1000 – 1200)							
BS-7	9	115.16	496.39	198.61	397.43	116.67	0.58
BS-8	10	115.16	361.35	184.83	246.19	70.12	0.37
BS-9	10	115.16	361.35	184.83	246.19	70.12	0.37
Decline and Demise (AD 1200 – 1500)							
BS-10	4	2.88	572	269.29	569.12	265.76	0.98
BS-11	4	2.88	407.08	188.79	404.20	177.68	0.94
BS-12	2	2.88	38.00	20.44	35.12	17.56	0.85
BS-13	1	2.88	42.00	22.44	39.12	19.56	0.87
BS-14	1	2.88	53.2	28.04	50.32	25.16	0.89
BS-15	2	2.88	24	13.44	21.12	10.56	0.78

to 361.35 m² (BS-8 and BS-9). The coefficients of variation ranged from 0.58 (BS-7) to 0.37 (BS-8 and BS-9), suggesting the existence of a tightly enforced house-size standard during this period.

With the onset of the Decline and Demise period, the construction arrangements of the previous period started to disintegrate with the available space devoted to activities other than habitation. The concept of household unit mean size is far less meaningful during this period. Coefficients of variation ranging from 0.78 (BS-15) to 0.98 (BS-10) tend to indicate an absence of overarching standards.

The coefficients of variation suggest the long-term change in household unit size came in three waves, or modes. Mode 1, developed at the beginning of the settlement on Awdaghost Acropolis, was characteristically an emergent one with random variations leading to a sustained reduction in the average size of the household units. Mode 2 took shape during Accelerated Growth, and was in operation until the very end of the Unsteady Post-Climax period. A certain house-size standard was devised and implemented during the climax of the town's history. And finally, mode 3, triggered by the unraveling of the Acropolis urban layout and a shift toward livestock space, was characterized by an absence of detectable standards.

Variations in Courtyard Size

During the Pioneer period, the arrangement of courtyards followed two distinct models. One, found in HC-V, consists of an extensive courtyard space with habitation facilities situated at the opposite end of a northwest-southeast diagonal axis. The other, documented in HC-IV, consists of a smaller but secluded courtyard. The descriptive statistics of the Pioneer period, shown in Table 24, are but illustrative; the means, varying from 202.60 m^2 (BS-2) to 134.88 m^2 (BS-4), describe a trend toward decreasing size in courtyards but are hardly more informative, as strongly suggested by the coefficients of variation (1.12 to 1.40). In fact, during the Pioneer period, each of the habitation complexes had its own spatial layout that probably depended on the socioeconomic status of its inhabitants. Craftpeople had an extensive courtyard subdivided into distinct workshop areas with intermingled domestic activity areas. The socioeconomic group comprising merchants, scholars and civil servants was, in general, wealthier. Their residences included secluded courtyards, the core of domestic life which was off limits for all strangers, and which ranged in size from 75.90 to 62.32 m^2 (BS-2), and 70 to 34.72 m^2 (BS-3 and BS-4).

The situation changed radically during the Accelerated Growth and Unsteady Post-Climax periods. All household units included at least one courtyard, generally secluded and located away from the main entrance, reached through a maze of hallways, corridors and alleys. During the Accelerated Growth period, the courtyard mean size varied from 72.22 m^2 (BS-5) to 87.47 m^2 (BS-6). The standard deviations and coefficients of variation (see Table 24) indicate a slight shift toward homogenization. In fact, 9 out of a total of 11 courtyards extended over less than 75 m^2, with two measuring more than 100 m^2 (see Chapter 5).

The trend outlined above continues through the Unsteady Post-Climax period that followed. The courtyard mean size rose to 99.12 m^2 (BS-8 and BS-9). The standard deviations (57.87-53.86) and coefficients of variation (0.58-0.54) tend to indicate relatively narrow margins of variation.

There are new developments at the end of the Acropolis settlement history during the Decline and Demise period. With the shift toward the creation of extensive but walled spaces for livestock management, courtyards ceased to exist, and became, strictly speaking, an unimportant element of the urban Acropolis landscape.

Variations in Room Distribution

The pattern of room distribution within household units is a good indicator of the Acropolis settlement history (Table 25). During the Pioneer period, the total number of rooms per building sequence grew from 28 (BS-2) to 46 (BS-4), indicating a more or less constant growth rate if the number of rooms is factored with the number of household units. The mean number of rooms per household unit fluctuated only from 6.75 (BS-2) to 6.83 (BS-3), to 6.57 (BS-4). Rooms per household unit varied from small household units of 2 or 3 rooms to an upper limit of 9 (BS-2) to 11 (BS-3 and BS-4).

In architectural terms, the household units were generally much more elaborate during the Accelerated Growth period, with the total number of rooms peaking at 81 (BS-5) and 72 (BS-6). The mean number of rooms per household unit witnessed sharp fluctuations. First, there was a sharp increase from 6.57 during BS-4 at the end of the Pioneer period to 7.36 during BS-5. This is followed by a sharp fall to 5.44 during BS-6 at the end of the period. The number of rooms varied from 1 to 4 at the low end of the spectrum and from 11 to 13

Table 24: Variation in courtyard size

Building Sequence	n	Min.	Max.	Mean	Range	Standard Deviation	Coefficient of Variation
Pioneer (?AD 600 – 900)							
BS-1	—	—	—	—	—	—	—
BS-2	4	62.32	598	202.60	535.68	228.34	1.12
BS-3	6	34.72	598	146.52	563.28	202.27	1.38
BS-4	7	34.72	598	134.88	563.28	189.42	1.40
Accelerated Growth (AD 900 – 1000)							
BS-5	11	34.72	167.24	72.22	132.52	35.09	0.48
BS-6	10	38.40	160.60	87.47	122.20	53.16	0.60
Unsteady Post-Climax (AD 1000 – 1200)							
BS-7	8	38.40	160.60	98.40	122.20	57.87	0.58
BS-8	10	38.40	160.60	99.12	122.20	53.86	0.54
BS-9	10	38.40	160.60	99.12	122.20	53.86	0.54
Decline and Demise (AD 1200 – 1500)							
BS-10	3	60.00	510	284.36	450	225	0.79
BS-11	3	60.00	283.08	181.02	223.08	112.74	0.62
BS-12 – 15	2	—	—	—	—	—	—

Table 25: Patterns of room distribution

Building Sequence	n	Min.	Max.	Mean	Range	Standard Deviation	Coefficient of Variation	No. of Household Units
Pioneer (?AD 600 – 900)								
BS-1	—	—	—	—	—	—	—	—
BS-2	28	2	9	6.75	6	2.27	0.33	5
BS-3	42	2	11	6.83	9	2.79	0.40	7
BS-4	46	2	11	6.57	9	2.92	0.44	8
Accelerated Growth (AD 900 – 1000)								
BS-5	81	5	12	7.36	9	2.53	0.34	11
BS-6	72	1	8	5.44	8	2.79	0.51	10
Unsteady Post-Climax (AD 1000 – 1200)								
BS-7	54	1	21	4.85	18	3.56	0.73	9
BS-8	55	1	12	5.88	11	3.87	0.65	10
BS-9	53	1	12	5.88	11	3.87	0.65	10
Decline and Demise (AD 1200 – 1500)								
BS-10	18	1	8	4.50	7	2.69	0.59	4
BS-11	14	1	8	3.75	7	2.58	0.68	4
BS-12 – 15	3	1	2	1.50	1	0.50	0.33	2

at the upper end. The standard deviations and coefficients of variation confirm the relatively narrow range in the frequency distribution of rooms per household unit.

The situation was totally different during the Unsteady Post-Climax period despite the stability in the total number of rooms (53-55). The distribution gap between household units is the largest, with ranges of 11 to 18 recorded in BS-7, BS-8, and BS-9 constructions. The mean number of rooms per household unit dropped to 4.85 in BS-7 from 5.44 in the previous BS-6, to rise to 5.88 during the rest of the period, during BS-8 and BS-9. The standard deviations and coefficients of variation are the highest of the whole sample, suggesting the absence of any overarching standard. Some of the units were completely devoted to livestock management; others were partially remodeled to include a larger livestock space; and others were still densely inhabited.

Finally, the trend triggered during the Unsteady Post-Climax period continued unabated during BS-10 and BS-11, at the very beginning of the Decline and Demise period. There were only four household units left, with the frequency of rooms varying from 1 to 8, and much smaller mean numbers of 4.50 (BS-10) and 3.75 (BS-11). The later part of the Decline and Demise period, from BS-12 to the end in BS-15, presented a completely different "urban" layout, with a probable caranvansérail during BS-13, and smaller single-room-with-courtyard houses during BS-14 and BS-15.

In summary, the Awdaghost Acropolis settlement went through a long one thousand years of architectural and demographic transformations. The earliest settlers were very likely part of pastoral-nomadic groups who used the area as a seasonal camping ground. Their dwelling features that consisted of movable elements may have included wood, straw, and/or tents made of animal hides. The postholes, pits, and hearths from the pre-urban BS-1 occupation are the clearest indication of this early settlement. Unfortunately, these early pastoral-nomadic deposits were not investigated as carefully as the later urban deposits. It is not known when the area was settled for the first time, and how they shifted to urban life, if they did. A number of interesting issues can be raised at this juncture. Did the first pastoral-nomadic people from the Noudache circus shift to an urban life style? Was the town created and built by a new group of foreigners? Were both sets of settlers distinct or were they complementary parts of the same sociocultural system? Did an originally native cultural group absorb foreign influences and later welcome a wealthy merchant diaspora flocking in from the Arabo-Muslim world? These different issues were touched on periodically throughout this book. Scenarios for the ultimate origins of the earliest settlers from Awdaghost has been suggested in several places (Holl 1985; McDonald 1996; Munson 1980). The agro-pastoral societies of the Dhar Tichitt and surrounding areas collapsed at the end of the first millennium BC, partly because of an enduring arid spell. Settlement systems were disrupted, and the area completely abandoned by the end of the first millennium BC. Using patterns of pottery decoration from a handful of sherds, McDonald (1996) claims to trace the connection between the Dhar Tichitt Tradition and the early settlements of the Inland Niger Delta. The "scramble" for wetter regions that may have characterized the redistribution of human population after the disintegration of the Dhar Tichitt-Walata settlement systems may have resulted in a wide dispersal of previously linked groups. The early settlers of Awdaghost may have been the descendants of the Late Stone Age agro-pastoral "Tichittians," turned pastoral nomads (Holl 1985). They were later the core element in the emergence of the Ghana Kingdom (Holl 1985; Munson 1980).

The shift from an intermittent seasonal camping ground to a permanent urban center took place during the Pioneer period. Mud-brick was the predominant building material during the early stages of urban life. It was progressively replaced and supplanted by stone.

The climax of the town's economic, social, and political life appears to have occurred in the tenth and eleventh centuries AD. Wealthy and probably large households took control of the Acropolis and built their homes following a cultural script that can be linked to the central Muslim concern for privacy. The Acropolis inhabitants were very likely linked to the "international" merchant diaspora. From AD 1200 onwards, with the collapse of Ghana, the rise to regional primacy of Mali, and the eastward shift of major trade roads, the Awdaghost urban layout entered its final demise. New economic initiatives like the opening of camping grounds, and the creation of caravansérail, altered the urban landscape in a significant way. Prosperity was however part of the past. At the very end of its medieval history, Awdaghost Acropolis was settled by modest nuclear family units, living in small one-room-courtyard houses. The area was finally deserted at the very end of the fifteenth or very beginning of the sixteenth century. A hundred years later, in the seventeenth century, a Moorish group, the ancestors of the Tegdaoust, moved south to the medieval ruins and built a new, if smaller, town in the west of the former medieval Awdaghost. The forgotten ruins of this famous medieval trade entrepot were rediscovered in the 1920s.

References Cited

IFAN Archives

File XV-5-MAU *"Sites Archéologiques et Historiques de Mauritanie"*
1. "A la Découverte d'Aoudaghost: Vingt-quatre étudiants et quatre professeurs Dakarois recherchent dans le sable le passé de l'Afrique." *Afrique Nouvelle* 29, Mars 1961, No. 712:1, 8, 9, 16.
2. Lettre de H. Masson, recteur de l'Université de Dakar au Ministre Mauritanien de l'Éducation Nationale, Juin 1960.
3. Lettre de R. Mauny a T. Monod, Directeur de l'IFAN, 18 Janvier 1961.
4. R. Mauny, 1961, Compte Rendu de Mission a Tegdaoust (Rkiz, Mauritanie). (4 pages)
5. R. Mauny, n.d., Fouilles de l'université de Dakar en Mauritanie. (96 pages)
6. S. Robert parle de la Campagne 1963 de fouille archéologiques de Tegdaoust. *Dakar Matin*, 21 Mai 1963.

References

Amilhat, P.
1937   Notes sur Aoudaghost et les Villages a l'Est du Tagant. *Revue d'Études Islamiques* 1937:123-28.

Ardener, S.
1981   Ground rules and social maps for women: an introduction. In *Women and Space: Ground Rules and Social Maps*, edited by S. Ardener, pp. 11-34. London: Croom Helm.

Arnould, E.J.
1984   Marketing and social reproduction in Zinder, Niger Republic. In *Households: Comparative and Historical Studies of the Domestic Group*, edited by R. McC. Netting, R.R. Wilk, and E.J. Arnould, pp. 130-62. Berkeley: University of California Press.

Bah, T.
1966   *Fouille d'un Quartier de Tegdaoust*. Advanced Studies thesis, Dakar, Faculté des Lettres.

Bedaux, R., K. MacDonald, A. Person, J. Polet, K. Sanogo, A. Schmidt, and S. Sidibé
2001   The Dia archaeological project: rescuing cultural heritage in the inland Niger delta (Mali).
       Antiquity 75:837-48.

Bernus, S., and P. Gouletquer
1976   Du Cuivre au Sel. *Journal des Africanistes* 46(1-2):7-68.

Bernus, S., and P. Cressier (editors)
1991   *La Région d'In Gal–Tegidda n Tesemt (Niger) IV: Azelik-Takadda et l'implantation séden-
       taire médiévale.* Niamey: Institut de Recherches en Sciences Humaines.

Berthier, S.
1997   *Recherches Archeologiques sur la Capitale de l'Empire de Ghana.* Oxford: British Archaeo-
       logical Reports.

Binford, L.R.
1981   Behavioral archaeology and the "Pompei premise." *Journal of Anthropological Research*
       37:195-208.

Bivar, A.D.H., and P.L. Shinnie
1962   Old Kanuri capitals. *Journal of African History* 3(1):1-10.

Bocoum, H., and S.K. McIntosh
2002   *Fouilles a Sincu Bara, Moyenne Vallée du Sénégal.* Dakar/Nouakchott: IFAN-Cheikh Anta
       Diop and Université de Nouakchott.

Blanton, R.E.
1994   *Houses and Households: A Comparative Study.* New York: Plenum Press.

Boery, Lt.
1923   Le Rkiss (Mauritanie): essai de monographie locale. *Bulletin du Comité d'Études Histo-
       riques et Scientifique de l'Afrique Occidentale Française,* 6.

Bohannan, P., and L. Bohannan
1968   *Tiv Economy.* London: Longmans.

Chayanov, A.V.
1966   *The Theory of Peasant Economy,* edited by D. Thorner, B. Kerblay, and R.E.F. Smith.
       Homewood, IL: R.D. Irwin, Inc.

Connah, G.
1981   *Three Thousand Years in Africa.* Cambridge: Cambridge University Press.

Conrad, D.C.
1994   A town called Dakajalan: the Sunjata tradition and the question of ancient Mali's capital.
       Journal of African History 35:355-77.

Cros, M.C.
1968   *Rapport de Fouilles Archaéologiques. Maison du Quartier Nord de la ville supérieure de
       Tegdaoust.* Maitrise thesis, Université de Paris I.

DeCorse, C.
2000 *Archaeology of Elmina.* Washington, D.C.: Smithsonian Institution Press.

Deetz, J.F.
1982 Households: a structural key to archaeological explanation. *American Behavioral Scientist* 25:717-24.

De Gironcourt, G.R.
1920 *Missions De Gironcourt en Afrique Occidentale, 1908-1909, 1911-1912.* Paris: Société de Géographie.

Delafosse, M.
1912 *Haut–Sénégal–Niger.* Paris: Larose.
1924 Le Gana et le Mali et l'emplacement de leurs capitales. *Bulletin du Comite d'Etudes Historiques et Scientifiques de l'Afrique Occidentale Française* 7:479-542.

Desplagnes, L.
1907 *Le Plateau Central Nigérien.* Paris: Larose.

Devisse, J. (editor)
1983 *Tegdaoust III: Recherches sur Aoudaghost, Campagnes 1960-1965 Enquetes Generales.* Paris: Editions Recherche sur les Civilisations.
1993 *Vallées du Niger.* Paris: Reunion des Musées Nationaux.

Digard, J.P.
1981 *Les Techniques des Nomades Baxtyari d'Iran.* Paris/London: Miason des Sciences de l'Homme/Cambridge University Press.

Dumas-Champion, F.
1983 *Les Massa du Tchad: Bétail et Société.* Paris/London: Maison des Sciences de l'Homme/Cambridge University Press.

Durrenberger, E.P.
1984 Operationalizing Chayanov. In *Chayanov, Peasants and Economic Anthropology,* edited by E.P. Durrenberger, pp. 39-50. London: Academic Press.

Filipowiak, W.
1966 L'Expédition Archéologique Polono-Guinéenne a Niani (Guinée). *Africana Bulletin* 4:116-27.
1969 L'Expédition Archéologique Polono-Guinéenne a Niani en 1968. *Africana Bulletin* 11:107-17.
1977 Les Recherches Archéologiques a Niani et le Probleme de la Capitale du Mali. In *Actes du colloque International de Bamako (16-22 Février 1976),* pp. 287-93. Paris: Fondation SCOA pour la Recherche Scientifique en Afrique.
1979 *Études Archéologiques sur la capitale Médiévale du Mali.* Szczecinie: Muzeum Narodowe.

Finley, M.I.
1998 *Ancient Slavery and Modern Ideology,* expanded edition, edited by Brent D. Shaw. Princeton: Marcus Wiener Publishers.

Flight, C.
1975a Gao 1972: first interim report: a preliminary investigation of the cemetery at Sané. *West African Journal of Archaeology* 5:81-90.
1975b Excavations at Gao (Republic of Mali) in 1974. *Nyame Akuma* 7:28-29.
1979 Excavations at Gao (Republic of Mali) in 1978. *Nyame Akuma* 14:35-37.
1981 The medieval cemetery at Sané. A history of the site from 1939 to 1950. In *Le Sol, La Parole, et L'Écrit. Mélanges en hommage a Raymond Mauny*, pp. 91-107. Paris: Société Française d'Histoire d'Outer-Mer.

Friedman, J., and M.J. Rowlands
1977 Notes towards an epigenetic model of the evolution of "civilization." In *The Evolution of Social Systems*, edited by J. Friedman and M.J. Rowlands, pp. 201-76. London: Duckworth.

Grébénart, D.
1985 *La Région d'In Gall–Tegidda n Tesemt (Niger) II: Le Néolithique Final et les Débuts de la Métallurgie*. Niamey: Institut de Recherches en Sciences Humaines.
1993 Marandet. In *Vallées du Niger*, edited by J. Devisse, pp. 375-77. Paris: Reunion des Musées Nationaux.

Hammel, E.A.
1980 Sensitivity analysis of household structure in medieval Serbian censuses. *Historical Methods* 13:105-18.

Hill, P.
1982 *Dry Grain Farming Families: Hausaland (Nigeria) and Karnataka (India) Compared*. London: Cambridge University Press.

Holl, A.
1985 Background to the Ghana Empire: archaeological investigations on the transition to statehood in the Dhar Tichitt region (Mauritania). *Journal of Anthropological Archaeology* 4:73-115.
1986 *Economie et Societe Néolithique du Dhar Tichitt (Mauritania)*. Paris: Editions Recherches sur les Civilizations.
1988 Review of *Tegdaoust IV* (see Polet 1985). *Les Nouvelles de l'Archéologie* 30:72.
1990 Unité de Production et unité de consommation dans le neolithique du Dhar Tichitt. *L'Anthropologie* 94:535-58.
1993 Late neolithic cultural landscape in southeastern Mauritania: an essay in spatiometrics. In *Spatial Boundaries and Social Dynamics*, edited by A. Holl and T.E. Levy, pp. 95-133. International Monographs in Prehistory. Ann Arbor.
2000 *The Diwan Revisited: Literacy, State Formation and the Rise of Kanuri Domination (AD 1200-1600)*. London and New York: Kegan Paul International.
2002 *The Land of Houlouf: Genesis of a Chadic Polity 1900 BC-AD 1800*. Memoirs, no. 35. Museum of Anthropology, University of Michigan. Ann Arbor.

Hunwick, J.O.
1973 The mid-fourteenth century capital of Mali. *Journal of African History* XIV(2):195-208.

Hunwick, J., and E. Troutt Powell
2002 *The African Diaspora in the Mediterranean Lands of Islam*. Princeton: Marcus Wiener Publishers.

Hrbek, I., and J. Devisse
1990   Les Almoravides. In *Histoire Générale de l'Afrique III: L'Afrique du VIIe au XIe siecle*, edited by M. El Fasi, pp. 365-95. Paris: UNESCO/NEA.

Insoll, T.
1996   *Islam, Archaeology and History: Gao Region (Mali) ca. AD 900-1250*. Oxford: British Archaeological Report.
2000a The origins of Timbuktu. *Antiquity* 74:483-84.
2000b *Urbanism, Archaeology and Trade: Further Observations on the Gao Region (Mali)*. Oxford: British Archaeological Reports.
2003   *The Archaeology of Islam in Sub-Saharan Africa*. Cambridge: Cambridge University Press.

Kent, S. (editor)
1990   *Domestic Architecture and the Use of Space*. Cambridge: Cambridge University Press.

Kiethega, J.B.
1973   *Fouille d'une Maison de Tegdaoust Est*. Maitrise thesis, Université de Dakar.

Kramer, C.
1982a Ethnographic households and archaeological interpretation: a case study from Iranian Kurdistan. *American Behavioral Scientist* 25:663-75.
1982b *Village Ethnoarchaeology: Rural Iran in Archaeological Perspectives*. New York: Academic Press.

Kunstadter, P.
1984   Cultural ideals, socioeconomic change, and household composition: Karen, Lua, Hmong, and Thai in northwestern Thailand. In *Households: Comparative and Historical Studies of the Domestic Group*, edited by R. McC. Netting, R.R. Wilk, and E.J. Arnould, pp. 299-329. Berkeley: University of California Press.

Laforgue, P.
1940   Notes sur Aoudaghost. *Bulletin de l'IFAN* 217-236.
1943   Notes sur Aoudaghost. *Bulletin de la Société Geographique et Archéologique d'Oran*, pp. 26-42.

Lebecq, S.
1966   *Fouille de deux maisons et des strates inférieures dans le tell méridional de Tegdaoust*. Advanced Studies thesis, Université de Lille III.
1983   Tegdaoust: Sondage dans un tell situé au sud du tell principal. In *Tegdaoust III: Recherches sur Awdaghost*, edited by J. Devisse, pp. 311-26. Paris: ADPF.

Levtzion, N.
1968   Ibn Hawqal, the Cheque and Awdaghost. *Journal of African History* 9:223-33.
1973   *Ancient Ghana and Mali*. London: Methuen.

Levtzion, N., and J.F.P. Hopkins (editors)
1981   *Corpus of Early Arabic sources for West African History*. Cambridge: Cambridge University Press.

Levtzion, N., and J. Spaulding (editors)
2003   *Medieval West Africa: Views from Arab Scholars and Merchants.* Princeton: Markus Wiener Publishers.

Lhote, H.
1942   Découverte d'un Atélier de Perles dans la Région de Gao (Soudan Français). *Bulletin de la Société Préhistorique Française* 39:277-92.
1943   Découverte d'un Atélier de Perles dans la Région de Gao (Soudan Français): Techniques de Perforation des Perles. *Bulletin de la Société Préhistorique Française* 40:24-36.
1972a Recherches sur Takkeda, ville décrite par le voyageur Arabe Ibn Battouta et située en Aïr. *Bulletin de l'IFAN, Série B* 34(3):435-70.
1972b Une Étonnante découverte archéologique au Niger. *Archeologia* 51:63-67.

Linares, O.F.
1984   Households among the Diola of Sénégal: should norms enter by the front or the back door? In *Households: Comparative and Historical Studies of the Domestic Group*, edited by R. McC. Netting, R.R. Wilk, and E.J. Arnould, pp. 407-45. Berkeley: University of California Press.

MacDonald, K.C.
1996   Tichitt-Walata and the middle Niger: evidence for cultural contact in the second millennium BC. In *Aspects of African Archaeology*, edited by G. Pwiti and R. Soper, pp. 429-40. Harare: University of Zimbabwe Publications.

Mauny, R.
1950a La Tour et la Mosquée de l'Askya Mohammed a Gao. *Notes Africaines* 47:66-67.
1950b Les Ruines de Tegdaoust et la Question d'Awdaghost. *Notes Africaines* 48:107-9.
1951   Notes d'Archéologie au Sujet de Gao. *Bulletin de l'IFAN, Série B* 13:837-52.
1952   Découverte a Gao d'un Fragment de Poterie émaillée du Moyen-Age Musulman. *Hesperis* 34:514-16.
1953   Découverte d'un atelier de fonte du cuivre a Marandet (Niger). *Notes Africaines* 58:52-57.
1961a Les Fouilles de l'Université de Dakar en Mauritanie. *Tropiques*, Aout-Septembre 1961:19-21.
1961b *Tableau Geographique de l'Ouest Africain au Moyen-Age.* Dakar: Institut Fondamental d'Afrique Noire.
1983   Les peintures rupesteres de l'Abri d'Ageuntrou el-Abiod a Tegdaoust. In *Tegdaoust III: Recherches sur Awdaghost*, edited by J. Devisse, pp. 71-76. Paris: ADPF.

McIntosh, R.J.
1998   *The Peoples from the Middle Niger.* Oxford: Blackwell.

McIntosh, S.K.
1999   Modelling political organization in large scale settlement clusters: a case study from the inland Niger delta. In *Beyond Chiefdoms: Pathways to Complexity in Africa*, pp. 66-79. Cambridge: Cambridge University Press.

McIntosh, S.K. (editor)
1995   *Excavations at Jénne-jeno, Hambarketolo and Kaniana: The 1981 Field Season.* Berkeley: University of California Press.

McIntosh, S.K., and H. Bocoum
2000   New perspectives on Sincu Bara, a first millennium site in the Sénégal Valley. *African Archaeological Review* 17(1):1-43.

McIntosh, S.K., and R.J. McIntosh
1980   *Prehistoric Investigations at Jénne, Mali.* Oxford: British Archaeological Reports.
1984   The early city in West Africa: toward an understanding. *The African Archaeological Review* 2:73-98.
1986   Archaeological reconnaissance in the region of Timbuktu, Mali. *National Geographic Research* 2:302-19.
1993   Cities without citadels: understanding urban origins along the middle Niger. In *The Archaeology of Africa. Food, Metals, and Towns*, edited by T. Shaw, P. Sinclair, B. Andah, and A. Okpoko, pp. 622-41. London: Routledge.

McNaughton, P.R.
1988   *The Mande Blacksmiths: Knowledge, Power, and Art in West Africa.* Bloomington: Indiana University Press.

Meillassoux, C.
1972   L'Itinéraire d'Ibn Batouta de Walata a Mali. *Journal of African History* XIII(2):389-95.
1983   A propos de deux groupes Azer: Les Giriganko-Tegdaoust et les Maxanbinnu. In *Tegdaoust III: Recherches sur Awdaghost*, edited by J. Devisse, pp. 525-30. Paris: ADPF.

Moraes-Farias, P. de
1990   The oldest extant writing of West Africa: medieval epigraphs from Essuk, Saney, and Egef-n-Tawaqqast (Mali). *Journal des Africanistes* 60(2):65-113.
1999   Tadmakkat and the image of the Mecca: epigraphic records of the work of the imagination in 11th century West Africa. In *Case Studies in Archaeology and World Religions: The Proceedings of the Cambridge Conference*, edited by T. Insoll, pp. 105-15. Oxford: BAR, Archaeopress.

Munson, P.J.
1980   Archaeology and the prehistoric origins of the Ghana Empire. *Journals of African History* 21:457-66.

Netting, R. McC., R.R. Wilk, and E.J. Arnould
1984   Introduction. In *Households: Comparative and Historical Studies of the Domestic Group*, edited by R. McC. Netting, R.R. Wilk, and E.J. Arnould, pp. xiii-xxxviii. Berkeley: University of California Press.

Oswald, D.
1984   The use of site structure to infer social and technological organization from the archaeological record. In *Frontiers: South African Archaeology Today*, edited by M. Hall, G. Avery, D.M. Avery, M.L. Wilson, and J.B. Humphreys, pp. 297-309. Oxford: BAR.

Person, A., and J.S. Saliege
1991   Pates, Dégraissant et Chronologie: Contribution Analytique a l'étude des Céramiques d'Azelik. In *La Région d'In Gall–Tegidda n Tesemt (Niger) IV: Azelik-Takadda et l'implantation sédentaire médiévale*, edited by S. Bernus and P. Cressier, pp. 89-118. Niamey: Institut de Recherches en Sciences Humaines.

Polet, J.
1967   *Fouille d'un Quartier du tell Principal de Tegdaoust.* Advanced Studies thesis, Université de Lille III.
1985   *Tegdaoust IV: Fouille d'un Quartier de Tegdaoust (Mauritanie Orientale: Urbanisation, Architecture, Utilisation de l'espace construit).* Paris: Editions Recherche sur les Civilisations.

Tamari, T.
1991   The development of caste systems in West Africa. *Journal of African History* 32:221-50.

Thilmans, G., and A. Ravisé
1980   *Protohistoire du Sénégal II: Sintiou-Bara et les Sites du Fleuve.* Dakar: IFAN.

Richir, C.
1983   Les Peintures rupesters a Tegdaoust. Topographie, constructions lithiques, peintures rupestres dans le Rkiz. In *Tegdaoust III: Recherches sur Awdaghost*, edited by J. Devisse, pp. 77-94. Paris: ADPF.

Robert-Chaleix, D.
1983a Céramiques découvertes a Tegdaoust. In *Tegdaoust III: Recherches sur Awdaghost*, edited by J. Devisse, pp. 245-94. Paris: ADPF.
1983b Fusaioles décorés du Site de Tegdaoust. In *Tegdaoust III: Recherches sur Awdaghost*, edited by J. Devisse, pp. 447-513. Paris: ADPF.
1989   *Tegdaoust V: Une Concession Medievale a Tegdaoust—Implantation, Evolution d'une unite d'Habitation.* Paris: Editions Recherche sur les Civilisations.

Robert-Chaleix, D., and C. Richir
1983   Un Site jusqu'a présent inconnu dans le Rkhiz: Moulay arbad. In *Tegdaoust III: Recherches sur Awdaghost*, edited by J. Devisse, pp. 335-55. Paris: ADPF.

Robert, D., S. Robert, and J. Devisse
1970   *Tegdaoust I: Recherches sur Awdaghost.* Paris: Arts et Metiers Graphiques.

Sahlins, M.
1968   *Tribesmen.* New Jersey: Prentice Hall.
1976   *Age de Pierre, Age d'Abondance: L'Économie des Sociétés Primitives.* Paris: Gallimard.

Saison, B.
1970   *Fouille d'un Quartier Artisanal a Tegdaoust.* Maitrise thesis, Université de Lille III.
1979   *Fouille d'un Quartier Artisanal a Tegdaoust (Mauritanie Orientale).* PhD thesis, Université de Paris I.
1981   Azugi: Archéologie et Histoire en Adrar Mauritanien. *Recherche, Pédagogie et Culture* XI (55):66-74.

Sauvaget, J.
1950   Les Épitaphes Royales de Goa. *Bulletin de l'IFAN* XII(2):418-40.

Schiffer, M.B.
1972   Archaeological context and systemic context. *American Antiquity* 37:156-65.
1987   *Formation Processes of the Archaeological Record.* Albuquerque: University of New Mexico Press.

Smith, R.
1984   Preface. In *Land, Kinship and Life-Cycle*, edited by R. Smith, pp. ix-xiii. London: Cambridge University Press.

Stevenson, M.G.
1982   Toward an understanding of site abandonment behavior: evidence from historic mining camps in the southwest Yukon. *Journal of Anthropological Archaeology* 1:237-65.

Tamari, T.
1995   Linguistic evidence for the history of West African "castes." In *Status and Identity in West Africa: Nyamakalaw of Mande*, edited by D.C. Conrad and B.A. Frank, pp. 61-85. Bloomington: Indiana University Press.

Thilmans, G., and A. Ravise
1980   *Protohistoire du Sénégal–2: Sintiou Bara et les Sites du Fleuve.* Dakar: IFAN.

Tringham, R.
1983   *The Development of the Household as the Primary Unit of Production in Neolithic and Eneolithic South-East Europe.* Paper presented at the annual meeting of the Society for American Archaeology, Pittsburgh, PA.

Vanacker, C.
1975   *Fouille d'un Quartier Artisanal du Site de Tegdaoust.* Maitrise thesis, Université de Lille III.
1979   *Tegdaoust II: Fouille d'un Quatier Artisanal.* Memoires de l'Institut Mauritanien de la Recherche Scientifique, No. 2. Paris.
1983a   Sondage au Sud-ouest du cirque de Noudache, Janvier 1969. In *Tegdaoust III: Recherches sur Awdaghost*, edited by J. Devisse, pp. 297-310. Paris: ADPF.
1983b   Verres a Décor géometrique retrouvés a Tegdaoust. In *Tegdaoust III: Recherches sur Awdaghost*, edited by J. Devisse, pp. 515-24. Paris: ADPF.

Wilk, R.R.
1984   Households in process: agricultural change and domestic transformation among the Kekchi Maya of Belize. In *Households: Comparative and Historical Studies of the Domestic Group*, edited by R. McC. Netting, R.R. Wilk, and E.J. Arnould, pp. 217-44. Berkeley: University of California Press.

Wilk, R.R., and R. McC. Netting
1984   Households: changing forms and functions. In *Households: Comparative and Historical Studies of the Domestic Group*, edited by R. McC. Netting, R.R. Wilk, and E.J. Arnould, pp. 1-28. Berkeley: University of California Press.

Wilk, R.R., and W.L. Rathje
1982   Household archaeology. *American Behavioral Scientist* 25:617-39.

Wolf, A.P.
1984   Family life and the life cycle in rural China. In *Households: Comparative and Historical Studies of the Domestic Group*, edited by R. McC. Netting, R.R. Wilk, and E.J. Arnould, pp. 279-98. Berkeley: University of California Press.